Automatic

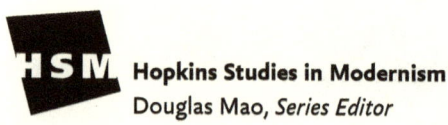

Hopkins Studies in Modernism
Douglas Mao, *Series Editor*

Automatic

Literary Modernism and the Politics of Reflex

Timothy Wientzen

Johns Hopkins University Press
Baltimore

© 2021 Timothy Wientzen
All rights reserved. Published 2021
Printed in the United States of America on acid-free paper
9 8 7 6 5 4 3 2 1

Johns Hopkins University Press
2715 North Charles Street
Baltimore, Maryland 21218-4363
www.press.jhu.edu

Library of Congress Cataloging-in-Publication Data

Names: Wientzen, Timothy, 1981- author.
Title: Automatic : literary modernism and the politics of reflex / Timothy Wientzen.
Description: Baltimore, Maryland : Johns Hopkins University Press, 2021. | Series: Hopkins studies in modernism | Includes bibliographical references and index.
Identifiers: LCCN 2020045437 | ISBN 9781421440873 (hardcover ; acid-free paper) | ISBN 9781421440880 (paperback ; acid-free paper) | ISBN 9781421440897 (ebook)
Subjects: LCSH: English literature—20th century—History and criticism. | Modernism (Literature) | Automatism in literature. | Politics and literature. | Literature and society.
Classification: PR478.M6 W49 2021
LC record available at https://lccn.loc.gov/2020045437

A catalog record for this book is available from the British Library.

Special discounts are available for bulk purchases of this book. For more information, please contact Special Sales at specialsales@ jh.edu.

Johns Hopkins University Press uses environmentally friendly book materials, including recycled text paper that is composed of at least 30 percent post-consumer waste, whenever possible.

Contents

Acknowledgments vii

Introduction. Prescribed Tracks 1

1. **Automatic Man: A Genealogy** 16

2. **Vibrant Bodies, Automatic Minds: Vitalism, D. H. Lawrence, and the Politics of Spontaneity** 41

3. **Public Reflex: Wyndham Lewis, Public Relations, and the Invisible Government** 72

4. **Pavlovian Nationalism: Rebecca West's Reflex Communities** 105

5. **Higher Degrees of Automaticity: Habitus, Samuel Beckett, and Late Modernism** 139

Afterword. Choice Architects, Where Is Your Vortex? The Politics of Reflex in the Twenty-First Century 170

Notes 191
Works Cited 231
Index 249

Acknowledgments

This book is the product of eleven years of labor. It has been nourished by friends and colleagues in Kansas City, Albuquerque, North Carolina, Boston, and New York, and energized by the example and generosity of many mentors. The people who have populated my professional and personal orbit over the years have contributed to the making of this book, even when they did not know it. My debts are many and deep.

Before I could learn about academic books, I had to learn about academia. As an undergrad at Boston College, my teachers were so smart and interesting that I decided I wanted to be just like them. Marjorie Howes guided me through Dublin 1904, Bob Chibka allowed me to glimpse something almost metaphysical about fiction, and the late Andrew Von Hendy introduced me to a thing called "modernism." I remain humbled by their kindness to me and inspired by their example. And to Carlo Rotella I owe a particularly profound thanks; he gave me simple and powerful advice as I was entering academia, and I regularly plagiarize his words with my own students now.

In the fall of 2006, I began graduate study in the English Department at Duke—an incredible stroke of fortune. In Michael Valdez Moses, I met an adviser who seemed to know every text a scholar of modernism might ever want to read. Traces of his advice can be found in each chapter of this book. As my dissertation on automatic behaviors took shape, I benefited from the wisdom and counsel of three additional advisers. Fredric Jameson turned me on to D. H. Lawrence, Priscilla Wald taught me about the history of brainwashing, and Ian Baucom pushed me to see the philosophical entailments of it all. I owe particularly deep gratitude to Nancy Armstrong. Upon arriving at Duke, she took me on as a member of the editorial team at *Novel: A Forum on Fiction*. There, I learned what an academic article is and how academic publishing works. I am grateful to her for giving me a panoramic view of the profession and for always taking me seriously as a scholar.

Nancy often said that the most important intellectual work at academic conferences happens not in the panels but over drinks at the end of the day. Among the graduate students at Duke, I entered a community of scholars whose company proved the wisdom of her observation. In Nathan Hensley, Gerry Canavan, Erica Fretwell, Lindsey Andrews, Keith Jones, Calina Ciobanu, Mitch Fraas, Orion Teal, Alex Ruch, Azeen Khan, and many others, I found a dynamic intellectual community. Each of these people had a hand in shaping this work at its earliest stages (and some at late stages). Nathan and Gerry, in particular, improved the rigor of my dissertation, and in the years since lent precious hours and attention to making this book sharper and more interesting.

By dumbest of dumb luck, 2012 saw me begin a lectureship in Harvard's History and Literature Program. I owe debts of the highest order to several friends and colleagues from my Cambridge years. In Jennifer Spitzer, I found a co-traveler in modernist studies—and an eager interlocutor. And my fellow *Novel* alum Wendy Allison Lee made the bowels of the Barker Center brighter every day. Above all, I want to thank Lauren Kaminsky, who not only made me a better teacher but explained to me in great detail how to interpret the vague parameters of a job talk.

Since 2015, I have taught at Skidmore College with a wonderful group of colleagues. Wendy Lee (again!), Maggie Greaves, Andrew Bozio, Paul Benzon, Nick Junkerman, and Barbara Black all read portions of this book and helped me navigate the late stages as it neared publication. And my former student Kallan Dana allowed me to avoid learning the intricacies of *The Chicago Manual of Style*. Deep gratitude!

This book was also shaped by colleagues in the world of modernist studies. I started attending the Modernist Studies Association's annual meeting in 2007, and it has served as an intellectual home base for me ever since. Lisi Schoenbach, Aarthi Vadde, Tommy Davis, Debra Rae Cohen, Gayle Rogers, Paul Saint-Amour, Chris Holmes, and many others gave me encouragement, invited me to talk on panels, and generally gave MSA that summer camp vibe. To Scott Selisker and Andrew Gaedtke I owe special thanks, not only for their generosity in reading chapters of this book in draft but also for serving as critical interlocutors. Their own work is cited throughout this book, though not nearly as much as it should be. And my deepest gratitude

Acknowledgments

to Douglas Mao, who supported this project from the first, and whose acumen made every idea in this book better.

Every graduate student hopes that their dissertation will one day see life as a book, but the process is fraught with self-doubt. I received encouragement along the way from journals and editors that saw virtue in the ideas at the heart of this book. An early version of chapter two appeared in the journal *Genre: Forms of Discourse and Culture* 46, no. 1 (2013), and portions of chapter four appeared in *Journal of Modern Literature* 38, no. 4 (2015).

Last but not least I want to thank my friends and family. My parents were supportive of me even when they were skeptical about my ambitions to study literature. For the freedom to be myself, I owe them everything.

And to Kendra Sena, love of my life, who made this thing worth doing. In the time that it has taken to write this book, we got married, climbed mountains, planted gardens, were robbed once at gunpoint, and brought a Smokey and a Bicho into this world. Whatever is good in this book is owed entirely to her love and support. This book is dedicated to her.

Automatic

Introduction
Prescribed Tracks

By the time the hostilities of the First World War were officially concluded, modernism was over. Or so Wyndham Lewis seemed to think. The political and cultural ferment of 1913 and 1914 that had given rise to England's lone avant-garde movement, Vorticism, had been checked by a war that "meant nothing" and was "grotesquely out of scale" with what it was meant to settle, as Lewis put it.[1] Those members of the Vorticist movement who were not killed in action were physically dispersed and creatively sapped. Whatever momentum a nascent modernist movement might have had before the war was gone, and Lewis, its self-proclaimed leader, returned from the front bereft of a clear vision for renewing it. Part of the challenge for Lewis and his contemporaries was that while the return of peace offered the opportunity for creative consolidation, the war had given birth to a set of political realities for which the British avant-garde was unprepared. The usually prolific Lewis entered a period of relative quiet during which he studied and reevaluated the forces that had produced the war and its aftermath. His readings in contemporary politics, philosophy, and science culminated in a torrent of books published between 1926 and 1931, in which he offered a sprawling critique of the intellectual and aesthetic underpinnings of mass modernity.

Of particular concern to Lewis was the status of individuality within mass society. In nonfiction works like *The Art of Being Ruled* (1926) and *Time and Western Man* (1927), as well as novels like *The Childermass* (1928) and *Apes of God* (1930), he would describe a society that, while outwardly celebrating individuality and creativity, covertly enforced a uniform set of habits among citizens. In the preface to *Time and Western Man*, he described this apparent contradiction as a political paradigm that required a new critical sensibility: "Everyone, I am persuaded, must today fit themselves for thinking more clearly about the problems of everyday life, by accustoming themselves to think of the abstract things existing, more distinctly than ever before, behind such problems." As Lewis understood it, "everyday life" could no longer be understood as politically neutral. His readings in politics and science in particular suggested that everyday social experience in its most varied forms acted as a kind of stimulus, conditioning thought and action in predetermined ways. Every facet of modern life, Lewis averred, imposed political and aesthetic values on citizens without ever registering on the conscious mind. Passively conditioning people to vote and consume according to predetermined protocols, mass society promoted the illusion of agency, all the while inculcating the most rote and unconscious kinds of behaviors. "Everything in our life today conspires to thrust most people into prescribed tracks," he warned.[2] Lewis discerned these prescribed tracks—reflexive ways of doing and thinking—everywhere he looked. In lieu of creativity, agency, and individuality, he saw a race of robots and automata, masses of people reduced to simple reflex actions and incapable of escaping the grooves provided by culture—indeed, unaware that such grooves existed at all.

Lewis's analysis of everyday life might be interpreted as an anxious desire to blast rising artistic and intellectual trends of the era or as a paranoid response to the changing political landscape of the interwar period. But his sense that life was increasingly dominated by reflexive, habitual, and automatic behaviors was widely shared by his contemporaries. Literary modernism followed a century during which questions about the mechanistic basis of human life found experimental validation in the work of physiologists, who stressed the power of environments to shape and delimit thought and action. By the late nineteenth century, the hypothesis that humans were "automata," as Descartes had conjectured in 1637, began to seem much more than philosophical speculation, as statesmen and industrialists appropriated blueprints of the human machine originally mapped by the sciences. Already by the last years of the nineteenth century, physiological inquiry into reflex had begun to filter into an array of disciplines, becoming a key term in emerging theories of mass modernity. Writing in the journal *Mind* in 1899, British political theorist Bernard Bosanquet surveyed the findings of physiologists and confidently concluded that automatic behaviors were necessary for progress in an age of political and economic dislocation. Social life, he explains, is necessarily and increasingly constituted by adjustments which have become automatic, and are in a large measure withdrawn from public attention. The formation of such adjustments would then appear to be the condition of social progress. A definite habit of orderly action, which receives the *imprimatur* of the State, and is thus put beyond the range of discussion, effects an economy of attention. The public mind is no longer pre-occupied with it; it becomes part of the rationalised sub-structure of conscious life, and subserves the social end, while, so far as it is concerned, setting free the social mind for new ideas.[3]

Speaking in a physiological idiom, Bosanquet made an argument that would prove extremely influential in the first half of the twentieth century. The notion that mass modernity was increasingly characterized by automatic behaviors was a sentiment common to writers of diverse political persuasions and a topic much debated by philosophers, sociologists, political scientists, and psychologists in the early twentieth century. Bosanquet's sentiment is illustrative of the stakes of these debates. He believed that by incorporating the empirical findings of physiologists into its political tactics, the state could guarantee order and enforce a set of socially beneficial habits, thus safeguarding itself against the tumult of rapid social change. Just as industrialists like Frederick Winslow Taylor and Henry Ford attempted to economize the actions of workers for the better functioning of the factory, Bosanquet imagined a regularized form of social life in which the values at the heart of society were managed through a regime of reflex. "Put beyond the range of discussion," the habits of the populace would become automatic, setting minds free for other, more important tasks. Or, as Lewis would explain in a more critical mode, such tactics would provide citizens "with a system of habits which agree with their neighbor's habits, and from this coma they [would] seldom wake."[4]

Of course, the imagery and language of automatism has long been a part of the mythos of modernism. Visions of robots, hollow men, and dehumanized laborers circulated widely in the cultural imagination of the early twentieth century, reflecting widespread societal concern about the status of spontaneity and agency within mass society. From the very beginnings of the modernist era, the aesthetics of futurists, surrealists, and other avant-garde groups were specifically geared toward breaking habits of perception among consumers of art—a project that always carried a political agenda. Bertolt Brecht's *Verfremdungseffekt* famously tied the aesthetic perception of audiences to their political habits, while Pound's "make it new" similarly regarded rote engagement with the world as a pernicious problem of mass modernity, one to be broken by the power of modernist literature. Indeed, even early critical schools like Russian Formalism and New Criticism positioned literature in opposition to what Victor Shklovsky termed the "automatism of perception."[5] If none of these can be taken as definitive of modernist aesthetics as a whole, they collectively reflect a cultural sensitivity to the place of automaticity in twentieth-century life. As Lisi Schoenbach has explained, modernism was broadly underwritten by a desire to put a spanner in the works of human perception: "Breaking free of habit and beginning anew is [modernism's] signal gesture. . . . [T]he modern moment of newfound wakefulness is always linked, explicitly or implicitly, to the destruction of habit."[6] The language of automaticity in these assorted definitions of modernism does not in all cases map on to Lewis's anxieties about the stimuli of everyday life. But it does reflect a broad cultural preoccupation with automatic behaviors, one that became a key problem in efforts to forge literary forms adequate to mass society.

I argue in this book that reflex played a decisive role in configuring the political dimensions of literary modernism. Writing in the wake of a half-century of scientific inquiry about the inherent susceptibility of bodies to the stimuli of everyday life, modernists were deeply anxious about the role of reflex in the new political structures of the twentieth century—and with good reason. Throughout the early part of the century, experts in government and industry theorized the behavior of citizens and consumers in terms of reflexes that could be molded through the careful manipulation of culture. The physiological certainty that our behaviors are influenced by stimuli that we do not consciously apprehend allowed political theorists to envision a mode of political life characterized less by appeal to the rational agency of citizens than by environmental conditioning. While an older political tradition emphasized Enlightenment values of individuality, agency, and rationality, the twentieth century witnessed the maturation of fields that understood unreasoned habits and reflexes as the foundation of collective life. For modernist novelists, nonfiction writers, poets, and critics, as well as political theorists, strategists, and philosophers, the twentieth century stood as a historical moment in which new knowledge about the human body's susceptibility to its environment was fundamentally reshaping the nature of political life. As a result, categories of automaticity became a shared language for understanding mass modernity across political, scientific, and cultural fields—a fact that directly influenced modernist writers and the literary forms they employed.

This book demonstrates some of the many ways that the science of reflex informed the political conditions of modernist literature. In so doing, it offers an account of modernism that conflicts with one narrative that has proven surprisingly durable across decades of scholarship, namely modernism's emphasis on the mind. In her 1926 essay, "On Being Ill," Virginia Woolf noted literature's seeming allergy to bodily matters. Literature, she writes, "does its best to maintain that its concern is with the mind; that the body is a sheet of plain glass through which the soul looks straight and clear, and, save for one or two passions such as desire and greed, is null, and negligible and non-existent."[7] Woolf's sense of the non-place of the body within literature has long been a staple of critical surveys of modernism. Conventional wisdom holds that modernism was profoundly indebted to Freud and psychoanalysis, and driven by a desire to forge new modes of depicting a consciousness. Modernist literature was to "record the atoms as they fall upon the mind in the order in which they fall" and "to trace the pattern, however disconnected and incoherent in appearance, which each sight or incident scores upon the consciousness," as Woolf famously proposed in "Modern Fiction."[8] The idea that modernism was fundamentally a literature of the mind owes much to the proximity between the institutions of modernist literature and psychoanalysis. However, approaches to consciousness as a disembodied phenomenon were somewhat foreign to the modernist era. Indeed, the early twentieth century was replete with disciplines that drew on the sciences to see consciousness as a direct manifestation of material forces. For those psychologists working within the empirical tradition in particular, the bodily economies of reflex action much more powerfully explained human behavior than narrowly cognitive categories or structural models of the psyche. In fact, Woolf herself rarely adhered to the program laid out in "Modern Fiction." A vocal critic of Freudian models of consciousness, she treated subjectivity as an embodied phenomenon. From *Mrs. Dalloway* (1925) to *Three Guineas* (1939), her work depicts selves as rooted in iterative, bodily habits, and susceptible to influence by material stimuli—often with politically damning consequences.[9]

The fact that even Woolf, a paragon of the modernist mind, persistently dwelled on the body suggests just how central it was to modernist writers. Scholars have been sensitive to the role of the body within modernism, with several studies appearing over the last twenty years that have attempted to recover this other side of the traditional mind-body dualism. Tim Armstrong's *Modernism, Technology, and the Body* (1998) and Sara Danius's *The Senses of Modernism* (2002) stressed the interface between the body and technology in the emergence of modernist aesthetics. More recently, Jessica Burstein's *Cold Modernism: Literature, Fashion, Art* (2012) and work by Joshua Gang have argued for an iteration of modernist art and literature in which interiority is supplanted entirely by the corporeal.[10] In many of these studies, the body enters the nexus of modernist thinking as a kind of reaction against the fetish of the mind, thereby nuancing well-established narratives of modernism but effectively affirming Woolf's assessment in "Modern Fiction." A more compelling account comes from Douglas Mao, who placed the body at the center of an emergent understanding of aesthetics at the turn of the century. In *Fateful Beauty: Aesthetic Environments, Juvenile Development, and Literature 1860-1960* (2008), Mao traces the development of late nineteenth-century aesthetic theories through changing attitudes about the susceptibility of organisms to the environments they inhabit. According to Mao, the idea that beautiful environments could lead to improved social adjustments of children informed an array of literary and social fields in the era, including criminology, child-rearing, and education, becoming, as he writes, "a cornerstone of Western approaches to social problems and indeed of inquiry into the nature of the universe."[11] Crucially, such aesthetic environments did not need to impinge on the consciousness of children in order to be successful. Because physiologists and early psychologists had begun to develop ideas of an unconscious grounded in the material body, writers and artists didn't necessarily gear their aesthetic projects toward actively shaping the behavior of children; instead, they conceived artistic projects that either reflected the power of environments to shape behaviors or themselves became part of the cultural environment. Mao's work is less invested in the trappings of modernity (technology, warfare, labor, and so forth) than it is in the broad intellectual climate that informed the literary period. As a result, his analysis opens onto a larger vista of inquiry than previous studies, reframing a critical history of the body to encompass the fluid interaction between disciplines, institutions, and cultural production. The body appears in Mao's study as an object undergoing critical reassessment in ways that challenged entrenched ideas about development, social programs, and agency in the decades preceding modernism—forces crucial to the political conditions of twentieth-century literature.

While embodiment has animated some recent work in modernist studies, it is probably outside of this field that these questions have been given their most extensive treatment. Recent critical debates about matter, particularly those classed under the term "new materialisms," have done particularly important work in this area. In contrast to critical emphases on language, discourse, and values, new materialist critics have emphasized the material construction of collective and individual identities, particularly what Samantha Frost and Diana Coole call the relationship between "the material details of everyday life and broader geopolitical and socioeconomic structures."[12] While "new materialisms" describes a variety of critical methodologies and orientations, its emphasis on matter has prompted a renewed interest in a critical tradition that understood habit as an important instrument of ideology.[13] New materialist criticism as a whole sits between contrary poles of thinking about embodiment; it both affirms the power of matter in conditioning behavior, attitudes, and political identities, while resisting the temptation to see matter in deterministic ways. In this sense, new materialist critics are inheritors of two traditions that figure prominently in this book—the vitalist tradition and those that drew on physiology in their analyses of twentieth-century life. As we will see, both were major intellectual forces in redefining the nature of politics for modernist writers.

This book takes inspiration from work in critical theory and modernist studies to define what I call the "politics of reflex." As physiologists developed models of human behavior that prioritized the preeminent role of the body, their work crossed disciplinary boundaries, inspiring specialists in numerous fields to understand how reflex could promote the cohesion of national communities, ensure the endurance of tradition, and produce citizens with predictable buying and voting habits. Enthusiasm for and anxieties about automatic behaviors had a vast intellectual life in the twentieth century and touched a remarkably diverse array of disciplines, including marketing, economics, propaganda, sociology, studies of industrial labor, philosophy, and literary criticism. In this book, I foreground some of the most important disciplinary formations that made reflex an object of inquiry and the institutions of mass modernity that traded in new knowledge about automaticity. By so doing, I map a set of concerns about how automatic behaviors were changing political life in the early twentieth century, concerns that lie at the heart of manifold modernist projects. Like these disciplines, literary modernism was substantially concerned with what many perceived as the increasing role of regularized, unreasoned behaviors in public life. Though, as we will see, in some cases modernists worked to expose the dangers inherent in automaticity, the period also produced cultural forms and political fields that saw potential—even utopian potential—in the politics of reflex.

This book's principal argument is that modernist literature mediated and responded to a twentieth-century public sphere understood to be increasingly geared toward automatic behaviors. This mediation took many forms. The modernists under examination here responded to the politics of reflex by variously critiquing and embracing them. For some, like D. H. Lawrence, literary form offered a way of challenging the political distortions wrought by reflex, while others, like Rebecca West, elaborated literary experiments that affirmed the place of reflex in the preservation of national traditions. Plotting the thinking of these and other modernists within a broader network of writing about reflex behaviors demonstrates the myriad ways in which early twentieth-century writers negotiated the conflict between scientific knowledge and political values of individuality, autonomy, and agency.

Like many academic books, then, this one makes a historical claim about literary modernism and the political currents that animated it. But the politics of reflex should not be regarded as a matter of mere academic interest or a curiosity locked safely away in the past. Reflex has come to play a central role in twenty-first-century political life. Today, experts in a vast array of commercial and electoral fields operate under the assumption that human behaviors should be mapped, anticipated, channeled, or conditioned—in short, that most human behaviors are automatic and merely waiting for proper management. Aided by sprawling data networks, real-time analytics, AI, and the vast machinery of digital life, contemporary politics has become a cutting-edge laboratory of human reflex. As the human sensorium becomes an ever more urgent site of competition (taking place almost always beyond the ken of the public), the politics of reflex threaten to have dramatic and often unrealized consequences for the future of democratic practice. Modernism, this book will show, invented ways of mediating, explaining, and answering the prescribed tracks of action demanded of mass modernity. As contemporary institutional forces vie to record, analyze, and nudge human behavior for political and commercial gain, this grammar stands as the first and most substantial body of thinking about the collective consequences of reflex. The political and aesthetic categories of modernism are, in this sense, probably more necessary to contemporary political life than ever.

The politics of reflex were not created out of whole cloth in the opening decades of the twentieth century. They were the outgrowth of diverse intellectual currents that reached maturity as the First World War was ignited. Chapter one traces these currents and their arrival on the shores of literary modernism. Sketching the philosophical and practical preoccupation with embodiment, reflex, and automaticity from the Enlightenment to the modernist era, this chapter shows how the science of reflex surfaced long-standing, unresolved anxieties about the role of rationality and agency in human affairs. These concerns would be taken up by an array of nineteenth-century empirical thinkers who saw reflex as crucial to political life—a trend that would find its culmination in the research of scientists like Ivan Pavlov and John B. Watson. Their work represents a distillation of thinking about automaticity, but cognate attitudes about reflex were simultaneously animating experts from across the political spectrum. Automaticity represented a problem for Enlightenment philosophers, but for capitalists and socialists alike, studies of reflex offered to solve an array of modern problems, including matters of industrial production, consumer desires, and the manufacture of political consent. For modernist writers, too, the science of reflex had profound implications. Just as twentieth-century fields like sociology, pragmatism, and public relations placed reflex behaviors at the center of mass society, modernists and their critical peers believed that literature had the power to both intervene and participate in the politics of reflex. Whether these writers understood themselves as critics of this new political reality or participants who worked to shape the automatic behavior of reading subjects, in all cases they used discourses of reflex to forge literary forms that responded to the political realities of twentieth-century life. Both mirroring and contesting major disciplinary engagements with reflex, modernism offered readers the ability to see themselves within a new kind of political sphere, one that sought to produce order out of the chaos of modernity by leveraging the innate automatisms of bodily life.

The remaining chapters focus on specific modernist writers, but each places literature in conversation with the principal disciplines and cultural fields within the politics of reflex. By foregrounding the institutional and disciplinary contexts of modernism, I map some of the major lines of debate—both theoretical and practical—that underpinned the politics of reflex. These disciplines offer valuable context for understanding modernists' own efforts to interpret the changing nature of political life and to situate their own endeavors within it. Even as most of the authors I examine here come from

England and Ireland, I focus on writers whose concerns reflect the depth and diversity of engagements with the politics of reflex within the modernist era as a whole. In each case, these authors forged literary works that mirrored or responded to their disciplinary contemporaries in illuminating ways. This process of selection has meant that some modernists whose aesthetics are important to the politics of rupture but stand outside of a larger network of disciplinary concerns—particularly avant-garde figures like Brecht—have been omitted. By the same token, while the philosophy of pragmatism appears throughout this book as one among a variety of disciplines within the politics of reflex, I have largely ignored writers like Proust, Henry James, and Gertrude Stein for whom pragmatism motivated aesthetic experiments.[14] I have instead highlighted authors who shared pragmatists' optimism about the virtues of automaticity in the modern world but did so with a more robust attention to the specifically political valences of reflex.

The chapters of this book are arranged with an eye toward understanding how the science of reflex generated dispute across fields of inquiry. For example, while vitalist philosophy (the topic of chapter one) offered a thoroughgoing critique of the science of reflex, contemporaries in a burgeoning field known as public relations (the topic of chapter two) were all too eager to take advantage of human automatism. Modernists themselves participated in these debates, often assailing each other's analyses of reflex and countering with their own. While these chapters do not adhere to a strictly dialectical rhythm, I have endeavored to show how questions about reflex and mass life preoccupied modernists and their contemporaries, generating a multifaceted cultural conversation about the role of agency and rationality within an automatic age.

Chapter two, "Vibrant Bodies, Automatic Minds," explores one of the earliest and most tenacious reactions to the science of reflex—the philosophy of vitalism. Though it was rooted in earlier Enlightenment theories, this philosophy was principally shaped by dissatisfaction with ascendant models of human automatism that Henri Bergson called "radical mechanism." Rejecting ideas of automatism advanced by physiologists, Bergson and his followers argued that the material body exhibited a deep intransigence to the total domination of physical stimuli. By investing organic matter with creative potentiality, they attempted to excavate conceptual space for individual agency without recourse to outmoded notions of a transcendental ego or the determinisms of positivist thought. This philosophy took on a strongly political dimension in the writings of Georges Sorel, whose *Reflections on*

Violence (1908) made its way into modernist circles through translation by British critic and poet T. E. Hulme in 1915. Drawn to the critique of positivism, Sorel extended Bergson's understanding of spontaneity into the political realm by theorizing its role in modern mass movements. This attempt to counter the politics of reflex was to find an echo in the writings of D. H. Lawrence, whose work persistently takes aim at the collusion of science and the institutions of modern life. Because mass society treats the human as an "automaton working in certain automatic ways when you touch certain springs," Lawrence argued that it engendered socially orthodox reflexes that undermined people's genuine individuality.[15] But rather than insisting on the free agency of individual minds, Lawrence echoed vitalists in placing the material body at the center of his vision of better collectives. Looking at his nonfiction works of the 1920s, as well as both late and early novels, I argue that Lawrence's thinking mirrors Bergson's and Sorel's ideas of material spontaneity and presents a literary version of vitalist politics. This analysis centers on Lawrence's much-neglected late novel *The Plumed Serpent* (1926), which rehabilitates the role of bodies in political life by employing formal qualities drawn from vitalist discourse. Affirming the centrality of the material body while simultaneously rejecting materialist doctrine, Lawrence's vitalism threads a conceptual needle that would continue to inform modernist reactions to the politics of reflex.

If "radical mechanism" threatened to make the twentieth century intellectually sterile and, as Lawrence averred, politically complicit, public relations is in many ways its institutional antithesis. The American behavioral psychologist John B. Watson maintained that the progress of science would allow psychologists to not just map the human machine but manipulate and control it. Such control was the very project of public relations. Born of First World War propaganda efforts and rooted in the physiology of conditioned reflex, public relations became by the late 1920s an industry intent on deploying the lessons of behaviorism for concrete political ends. Chapter three, "Public Reflex: Wyndham Lewis, Public Relations, and the Invisible Government," examines the role of PR within the politics of reflex and situates its impact on the culture of modernism. Though PR was originally an American product, it was to have a pronounced influence on the thinking of British intellectuals in the 1920s, including pioneers at the BBC and within the burgeoning British Documentary Film Movement. Drawing on the writings of PR experts like Walter Lippmann and Edward Bernays as well as their British followers, I argue that Wyndham Lewis's work offers a stinging rebuke of how this emerging industry skewed values of individual creativity while forestalling the possibility of political dissent. Lewis's work consistently diagnoses the effect of "publicity" in producing political and intellectual habits, with Bergson, Sorel, and Lawrence representing the worst of the early twentieth-century's faux rebellions. But his work speaks to a much larger frame than vitalism alone. Reading Lewis's novels and nonfiction—including *The Art of Being Ruled* (1926), *Time and Western Man* (1927), and *The Childermass* (1928)—I show that Lewis's work mirrors in formal terms the vision of mass modernity propounded by PR experts. Bernays claimed that public relations experts constituted the "invisible government" of the twentieth century. I argue that Lewis's interwar work formally mediates the covert manipulation of behavior by mass "manipulators."[16] While critics have often seen Lewis's opus in terms of political paranoia, I see a literary project firmly rooted in a prescient understanding of how the politics of reflex were finding footing in institutions that would endure long beyond the modernist era.

In vitalism and public relations we encounter two of the era's most significant disciplinary engagements with the politics of reflex. Though they represent opposite sides of the political spectrum—vitalism *opposing* theories of human automatism, and PR *employing* them—these fields were equally indebted to physiologists and psychologists who promised to map the human machine. Chapter four looks directly at the most notorious of these early twentieth-century scientific thinkers, Ivan Pavlov. Despite his own conservative politics, Pavlov's proximity to the Bolshevik revolution informed the reception of his work among laypeople abroad, who commonly associated conditioned reflexes with ideological indoctrination. Indeed, the very name Pavlov would become synonymous with the political techniques of totalitarianism and "brainwashing." Aldous Huxley placed "Pavlovian" conditioning at the center of his 1932 novel *Brave New World*, where individual agency and collective identity are centrally orchestrated by political elites. Yet, whereas writers like Lewis, Lawrence, and others understood conditioned reflex as an affront to individual volition, other modernists saw Pavlov's research as a solution to the weakening of collective tradition. I look in particular at the work of Rebecca West, a writer who viewed Pavlov's theories as a scientific extension of literary modernism's own concerns. Focusing on her ambitious, multigeneric work, *Black Lamb and Grey Falcon* (1941), this chapter suggests that West employed the language of reflex to both diagnose the sterile politics of fascism *and* to make an argument for the importance of British nationalism. For West, the nation is a kind of reflex community—an assemblage of individuals whose shared environment endows them with collective behaviors. In *Three Guineas*, Virginia Woolf asserted that it would take an epic of "ten or fifteen volumes" to adequately address the effects of atmosphere on "solid bodies."[17] I suggest that in *Black Lamb* West attempted precisely this epic. Extending her interest in Pavlov to her defense of nationalism in *Black Lamb*, West models in formal terms how environments preserve the collective reflexes of the nation amid the centrifugal forces of modernization.

The idea that a shared milieu engenders the reflexes of national communities was to have lasting value to West, who continued to explore related issues after the war. The idea, however, was not exclusively her own. Though she was unaware of it, a similar discussion was then underway in sociology, another discipline entrenched in the politics of reflex. While early sociologists like Max Weber and Émile Durkheim explicitly ceded the discipline's early interest in habit to thinkers like Pavlov and Watson, sociologists of the 1930s returned to these ideas to examine the role of automatic behaviors in collective life. In his 1939 study, *The Civilizing Process*, the German sociologist Norbert Elias suggested that mass modernity entailed a more refined system of political conditioning than any previous era, leading to "a higher degree of automaticity" in citizens.[18] In making this analysis, Elias was perhaps more in line with late modernist writers than West herself. Chapter five explores the convergence between late modernist ideas of reflex and the sociological discourse of "habitus." Informed by an interest in reflex psychology and behaviorism, Samuel Beckett's novelistic work characterizes twentieth-century life in ways consonant with earlier modernists—as an era in which automatic behaviors came to dominate social life. But Beckett's work also pursues the political and narrative entailments occasioned by these higher degrees of automaticity. Sociologists like Elias suggested that our political reflexes are so pervasive and seemingly natural that they often defy conscious apprehension. Starting with *Murphy* (1938) and culminating in *The Unnamable* (1953), Beckett's novels mediate those political dispositions that inhere in automatic behaviors and thus dwell below the threshold of conscious apprehension. In pursuing this aspect of automaticity, I show, Beckett's novels followed the course set by earlier modernists but also exhaust some of modernism's efforts to find solutions to the politics of reflex. But the same cannot be said of his dramatic work. Indeed, by midcentury he would come to share ground with those writers and thinkers who understood habitual behaviors as necessary to survival in a hostile and contingent cosmos.

Beckett's appreciation for habit in his later work reflects an important trend in the culture at large, which at midcentury started to lose interest in the political liabilities of embodiment. In key intellectual movements of the second half of the century, thinkers established the preeminence of categories like "discourse" and "information" without undue concern about their mediation through physical bodies. When reflex does appear in the cultural record of the postmodern era, it typically does so either within established generic conventions of the dystopia, or in efforts to explain the behavior of cult members and terrorists as "programmed" or "brainwashed."[19] But thinking about reflex in these terms misses the endurance of the fundamental insights into human behavior enabled by the science of reflex. The modernist era's sustained inquiry into bodily susceptibility may have seemed outdated in some quarters by midcentury, but it also birthed a number of industries that we take for granted today, including political industries that touch all of us in ways we are rarely capable of fully grasping.

What began in the modernist era as a crude attempt to map the human machine has become in our age a highly refined, multifaceted set of institutions that work to understand our behaviors as consumers and voters, and to subtly shape them without our knowledge. Producing behaviors that do not require our conscious deliberation, we could say, has become *the* major technology of twenty-first century politics, particularly as the media ecology of the internet and social networks has produced troves of data about how we perform as consumers, readers, and voters. In an afterword, I consider some of the ways that the politics of reflex manifest today, particularly in the use of behavioristic models in elections, statecraft, and advertising. Researchers and new media industries have gone several steps beyond the work of Pavlov and Watson by mapping exactly what kind of stimuli will most reliably produce effects desired by paying clients. While such efforts are not always partisan in nature, they reflect a commonly understood facet of modern democratic practice, namely that it takes very little to "nudge" people to behave in specific ways. This understanding of human susceptibility is so pervasive today that we rarely register the ways in which our behaviors are sounded and actuated by the digital architecture of our lives. Communication technologies, including major companies like Google and Facebook, depend more than ever on their ability to record our behaviors and monetize their future, processes that occur almost always without our knowledge. And while the economic imperative to herd and condition citizens has come to dominate many institutions that we interact with on a daily basis, we have almost no critical vocabulary for describing what, a hundred years ago, modernists recognized as historically novel.

Reading this volume returns us to the moment when knowledge about human susceptibility became widely available for the first time. Theories of bodily susceptibility touched the period in ways that were far-reaching, mandating new forms of disciplinary knowledge that in many cases reflected modernists' own concerns. The writers under examination here collectively developed a grammar for understanding the role of reflex in mass society. For them, the body was central to modern life, but then, as now, it occupied an ambiguous place. Modernist writers responded to the politics of reflex in myriad ways—often as critics, but also by appropriating physiological knowledge to theorize their own answers to the problems of mass modernity. Neither a literature intent on rupturing the automatisms of perception, nor a literature that mindlessly celebrated them, modernism was our culture's first attempt to reckon with a modern world that exploits the fact that we are less autonomous than we sometimes like to imagine.

1 Automatic Man

A Genealogy

In 1921, the Czech playwright Karel Čapek debuted his play, *R.U.R. (Rossum's Universal Robots)*. Set on a factory-island where humanoid machines are manufactured, the play imagines a future in which human labor has been almost entirely replaced by mechanical men. Over the course of the play, spectators learn about the effect of these machines on the global economy and witness an uprising against their frail human masters. Rehearsing themes about the rights of workers, the degradations of modern labor, and the usurpation of godly powers, the play was an immediate hit. Within two years of its initial performance, *R.U.R.* would be translated into thirty languages and see performances in London, New York, Chicago, and Los Angeles, while the figure at the center of the play—the "robot"—would find its way into dozens of languages. As compelling as Čapek's play was in its imagination of modern industry, contemporaries were arguably more captivated by its evocation of the thin line between the machine and the denizens of modernity. As soon as "robot" entered the English language, it became shorthand for describing citizens stripped of agency and dependent on rote behaviors of all kinds. By the early 1920s, modernist writers were complaining bitterly about the "robots" they encountered—in capitalist America, in communist Russia, and in individualistic societies where they should have been out of place.[1] While the robot proved to be a remarkably flexible figure, it was far from unusual. The cultural life of the twentieth century was saturated by visions of citizens behaving in mindless ways. Images of automatic behaviors—whether in the marketplace or at the ballot box, on the assembly line or on the front line—are part and parcel of diverse representations of mass modernity. Puppets, marionettes, hollow men, and automata of all sorts populated the cultural imagination of the modernist era, providing literary and rhetorical resources for a century anxious about agency and autonomy, particularly in the political realm. While these robots and mechanical men may have been at home in mass society, they were not, in fact, native to the twentieth century. They were the product of a long intellectual tradition in philosophy and the sciences, one that began at the outset of the Enlightenment.

Throughout the eighteenth and nineteenth centuries, all philosophical and scientific debates about automatic behaviors took place in reference to a single, original articulation of such concerns in the philosophy of René Descartes. In an effort to affirm the priority of human reason in *Discourse on Method* (1637), Descartes drew a strict line between human beings and the animal world on the basis of materiality. Arguing that animals are pure matter and devoid of souls, Descartes likened them to the "automata, or moving machines fabricated by human industry."[2] This was an important point for Descartes because by partitioning humans and beasts, he was able to elevate human rationality as the preeminent faculty of the creature made in God's image. Yet for later philosophers, Descartes's equation between animal life and machinery endangered the mind/body dualism upon which his philosophy had been founded. As Daniel Cottom has noted, what was important about Descartes's thought was not the implication that *animals* were machines, but "the evident failure in Descartes's attempt to forbid the image of the machine, once it was identified with animals and the workings of bodies, from trespassing into the image of human nature proper."[3] Though largely committed to human rationality, European thought following Descartes remained dogged by a body that seemed not only to transmit physical stimuli to the mind, but which often behaved independent of consciousness itself.

Descartes's assertion that animals were automata is an oft-cited source for later concerns with human "automatism," a term not coined until the 1830s.[4] Yet, in some ways, it was Descartes's interest in reflex that would have an even more pronounced influence on the history of science. In his posthumously published *Treatise of Man* (1662), he established the principal terms upon which physiological inquiry would proceed in the following two centuries by theorizing the transmission of stimuli within the body and our ability to respond to it without thinking. Inspired by the hydraulically animated statues he had seen as a child in the royal gardens at Saint-Germain-en-Laye, Descartes suggested that the involuntary action of humans and the behavior of all animals could be systematically understood through the work of nerves and "animal spirits." As Robert Boakes explains, "Descartes' idea was that when some sensory organ is excited by some external stimulus . . . delicate threads contained within the nerves are moved. The threads are attached to valves within the brain and such movement leads to the release of animal spirits, which pass through the nerves to appropriate muscles."[5] So, when we get too close to fire, for example, our sensory organs communicate that stimuli to the brain, which in turn communicates it to our muscles, causing us to withdraw from the fire before we have even thought to do so. This circuit of stimuli would later be termed "the reflex arc" by nineteenth-century physiologists, who refined Descartes's basic model of the nervous system.

Descartes's work in this area helped lay the foundation for eighteenth-century philosophers, many of whom suspected that the automaticity of the body might have a more significant role in human affairs than previously understood. Julien Offray de la Mettrie, for example, examined the effects of bodily experience, including the effects of alcohol and caffeine, on the mind; in so doing, he pushed Descartes's theory to its materialist extreme. In his 1748 book, *Man a Machine*, he affirmed Descartes's analysis of animals as automata, but agitated for including humans in this category as well. Inspired by eighteenth-century "androids"—mechanical figures that could do all manner of ostensibly human activities, such as play music, draw pictures, and even defecate—he posited that even the "higher" capacities of human life, such as learning, might be grounded in bodily reflex.[6] This account would be echoed by David Hartley, whose *Observations on Man, His Fame, His Duty and His Expectations* (1749) not only rejected the Cartesian split between humans and animal automata, but suggested that all ideas and mental activity were grounded in the automaticity of the nervous system. In his account, learned habits held the same status as the unlearned reflexes of the body, with reflexes establishing the necessary conditions for agency itself. For example, he suggested that while a child will initially reflexively grasp an object placed in its hand, in time repetition allows the child to associate this stimulus (and related stimuli, such as spoken language) with the action. A *will* to grasp thus emerges from what was originally an unwilled, reflex behavior.

In the case of both Hartley and de la Mettrie, we can see the logical progression of Descartes's model of the nervous system. Despite his efforts to cordon off the higher centers of the rational mind from the material world, the mind was incapable of remaining autonomous from the body. As Ruth Leys explains, though Descartes's "dualism fixed definite boundaries to a purely mechanistic biology," with the "growth of science the success of the experimental method, those limits were increasingly challenged by the view that *all* aspects of behavior were to be understood in mechanical terms."[7] This would become particularly apparent in the nineteenth century, as physiologists produced new experimental methods to test Descartes's hypotheses. One of the problems with Descartes's original theory was the importance he placed on the brain as a conduit for transmitting stimuli. Already in the seventeenth century, it was widely known that some animals will continue to respond to stimuli even after decerebration or decapitation. How could this be if the brain mediates reflexes? By the start of the nineteenth century, the Scottish physiologists Charles Bell and the French physiologist François Magendie independently demonstrated the role of the spinal cord in the nervous system, including its role in mediating specific kinds of involuntary actions. Importantly, they demonstrated that nerve fibers split into posterior and anterior roots along the spinal cord, and that posterior roots perform a sensory function and anterior roots a motor one. In 1833, the English physiologist Marshall Hall for the first time named "the reflex arc" and confirmed the importance of spinal marrow in sensory and motor nerves. By 1850, the German physiologist Hermann von Helmholtz was able to measure the speed of neural transmission. Along with German physiologists Johannes Müller, Carl Ludwig, and Emil du Bois-Reymond, Helmholtz not only affirmed the mechanistic parameters theorized by Descartes but helped establish an experimental agenda for the discipline that would prove to have important consequences for the fledging discipline of psychology.

The step from a physiology of reflex to a psychology of reflex proved to be a short one in spite of the fixed boundary Descartes instituted between body and mind. Thinkers like Hartley had understood the connection between bodily reflex and the automatism of the mind already in the eighteenth century, but it would take a full hundred years for scientists to move from theoretical speculation to practical experimentation. Such experiments were to be found across the discipline of physiology in the latter half of the nineteenth century, but it was perhaps the Russian physiologist Ivan Sechenov who offered the most sustained study of reflex as a cognitive phenomenon. Sechenov was a product of the best physiological education nineteenth-century Europe had to offer, studying in Germany with Ludwig, du Bois-Reymond, and Helmholtz, and, later, with Claude Bernard in Paris. His studies of reflex built on the findings of Eduard Weber, who in 1845 had demonstrated that certain kinds of stimuli could actually slow the operation of reflexes. Whereas physiologists had largely thought of stimuli in terms of "excitatory effects," these "inhibitory effects" helped physiologists construct a more complete model of the nervous system, in which some stimuli need not originate outside of the body. This distinction was crucial because it offered a bridge from the mechanistic body to the mind itself. It was now possible to see all human behavior—both private and public—under the rubric of reflex action. The result was a slim volume titled *Reflexes of the Brain* (1866), which not only made the case for a fully materialist model of the psyche but also laid out the social consequences that follow from understanding the role of environment in producing patterns of thought and action. As Sechenov saw it, the study of reflex would lead to man's liberation, releasing "him from the mental bonds that allowed a stiflingly repressive form of society to continue."[8] These ideas would become key to later theories of mass modernity that emphasized the role of the automaticity of citizens and would influence some of the most significant twentieth-century figures in the history of reflex, such as Ivan Pavlov.

This narrow history of reflex's development might suggest that attempts to understand human behavior in mechanical terms were a dominant concern of the sciences from Descartes until the twentieth century. However, the study of reflex stood in sharp contrast to traditions of thought that employed speculative reasoning about the nature of life over experimental methods of analysis—currents later energized by the politics of reflex in the twentieth century, as we will see in chapter two.[9] Indeed, it was only in the latter half of the nineteenth century that these ideas about reflex became anything like a scientific paradigm. In the 1890s, the editors of *The American Journal of Psychology* had to wonder why it was that "the simple rubric of reflexion, which now explains so much, was not suggested by the phenomena so often observed before the second quarter of our own century."[10] After the middle of the nineteenth century, not only did physiological concern with reflex enter into psychological and philosophical debate, but it began to spill over into a diverse array of disciplines and cultural fields as well.

Outside of the laboratory, reflex was endowed with social implications that it had to that point lacked, challenging traditional Enlightenment values of rationality, agency, and autonomy. While thinkers like Darwin had shown the importance of a physical environment in the development of *species*, the physiological tradition suggested environments might play a determinative role in forming *individuals*. For this reason, a large amount of cultural production in the latter half of the nineteenth century concerned itself with milieu. Inaugurated by Newton to explain the interaction between physical bodies separated by distance, "milieu" originally referred to the medium in which bodies are situated, and which functions as an intermediary between them—media such as water, air, or light. In the nineteenth century, writers began to think of milieu not simply as a physical medium, but as a cultural one as well. But this shift also occasioned a reorganization of the values attributed to a milieu. For Darwin, the relationship between an organism and its environment was largely reciprocal, defined by harmony and mutual conditioning. But as "milieu" became a useful way of thinking about an individual's relationship to society, this equanimity was replaced by a sense of the individual's insignificance amid a welter of stimuli. In this context, as Georges Canguilhem explains, "milieu becomes a universal instrument of the dissolution of individualized organic synthesis in the anonymity of elements and universal movements."[11] Far from affirming the autonomy of subjects from the material world, nineteenth-century thinkers often looked at subjects as the direct products, and even victims, of the environments they inhabited—creatures animated less by volition than by their environment.

The sociological implications of physiological research were to reach fruition in French letters by the latter half of the nineteenth century, particularly in literary naturalism. For French writers like Balzac and Zola, studies of milieu mandated a new orientation toward foundational literary categories like character. The Romantic individual—autonomous from the influence of social context, capable of forming himself—was simply incompatible with what contemporary science said about agency. As Zola explained in his 1868 preface to *Thérèse Raquin* (1867), he chose "protagonists who were supremely dominated by their nerves and their blood, deprived of free will and drawn into every action of their lives by the predetermined lot of their flesh."[12] A new sense of literary character would require dispensing with Enlightenment values in favor of automaticity. "The metaphysical man is dead," Zola exclaimed in "The Experimental Novel" (1880). "Our whole territory is transformed by the advent of the physiological man."[13] This note would be picked up by American naturalist writers like Jack London, Frank Norris, Stephen Crane, and Theodore Dreiser, among others, who emphasized an anti-humanistic aesthetic of determinism.[14] French naturalists saw milieu as a key to understanding human behavior in general. Illuminate the salient features of a milieu and you could explain the mechanism of society itself, they reasoned.

These impulses were registered equally in the British literary context.

George Eliot's approach to the novel form, for example, drew on the materialist sciences (including the work of Darwin, Herbert Spencer, and George Henry Lewes), as well as the proto-sociological theories of milieu propounded by Auguste Comte, whom she translated. Though she avoided the strict determinisms of later French writers, Eliot registered an early awareness of how physiology was undermining liberal conceptions of individuality grounded in rationality and agency. Her novels not only stress the placement of characters within larger social and material contexts—lives "woven and interwoven" in "this particular web," as she writes in *Middlemarch*—but they often prioritize the body at the expense of rational agency in much the same way her contemporaries in physiology did.[15] As Darwin's theories of physical adaptation gained a wide audience in the latter half of the nineteenth century, many Victorian intellectuals came to think of life itself as a process defined by the exchange between organisms and their environments. For some, an understanding of the susceptibility of bodies to their environments mandated rethinking the grand forces of populations, evolutionary phenomena, and the determining forces of social institutions. Herbert Spencer, for example, integrated evolutionary theories of material adaptation with a concern for social institutions, arguing that domesticity, religion, and economics are products of social intercourse and themselves form a social milieu that sediments ways of thinking and doing. Writing at the end of the Victorian period, Thomas Hardy would synthesize many of these ideas, particularly in his late fictions like *Tess of the d'Urbervilles* and *Jude the Obscure*, where social environments take on the power that Darwin imputed to natural ones. At the mercy of their social milieu, Hardy's characters often prove unable to adapt to the rapid transformations of a rising modernity and meet the ends suited for the least fit in the population.

Though not a precise analogue to French naturalism, the works of Eliot, Hardy, and their scientific contemporaries represent a Victorian mindset that increasingly understood the social implications of reflex, which was slowly eroding Enlightenment notions of individual sovereignty. As we will see, for twentieth-century writers these terms would become keywords for modernity itself, as the interface between bodies and environments took on a manifestly political dimension. Nineteenth-century writers, for their part, were somewhat ahead of what researchers were able to demonstrate about the role of automatic behaviors in social life. But in so doing, they were merely following the metaphors that physiologists themselves employed to describe human behavior. As the study of reflex developed, physiologists came to think of the human mind as a kind of recording instrument. For example, in *The Nature of Mind and Human Automatism* (1885), the American physician Morton Prince explained that "we are automata" and that "our mental processes are automatic" in the sense that "our thoughts, sensations, volitions, and actions follow in certain grooves or channels."[16] Much as a phonograph produces sound by following the grooves etched on a wax cylinder, human thought and action was understood to be constrained by the reflex arcs imprinted by our environments. This metaphor—which, as we will see, informed Rebecca West's analysis of fascism in *Black Lamb and Grey Falcon*—suggested that not only does the mind "record" sensory data in cognitive channels but that everyday life witnesses the re-inscription and reproduction of that data in the form of cognitive reflexes and behavioral habits. Robert Michael Brain has suggested that physiologists originally employed the mind-as-phonograph metaphor to study evolutionary phenomena, especially the body "as a matrix of surfaces upon which impulses were received from the milieu and stored in tissues as organic memory."[17] Physiologists like Étienne-Jules Marey in France and Michael Foster in England would later develop this perspective, seeing the human organism "in mechanical terms, emphasizing physiological functions and iterative habitual actions as the key features of life."[18] So strong was the conceptual link between the phonograph and studies of human automatism that Thomas Edison appended T. H. Huxley's 1874 essay "On the Hypothesis that Animals Are Automata, and Its History" to his first publication on the phonograph in 1878. The implication of such metaphors was that human belief and action were regular *and* that they were reproducible. Engineer a milieu and social reformers, educators, politicians, and businessmen could impress upon an entire populace the reflexes and habits most suitable to their aims—the "prescribed tracks" that Wyndham Lewis warned about in *Time and Western Man*.

Even without the specialized knowledge of physiology, the political implications of reflex were hard to miss. Working in the late nineteenth and early twentieth centuries, Russian physiologist Ivan Pavlov was instrumental in bridging the gap between politics and strictly scientific analyses of human automatism. An accomplished researcher of bodily automatisms (for which he won a Nobel Prize in 1904), Pavlov was inspired by Sechenov's *Reflexes of the Brain* to study the link between psychic and physical reflexes beginning around the turn of the century. As is well known, Pavlov was able to demonstrate that he could induce salivation in dogs, but more significantly, that arbitrary signals like lights and bells would produce the same results as the introduction of objects into the dogs' mouths. Pavlov, in effect, produced a well-tested theory of the mechanisms and environmental triggers of reflex behavior, what he called "conditioned reflex." In his early studies of salivation, Pavlov showed restraint in applying his findings to human life. But as his fame rose in the opening decades of the century, he began to suggest the utility of conditioned reflex in the political realm. As Pavlov saw it, the organized study of reflex behaviors offered an avenue for solving some of the largest challenges to modern life. In the preface to his *Lectures on Conditioned Reflexes* (1928) he explained, "Only science, exact science about human nature itself, and the most sincere approach to it by the aid of the omnipotent scientific method, will deliver man from his present gloom, and will purge him from his contemporary shame in the sphere of interhuman relations."[19] The "present gloom" of "interhuman relations" could encompass a vast array of distinctly modern phenomena, including relations between classes and genders, or those between nation and nation. In time, he asserted, the science of reflex would yield "incalculable advantages and extraordinary control over human behaviour."[20]

In principle, Pavlovian physiology offered the ability to mold habits of thought and action through regimes of conditioned reflex—a power that would appear variously utopian or dystopian in the opening decades of the century. As we will see in chapter four, by the Second World War many commentators asserted a direct link between the manufacture of consent in totalitarian countries and the work of the Russian scientist, an association that would be firmly cemented by American Cold War anxieties about "brainwashing" in the 1950s. However, it was not Pavlov whose work most strongly highlighted the political utility of reflex but his American follower, John B. Watson. Drawing on Pavlov's findings, Watson elaborated a new school of physio-psychological research that he termed "behaviorism." Eschewing psychologies that emphasized the nonobservable phenomena of consciousness, Watson hoped to rehabilitate psychology as an empirical science, one rooted in new experimental methods for studying the role of reflex in the life of the mind. This ambition, however, quickly turned into dogma about the nature of human behavior itself. The effort to restrict psychology to discernible behaviors and habit formation soon evolved into a belief that *all* behavior was the manifestation of an inherent human automatism. According to Watson, the entire ensemble of human belief and action—from simple forms of instinctual behavior like blinking, to the most complex emotions of love and

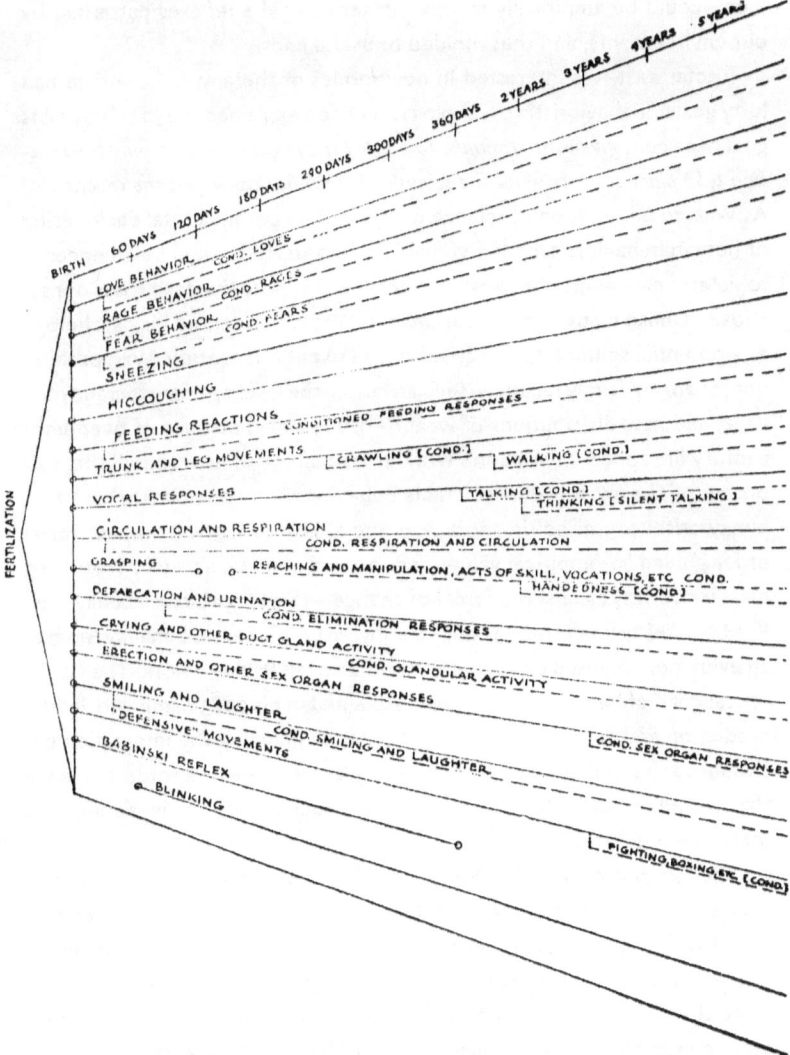

Watson's "The Activity Stream" illustrates the gradual accretion of reflex behaviors in the individual, building from less complex, unlearned ones (such as "feeding reactions" and "smiling and laughter") to more complexly conditioned reflexes necessary to society (including "thinking" and "fighting"). Watson, *Behaviorism*, 106 hate—could be empirically mapped in terms of the reflexes patterned by our environments, and thus molded to useful ends.

Insofar as it was interested in new modes of therapy, behaviorism had lofty goals. "Behavioristic psychology," Watson explained in 1924, "has as its goal *to be able, given the stimulus, to predict the response—or, seeing the reaction take place to state what the stimulus is that has called out the reaction.*"[21] As Watson understood it, science would in time permit a total deciphering of human behavior; each individual life, he asserted, could be engineered to determinate ends, or reverse engineered to expose the deep roots of psychoses. Unlike many of his predecessors, Watson presented his psychology as a potential solution to the crises of the twentieth century. War, prohibition, changing family relations, secularization, the leveling of aristocratic privilege, and new distributions of wealth—these signal features of twentieth-century life appear in Watson's work as an anarchy of new stimuli that had prompted the entirely unpredictable behavior of modern citizenries. What behaviorism promised, in short, was the ability to fabricate a new social order guided by empirical values and rational control, a way of stabilizing mass modernity against the forces of change—what the Harvard behaviorist R. M. Yerkes termed "human engineering."[22] In this sense, behaviorism had an even more pointed political register than even Pavlov's work. The "theoretical goal" of behaviorism, Watson explained in his 1913 manifesto, is "the prediction and control of behavior."[23] By fully mapping the interaction between bodies and their environments, Watson hoped to forge a science that would be useful to educators, jurists, sociologists, businessmen, and (of course) politicians.

Though Watson was likely unaware of it, the problems raised by industrial modernization had already called forth new political techniques that meant to manipulate the reflexes of the populace. The physiological model of the human subject, already theorized by the late nineteenth century, entered the cultural and political lexicon of the early twentieth century in diverse cultural fields, laying the groundwork for a politics geared toward the automaticity of citizens. Henceforth, "environment" would come to be the domain of political life—a way of shaping self and community amid the dislocations of mass modernity.

Everything Is Politics: Reflex and Mass Modernity

The implication of research conducted by thinkers like Pavlov and Watson was far-reaching. "Stimuli" encompassed a wide array of phenomena, including the information communicated by both the physical and cultural spaces we inhabit. And everything, they suggested, leaves a mark on us. What we read, what we hear on the radio, the education we receive, the norms of behavior that surround us, and even those elements of culture that we do not consciously record—these have as much of a physical effect on us as the lights and bells of Pavlov's laboratory. Indeed, it is perhaps those things that we most take for granted and that are most deeply ingrained as default habits of conduct that shape our sense of the world. The ego, once understood as autonomous from the world, was subject to perpetual and unending bombardment from all quarters. And the will, that metaphysical quality of self-actualization, was left aside as a notion of little practical value to the young century.

What gave these discussions a wide appeal in the twentieth century was not their scientific force, per se, but their utility within a rapidly changing political sphere. Amid mass enfranchisement, the rise of new media technologies, and the disintegration of long-standing political institutions, studies of reflex behavior found a receptive audience among writers and thinkers in their attempts to work the levers of the human machine. As the science of reflex eroded traditional Enlightenment emphases on rationality and agency, it precipitated a reevaluation of liberal democratic values and the notion of a "popular will." If our thoughts and actions are largely the product of the ways we have been conditioned by our environments, as Watson averred, the job of politics was not to *convince* citizens to vote or consume in particular ways; it was to create the conditions in which citizens would do so automatically, in response to a milieu acting upon them. In *Crisis of Parliamentary Democracy* (1923), the German jurist Carl Schmitt argued that within a liberal political order, "politics" is not a competition for the will of the people but rather a competition for "control over the means with which the will of the people is to be constructed."[24] Constructing political will is, of course, the explicit aim of propaganda; as we will see in chapter three, this field emerged from studies of reflex after the First World War and became a crucial context for modernism's own engagements with the politics of reflex. But shaping popular will could take many forms. Political theorists of the era believed ideological values could be rendered automatic by the material practices of everyday life. In this context, politics became linked to stimuli of all kinds—linked, indeed, to the totality of social institutions, cultural practices, and habits that constitute everyday life. When Wyndham Lewis argues in *Time and Western Man* that "much more has been put into 'politics' than the European of a hundred years ago would have considered appropriate to that term," he signaled an awareness of a shift in twentieth-century life.[25] "Politics," in effect, had infected "everyday life" at its roots, where it threatened to condition belief and behavior in determinate ways.

Perhaps the most famous example of this new understanding of political will came from Antonio Gramsci. His notion of "cultural hegemony," elaborated between 1929 and 1935, is symptomatic of a changing understanding of politics, one geared toward categories of reflex and automaticity rather than agency and rationality. Seeking to move beyond entrenched Marxist notions about the inexorable laws of historical necessity, Gramsci recognized that achieving a socialist revolution within modern nation-states would require more than just educating citizens about the economic conditions of capitalism. Instead, he believed that politics entailed the creation of "even physically new types of humanity" through the total work of a cultural environment.[26] The state could transform citizens through institutions like the law and education, but hegemony meant making political values so deeply engrained in citizens' worldviews that they would be second nature. The particular mechanism for forging these values was not the traditional domain of politics, but the transformation of social milieu itself. As he explained, "Every man, in as much as he is active, i.e. living, contributes to modifying the social environment in which he develops . . . in other words, he tends to establish 'norms,' rules of living and of behaviour."[27] These behaviors constitute for Gramsci key elements of a cultural environment, which along with institutions of power, normalize values and create "new subjects."[28] Like Watson, who argued that all domains of life enforce cognitive reflexes, Gramsci understood milieu as *the* domain of politics. In this sense, socialist strategy had already discovered what physiologists like Pavlov had attempted to show in their labs—that environment conditions action, and that reflex plays a more significant role in political life than the individual will does. Notably, however, Gramsci's major influence in conceiving politics in this way came not from physiology, but rather from another field, one actively involved in the politics of reflex: industry.

Engaging the writings of American industrial pioneer Frederick Winslow Taylor, Gramsci argued that earlier notions about the formation of subjects were mistaken. Socialists like Trotsky had insisted that society, like a factory, requires discipline, and that the "principle of coercion, direct or indirect, in the ordering of production and work" would lead to a fully realized socialist society.[29] Gramsci, on the other hand, argued that discipline was liable to impede the very unity of thought and action it sought to create. Taylor's system of "scientific management" presented a better model, one that sought to develop in the worker "the highest degree automatic and mechanical attitudes."[30] The work of Taylor and Henry Ford is well known for attempting to "rationalize" production by economizing the motions of workers; by reducing labor to its constituent parts, they helped usher in a new era of industrial efficiency. So influential was their thinking about the physical economies of labor that the assembly line would become a central trope for mass modernity's dependence on automatic behaviors. Yet it would be easy to overstate the centrality of the assembly line to the politics of reflex. Minsoo Kang, for example, has argued that labor regimes of the period were *the* source of twentieth-century anxieties about human automatism, with the machine standing as "the inexorable and destructive force of modernity itself."[31] But the importance of scientific management ultimately relied not simply on its efforts to turn workers into physical automata, but to translate the principle of reflex to society as a whole. Taylor himself objected to the idea that scientific management makes the worker "a mere automaton, a wooden man," as he wrote in *Principles of Scientific Management* (1919). But it is no exaggeration to say that industrialists saw the automaton as something like a model citizen, at least among the working classes.[32] Beyond economizing physical motions, scientific management sought to make the conditions of a hierarchical class society *themselves* automatic. As experts in the emerging field of industrial psychology understood, scientific management was as much about creating political efficiencies outside of the factory as it was about creating physical ones on the assembly line.[33]

For Gramsci, the language of automatism was at the center of an altogether new understanding of politics. Drawing on what he called the "psychophysical" model of humanity employed by Taylor, Gramsci provided a framework for how cultural hegemony might work—the creation of new citizens not through discipline but through the work of culture in its most manifold forms.[34] Just as Lewis worried about the "much more" that had been injected into twentieth-century politics, Gramsci argued that all elements of culture—labor, institutions, media, norms—conspire to create in citizens the reflexes and attitudes of collective life. As he candidly put it in *The Prison Notebooks*, "everything is 'politics.'"[35] If Gramsci's theory of hegemony seems familiar to readers today, it is not due solely to its subsequent influence on critical theory. That Gramsci used the language of reflex to articulate a theory of political life suggests just how widely such concepts were circulating in the early twentieth century. Indeed, the idea of physiological conditioning as a way of creating behaviors and social attitudes transcended national contexts and ideological divides. At the same time that Gramsci, a Marxist, was filling up notebooks in an Italian jail cell, a decidedly capitalist theory of political reflex was emerging in full force in the United States, where experts were attempting to program the human automaton to conform to the demands of democratic society.

Just two years after Gramsci was arrested by Fascists in Italy, Edward Bernays, Sigmund Freud's American nephew, offered a cognate theory of how the science of reflex might be deployed in the realm of politics. In his 1928 book, *Propaganda*, Bernays outlined the nature and tactics of the public relations industry, a field that saw in a modern mass media the power to create beneficial reflexes in citizens. This industry, which emerged from Bernays's experience as a pioneer of propaganda techniques during the First World War, drew directly on Pavlov's theory of conditioned reflex to conceptualize citizens in terms of automaticity. As Bernays explained, because populations are affected by the stimuli of their environment, the collective "will" is something that can be molded, shaped, and even manufactured. *Propaganda* begins by making the same argument as Schmitt—that fabricating political will is the lifeblood of modern democracies. Bernays writes, "The conscious and intelligent manipulation of the organized habits and opinions of the masses is an important element in democratic society. Those who manipulate this unseen mechanism of society constitute an invisible government which is the true ruling power of our country."[36] Bernays believed that by strategically saturating the cultural milieu, PR experts could mobilize an inherent human automatism and shape citizens' habits to socially beneficial effect. In this respect, Bernays shared Gramsci's sense that politics should be conceived of in terms of conditioned behaviors. But for each thinker, the appeal of reflex lay specifically in its promise to help control the most unpredictable elements of mass society. While Gramsci looked to scientific management's attempt to rationalize production, Bernays hoped PR would be able to control that other facet of the modern economy—consumption. Although consumer tastes are by definition fickle, Bernays suspected that consumer "choices" could be effectively manipulated to bring supply and demand into harmony. By employing new technologies like the radio and the cinema, as well as established cultural institutions, public relations experts could effectively condition the reflexes of consumers in predictable ways. As he imagined the problem, producing such reflexes was simply a matter of knowing how to manipulate the human machine: "Touch a nerve at a sensitive spot and you get an automatic response from certain specific members of the organism."[37] But as Bernays would go on to suggest, PR promised to do much more than simply boost or control consumption; such techniques could be used to make specific kinds of *political* values automatic as well. Indeed, while Bernays achieved considerable notoriety as a corporate strategist, his skills were equally in demand in the political sphere. He is credited with single-handedly breaking the taboo on women's smoking in public (a corporate campaign for Lucky Strikes), as well as manufacturing public enthusiasm for the overthrow of a democratically elected government of Guatemala in 1954.[38] "Public relations," as he self-consciously termed his brand of political engineering, could in principle create public "will" for any kind of political ideology, given the right circumstances. All that was needed was a thorough understanding of which "nerves" to touch.

Gramsci and Bernays make for an unlikely fraternity of political theorists given their opposing ideological orientations. Yet, public relations and hegemony are two sides of the same historical coin—ideas that emerged concurrently to describe the task of adapting citizens and consumers to the necessities of mass society through an inherent human automatism. And in both cases, we can glimpse an understanding of something lost in many critical appraisals of the historical period that birthed literary modernism, namely the power of the unconscious as something rooted in the body. Though we tend to think of the unconscious primarily in reference to Freudian psychology, the unconscious grew out of diverse disciplines in the nineteenth century that emphasized the primacy of physical embodiment.[39] Douglas Mao has noted that in the half century prior to the First World War, "the unconscious covered a much wider range of elusive phenomena" than the Freudian unconscious, "including the unwilled operations by which we synthesize sense data into meaningful forms, the knowledge that we seem to store even while sleeping or thinking of other things, the cognitive operations that transpire away from the light of consciousness, the capacities that our bodies develop without explicit direction, and the neurophysiological changes that subtend experience and the evolution of personality."[40] Theories of a physical unconscious collided in the twentieth century with understandings of mass society as a welter of new stimuli. Georg Simmel, for example, regarded the twentieth century as unprecedented in the sheer bombardment it visited upon the human organism. While in "Metropolis and Mental Life" (1903) he wrote about "the swift and continuous shift of external and internal stimuli" of urban experience that threatened to desiccate individuality, not all commentators saw the stimuli of mass society in just this way.[41] Indeed, scientific currents at the turn of the century suggested just the opposite—the ease with which we are capable of synthesizing sensory data through the ordinary functions of the nervous system. By the twentieth century, physiologists like Pavlov and Watson were attempting to show how our bodies process information and provide us with the behavioral and cognitive reflexes that allow us to easily inhabit even the most "modern" of environments. The result of inquiry about reflex was not to fret for the individual who might be incapable of processing the deluge of stimuli that modern life entailed, but rather to stress that individuals were all too capable of processing these stimuli without conscious effort. As Gramsci and Bernays understood, the most effective way of achieving political aims was not to transform the ideologies that we consciously adhere to, but to touch that deeper, more fundamental part of us that exists below the threshold—the political unconscious, as it were. Here, the physical body's registration of cultural stimuli could produce efficiencies—cognitive and behavioral reflexes that were more reliable and effective than conscious belief alone.

In this context, categories of agency and rationality were shown to occupy a much less important role in political life than Enlightenment thinkers had imagined. But even more importantly for modernist writers, these understandings of the body and the unconscious posed difficult problems given the ongoing structural transformations of mass society. Bureaucratization, corporatization, the modernization of communication and transport, and the birth of a new mass media in their various ways presented new opportunities to shape the reflexes of citizens. Moreover, public relations specialists like Bernays could utilize these structures to influence citizens from a position of relative anonymity. As the seemingly unmasterable sprawl of the modern world obscured the human agents behind efforts to engineer political behaviors, citizens could almost never be certain that their actions were the products of their own conscious decision. The inability to fully distinguish automatic behaviors from agential ones, the unconscious from the conscious, often resulted in paranoia about the ability of ordinary people to make rational, autonomous decisions. However, if paranoia can be thought of as something like a constitutive affect of mass modernity, it represents just one consequence of the politics of reflex. Discourses of reflex acquired currency in the modernist period because they helped explain how the human organism might respond to the new conditions of modernity—whether for good or for ill. Behavioral psychology, the pragmatism of William James and John Dewey, the cinema of Chaplin, early documentary film, Henri Bergson's vitalist philosophy, studies of the mass media, the industrial psychology of Hugo Münsterberg and Elton Mayo, the sociology of Émile Durkheim, Max Weber, Norbert Elias, and Marcel Mauss: these represent only a fraction of the fields and disciplines that engaged studies of reflex in the first half of the twentieth century. These fields individually participated in the politics of reflex, either as practitioners (like Gramsci and Bernays), or as fields for which the political conditions of the period demanded new modes of knowledge. As we will see, in some cases debates about reflex frame automatic behaviors as a potential solution to the problems of mass modernity, while others balked at the loss of autonomy that the science of reflex implied. Whether these fields related to the politics of reflex as critics, enthusiasts, or detached observers, they collectively yoked images of automaticity to mass modernity and created conditions of cultural production in which categories of reflex were to play a central part.

Automatic behaviors are, by definition, those that do not require conscious thought. Literary modernism named mass modernity as the moment in history in which reflex behaviors became central to public life, bringing back in to consciousness those habits of thought and action that the architects of modern life worked so assiduously to produce. For modernist writers, the politics of reflex would become a key determinant for thinking about the goals of a genuinely new form of literature. Placing reflex at the center of modern life, they understood literature as a way of participating in a political sphere where bodily automatisms held new sway. Whether as critics or participants, modernists emphasized reflex as a feature of twentieth-century politics that presented distinct challenges to individual and collective life.

Modernism and the Dog Vomit

In 1931, when he was still several years away from publishing his first novel, a young Samuel Beckett wrote an extended essay on Marcel Proust. Focusing on memory and involuntariness in À la recherche du temps perdu, Beckett offered a philosophical analysis of habit that anticipated some of the major themes and formal concerns of his subsequent career while memorably articulating a common modernist perspective on automatic behaviors. Noting that automatic behaviors in Proust provide characters with a sense of existential balance, Beckett describes habit as a "compromise effected between the individual and his environment."[42] By regularizing our thoughts and our behaviors, he explains, habit allows us to endure the constant onslaught of sensory stimuli without being overwhelmed or forced to negotiate every common action anew. However useful this involuntary process is for Proust's characters, Beckett saw a more nefarious aspect to it since habit provides us with "a dull inviolability" to the world. In a memorable passage, he describes habit as the execrable condition of life: "Habit is the ballast that chains the dog to his vomit."[43] In lieu of Proust's model of useful habits, Beckett yearned for a mode of perception in which habits would be stripped away and "the boredom of living [would be] replaced by the suffering of being."[44] Though the rupture of habit exposes us to experience that is "dangerous, precarious, painful, [and] mysterious," the fall of habit replaces the vegetative "living" for the agonies and glories of "being." In the rupture of habit, every faculty is freed of atrophy, and the self is made vital again.

Beckett's description of habit could easily be taken as typical of modernist attitudes toward automatic behaviors of all kinds. As Lisi Schoenbach has demonstrated, the early twentieth century often coded "habit" as the historical baggage that "must be violently scarified in order for modernity to emerge," a mode of perception inhibiting the emergence of the new.[45] Beckett's emphasis on "being" would thus seem to fit in to this larger narrative, one that links modernism to the avant-garde and its aesthetics of shock. Part of the reason that this narrative, however flawed, became a part of the critical tradition of modernism has to do with the ambiguity of the word "habit" itself.[46] Though "reflex" and "habit" describe different phenomena, writers of the period readily collapsed the social economies of the latter into the neurological economies of the former. As we will see in chapter five, the ambiguity between these categories—already troubled by Watson's and Pavlov's research—would become a flashpoint in early sociology, as figures like Weber and Durkheim attempted to draw strict disciplinary boundaries around the fledgling discipline. Even when modernist writers used these terms interchangeably, they often did so with a robust awareness of ongoing arguments about reflex in the sciences, as was the case for writers like Lawrence, Beckett, and West. In this respect, modernist writers were in sync with early twentieth-century literary criticism, a field deeply enmeshed in the politics of reflex. For many literary critics of the period, the science of reflex augured a mass society deeply in need of the kinds of existential awakening that Beckett described—deliverance from the reflexes of thought engendered by mass culture at large.

Russian Formalism presents one of the best examples of the critical animus against reflex within early twentieth-century literary studies. In his 1917 essay, "Art as Technique," Viktor Shklovsky articulated a central doctrine of Russian Formalism—that genuine art "defamiliarizes" or "estranges" perception, delivering readers from the diurnal flattening of experience. The Formalist idiom of defamiliarization would go on to become so commonplace within the critical history of the twentieth century that its roots in the politics of reflex are easily forgotten. When Shklovsky wrote that art breaks "the automatism of perception," he directly invoked a physiological discourse that he and his collaborators had derived from Herbert Spencer's 1852 essay, "The Philosophy of Style."[47] Spencer's essay had attempted to outline a "general theory of [linguistic] expression" grounded in a model of cognitive and corporeal economy.[48] Arguing that the mind, like the body, inherently desires to conserve its energy, Spencer reasoned that linguistic style is always most powerful when it "economizes" the reader or listener's attention. He writes, "Regarding language we may say that, as in a mechanical apparatus, the more simple and the better arranged in its parts, the greater will be the effect produced."[49]

Shklovsky and his Formalist colleagues appropriated the language of physiological economy from Spencer but rejected the notion that art works best when it finds the path of least cognitive resistance. According to Shklovsky, the trademark of art is that it inhibits reflex. He explains, "The author's purpose is to create the vision which results from that deautomatized perception. A work is created 'artistically' so that its perception is impeded and the greatest possible effect is produced through the slowness of the perception."[50] According to the Formalist paradigm, art does not economize perception; it hinders it, stretches it out, and forces us to contend with it. It breaks our cognitive habits, allowing us to renew our perception of the phenomenal world. This understanding of literature as a check against reflex squares with many other modernist-era critical schools, though on the eve of the Russian Revolution, Formalists were anxious to avoid the sociological or political concerns that had dominated Russian literary criticism up to that point.[51] Indeed, the fact that Shklovsky looked to Victorian England in his citation of Spencer rather than Pavlov, his contemporary and countryman, was likely part of his effort to launder defamiliarization of political overtones. However careful Formalists were to avoid the appearance of politics, their signature concept, like the movement itself, was politically charged from the beginning. As critics like Fredric Jameson have noted, political ideologies depend on habits of perception: destroy perceptual foundations, and ideologies crumble as well.[52]

The purchase of reflex within Formalism is not a quirk of literary history. For modernist writers, the science of reflex provided a major intellectual framework for understanding the nature and problems of political modernity. In Beckett, for example, reflex and modern politics were always mutually entangled, a realization that emerged from his own study of materialist philosophy in the early 1930s, including the work of Pavlov and Watson. His emphasis on habit and reflex as *political* categories found a near analogue in British literary critics of the era, for whom (unlike Russian Formalists) the science of reflex provided a diagnostic lexicon of mass society. For F. R. Leavis, reflex stood as a political problem that required new forms of education. In their 1933 book, *Culture and Environment*, Leavis and Denys Thompson cast mass culture as a force that tended "to discourage all but the most shallow and immediate interests, the most superficial, automatic and cheap mental and emotional responses."[53] According to their view, the new "mass" media was an unprecedented phenomenon because it was capable of conditioning thought and action at scale, creating new tastes and values without impinging upon the consciousness of citizens. Thus, newspapers, film, and the wireless flatten cognition, causing citizens to "surrender, under conditions of hypnotic receptivity, to the cheapest emotional appeals," as Leavis argued in "Mass Civilisation and Minority Culture" (1930). All these media tend "to make . . . active use of the mind, more difficult"—to enforce an economy of perception.[54] Leavis's characterization of mass culture as a realm of economized perceptions, behavioral clichés, and cognitive reflexes was one that broadly populated the modernist period. As we will see, the growth of a mass media raised a particularly vexing problem for analysts of democracy, like the American writer Walter Lippmann, who saw the susceptibility of bodies to stimuli as a gateway to a public sphere in which conditioned reflexes dominated. Thinkers in other national contexts concurred. In *Escape from Freedom* (1941), the German philosopher Erich Fromm would attempt to diagnose an "atmosphere of subtle suggestion" that "pervades our whole social life," resulting in what he regarded as political "automatism."[55] Norbert Elias, a fellow Jewish refugee from Germany, offered a similar account in *The Civilizing Process* (1939), where he suggested that the twentieth century had led to "a higher degree of automaticity" than any previous era.[56] Like Leavis, these writers worried about the ways in which mass society played on the susceptibility of bodies and enforced reflexes at odds with democratic notions of rationality, agency, and individuality, creating what Leavis and Thompson called the "standardization of persons."[57]

Tellingly, Leavis was not the only cultural critic to situate literature within a public sphere increasingly ruled by reflex. British New Critics C. K. Ogden and I. A. Richards were steeped in a tradition of thinking about bodily reflex, which broadly informed their understanding of language, culture, and politics. Richards's work, for example, was directly influenced by Watson's *Behaviorism*, a text which he not only reviewed in *The New Criterion* in 1926 but which proved central to the creation of the techniques of "close reading." As Joshua Gang has demonstrated, works like *Principles of Literary Criticism* (1924) and *Practical Criticism* (1929) "present us with a translation of Watson's behaviorism into a protocol for reading literature."[58] Like Leavis, Richards worried that the environment of mass society mandated ever more reflexive behaviors that emptied life of its "fullness." In *Practical Criticism*, he acknowledged that the "stock responses" and "mental habits" of everyday life are at some level "necessary," but suggested that they pose a problem because they make for "a population easy to control by suggestion."[59] In the context of a mass media, he writes, "our performances, both as speakers (or writers) and listeners (or readers), are worse than those of persons of similar natural ability, leisure and reflection a few generations ago," a threat that will "only grow greater as world communications, through the wireless and otherwise, improve."[60] Literature enters here precisely because it promises to disrupt the "mental habits" and economies of perception promulgated by the environment of mass society. Richards writes:

> Nearly all good poetry is disconcerting, for a moment at least, when we first see it for what it is. Some dear habit has to be abandoned if we are to follow it. Going forwards we are likely to find that other habitual responses, not directly concerned, seem less satisfactory. In the turmoil of disturbed routines that may ensue, the mind's hold on actuality is tested. Great poetry, indeed, is not so safe a toy as the conventional view supposes. But these indirect effects of the overthrow of even a few stock attitudes and ideas is the hope of those who think humanity may venture to improve itself. And the belief that—on the whole and accidents apart—finer, subtler, more appropriate responses are more efficient, economical, and advantageous than crude ones, is the best ground for a moderate optimism that the world-picture presents.[61]

Richards's emphasis on the ability of literature to "overthrow" the "stock attitudes" engendered by the environment of mass society presents a politicized equivalent of Formalist ideas, one that echoed some of Leavis's own thinking. What is significant about figures like Richards, Leavis, and Shklovsky is that, despite their many ideological and methodological differences, each drew on the discourse of reflex to articulate the potential of literature to intervene in a society threatened by automatic behaviors. Engaging directly with the science of reflex, they collectively forged literary critical methodologies opposed to habit and reflex. In this way, Russian Formalism, New Criticism, and other early twentieth-century literary critical endeavors helped substantiate a narrative of literary modernism that rhymed with the thinking of writers like Beckett, who saw automaticity as the dog vomit of modern life.

However, not all modernists were swayed by efforts to paint the automaticity of the twentieth century in negative terms. Even a critic like Leavis, who broadly assailed the role of reflex in mass life, saw virtue in at least some kinds of habits.[62] Indeed, many saw automatic behaviors as crucially important to successfully navigating the politics of mass society. Pragmatism is perhaps the most significant intellectual field to occupy this position. For William James and John Dewey, the science of reflex suggested that habit was simply part of the biological makeup of humans, one that was necessary to everyday life. As Lisi Schoenbach has argued, "Pragmatism saw habit as constitutive of—and utterly necessary to—thought and social behavior."[63] For James, our ability to complete ordinary, routine tasks without conscious effort is a great aid because it allows our minds to focus on other, more important tasks. In contrast to literary critics of the modernist era, pragmatism focuses on the cultivation of economies of perception—the social necessity of *fostering* cognitive habits. In *Principles of Psychology*, James explains, "The great thing, then, in all education, is to *make our nervous system our ally instead of our enemy. . . . For this we must make automatic and habitual, as early as possible, as many useful actions as we can.*"[64] Unlike many fields of the era, pragmatism rejected the strict binary between reflex and agency, suggesting that some forms of habit may actually allow us to exercise better agency. But pragmatism was also one of the first disciplines to make explicit the connection between habit and politics. Already in 1890, James could write about habit as a major force in the sustenance of political ideologies. In a memorable passage, he explained:

> Habit is thus the enormous fly-wheel of society, its most precious conservative agent. It alone is what keeps us all within the bounds of ordinance, and saves the children of fortune from the envious uprisings of the poor. It alone prevents the hardest and most repulsive walks of life from being deserted by those brought up to tread therein. It keeps the fisherman and the deck-hand at sea through the winter; it holds the miner in his darkness, and nails the countryman to his log-cabin and his lonely farm through all the months of snow; it protects us from invasion by the natives of the desert and the frozen zone.... It keeps different social strata from mixing.[65]

When James claims that "the more of the details of our daily life we can hand over to the effortless custody of automatism, the more our higher powers of mind will be set free for their own proper work," it is easy to think of these automatisms as the mundane details of everyday life. The ability to, say, brush one's teeth or lock one's door without overt cognitive effort becomes, in his account, a marker of habit's preeminent value—a kind of naturalized economy of attention. But such economies are always subtended by ideological habits as well, he implies. Our social reflexes conserve society and fend off the agents of change. If for Beckett habit is the ballast that chains the dog to his vomit, for James it is the ballast of social existence; habit keeps the native population at bay, restrains the envious poor, and ensures that workers continue their thankless task. Habit is a kind of "insurance against the inevitable crises modernity will bring," Schoenbach writes, even if those crises may be politically desirable.[66] These habits may need to be ruptured, but for James they also have a political value because they prevent mass society from disintegrating into chaos. As in Bosanquet's analysis of automatism, James's pragmatism understood automatic behaviors as a way of maintaining an equilibrium amid the social tumult of economic modernization. For modernist writers, this dynamic between habit and its rupture would prove attractive, furnishing the intellectual foundation of aesthetic experimentation for numerous writers, including Gertrude Stein.[67]

What these liaisons between modernism and the discourses of reflex tell us is just how important such ideas were in attempts to understand the brave new world of mass society. However ambivalent modernists may have been about the politics of reflex, what is clear is that they were almost universally convinced of the claims of figures like Watson and Pavlov. Even when they lacked direct engagement with these thinkers, they saw susceptibility to our environments as constituting a new and important way of understanding public life. The figure of the robot may have generated vastly different responses, but all understood its diagnostic appeal. As the coming chapters demonstrate, modernist writers often depicted the modern world as one populated by automata, people whose autonomy and agency had been corrupted through regimes of conditioning, whether orchestrated or organic. While some saw ways of negotiating the problems inherent in human automatisms, others worked to fathom and undermine the institutions of reflex altogether. Taken as a whole, these responses to the politics of reflex represent a significant record of the entailments of human automatism *and* of potential responses to it. As we will see, modernist responses to the politics of reflex quite often founder; they veer into authoritarian thinking, nationalist thinking, paranoia, and the like. But these failures are also generative. In a world where our habits and reflexes are recorded and managed millions of times a day by the very architecture of our lives, understanding these successes and failures may allow us to better respond to the politics of reflex of our own century.

2 Vibrant Bodies, Automatic Minds
Vitalism, D. H. Lawrence, and the Politics of Spontaneity

By the start of the twentieth century, the doctrine of human automatism had settled into something like an orthodoxy. In the late nineteenth century, scientists in diverse national contexts had advanced theories of human behavior in which our thoughts, actions, and feelings are all dependent on the materiality of bodily life. Yet, throughout these debates, little consensus emerged about the philosophical conclusions to be drawn from such issues. Do the material economies of our bodies necessarily delimit freedom, or does consciousness somehow exceed gross matter? Does our susceptibility to our environment mean we lack agency, or does our freedom exist apart from the mechanisms of the body? These philosophical questions would be set aside by the early twentieth century, with scientists increasingly willing to treat the material bases of consciousness as established fact. In his 1905 book, *The Eternal Life*, industrial psychologist Hugo Münsterberg wrote that science is "not a mass of disconnected information, but the certainty that there is no change in this universe, no motion of an atom, and no sensation in a consciousness, which does not come and go absolutely in accordance with natural laws,—the certainty that nothing can exist outside of the gigantic mechanism of causes and effects. Necessity moves the stars in the sky, and necessity moves the emotions in my mind."[1] Münsterberg, who had joined the faculty at Harvard in 1892 and would later become president of the American Psychological Association, here expressed a view that was no longer controversial—that what we are, what we think, and what we feel are merely the manifestation of grand, material forces. Just as Enlightenment thinkers like Newton imagined the universe as a clockwork mechanism, Münsterberg and his peers saw consciousness as the product of "the gigantic mechanism of causes of effects" at work. Setting aside speculative questions about agency and free will, psychologists focused instead on solving the real-world problems of industry, domestic life, law, and much more. If thought and emotions are entirely the product of material processes, psychologists like Münsterberg proposed to be the mechanics of the new century, fine-tuning the machine to work at its highest, most efficient pitch.

But every dogma has its apostates, and by the early twentieth century a broad philosophical reaction against the doctrine of human automatism was beginning to consolidate in Europe and the United States in the form of vitalist philosophy. Building on earlier critiques of Enlightenment empiricism, twentieth-century vitalists broadly rejected orthodox views about the role of material forces in prompting human behavior. As Sanford Schwartz explains, "Whereas the positivist applies the mechanistic assumptions of the physical sciences to the study of human thought, feeling, and action, the vitalist maintains that the organic nature of 'life' is irreducible to mechanistic explanation, and that the methods appropriate to the investigation of the physical world lead only to a distorted understanding of human nature."[2] This mode of philosophical inquiry played a steady if latent role in most Enlightenment philosophy, but with the coterminous consolidation of mass society and mechanistic theory, vitalism became an influential force within American and European thought. By the first decade of the twentieth century, the work of Henri Bergson, Georges Sorel, and others would offer a robust answer to the philosophical and political entailments of materialism, becoming one of the most significant and popular interventions in the politics of reflex.

This chapter attempts to understand the role that vitalist thought played within the politics of reflex, particularly the convergence between early philosophers and writers who sought to escape the deterministic society that materialist theory augured. Vitalists like Bergson and Sorel played an important part in modernist culture by inventing a diagnostic vocabulary for the politics of reflex, one that saw materialist science as a dangerous force in promoting the reflexes of mass life. Their work found a large audience among early twentieth-century intellectuals, including modernists who gravitated toward their analysis of an automatic society and the scientific currents that animated it. But vitalism also gained adherents before the flourishing of those industries that would capitalize on materialist accounts of human behavior, like public relations. For this reason, while vitalist thinkers shared with later writers a concern about the role of reflex in mass life, they tended to associate automaticity with the unchecked operations of the mind, not with the mindless operation of the body. This critique of the intellect was central to vitalism's critical agenda as well as its reparative emphasis on the body, spontaneity, and intuition—elements that would be echoed in modernism's own response to the politics of reflex. I focus here on D. H. Lawrence, whose work represents an unusually strong (though rarely noted) form of vitalism.[3] For Lawrence, as for many other vitalists, the problem with materialist science was not that it laid bare the susceptibility of human bodies to conditioning, but rather that it taught people to see themselves as the dead matter of a material universe. Throughout his fiction and nonfiction, Lawrence drew on the imagery of the human automaton to diagnose the pernicious political consequences of materialist thought as an ideology that inhibits our spontaneity. But his work also shares with vitalism its reparative agenda, promoting the virtues of intuition and spontaneity as political alternatives to the rational, mind-driven, and automatic modes of social experience demanded by mass modernity.

In asserting the virtues of bodily spontaneity, Lawrence was in good company among his modernist peers, including the British poet and critic, T. E. Hulme. Described by Eliot as "the forerunner of a new attitude of mind," and by Wyndham Lewis as "one of the most promising intelligences produced by England," Hulme was an early champion of vitalism, which he helped spread throughout modernist circles via his translation of Bergson's *Introduction to Metaphysics* (1903, translated in 1912) and Sorel's *Reflections on Violence* (1908, translated in 1914).[4] Though Hulme would later disavow vitalism, his exegesis of Bergson proved immensely influential in poetic circles because it provided a way of understanding literary form's role in advancing a vitalist politics. As I will show, Lawrence's novels develop a vitalist understanding of literary form that closely resembles Hulme and Bergson's analysis of language and consciousness. Eschewing the intellect (or what he called "idealism") in favor of spontaneity, Lawrence attempted to imagine literary and political solutions to the routinizing forces of mass modernity. I focus in particular on his late novel, *The Plumed Serpent*, which depicts a political revolution grounded in vitalist principles of spontaneity. Understanding this neglected novel as the culmination of Lawrence's vitalism, I return to some of his earlier novels to uncover a vitalist current that runs throughout his oeuvre.

In vitalist philosophy and its literary extensions, we encounter some of the most robust critiques of the science of reflex and the institutions it enabled. Vitalism, and Bergson in particular, commanded adherents across every corner of the educated public in the early twentieth century. While we can think of vitalism as one of the most significant ripostes to an ascendant understanding of human automatism, it is important to note that vitalism was not successful in vitiating materialist science or overthrowing its political institutions. By the time Lawrence died in 1930, vitalist ideas had found fertile ground among some whose politics harmonized with the politics of reflex, including fascists. In Lawrence's own writing we can see how the desire to contest a culture of automaticity led him to ideas that, in retrospect, have an unmistakably fascist character. In this way, Lawrence's career demonstrates one of the tensions in vitalism as a response to the politics of reflex. While its celebration of the body, intuition, and spontaneity proved influential in both political and literary circles, vitalist thought shifted definitions of agency and the value of the intellect in ways that threatened the very political values that it sought to defend.

Vitalism, Intuition, and the Reflex of Ideas

At no point during the Enlightenment did strict materialism enjoy uncontested rule. For every model of the cosmos founded on brute materiality and fixed, mathematical rule, another proclaimed the higher law of the numinous, unknowable spirit. Twentieth-century vitalism is, in this sense, a latecomer to a much longer history of anti-empirical or spiritualist thought that arose in response to the Enlightenment. But Bergson and his followers enjoyed far more popularity than any of their predecessors because of the historical context in which they worked. Much of intellectual life at the end of the nineteenth century employed and propounded mechanistic models of organic life. In Darwin's evolutionary theory, readers encountered a model that treated species as the strict product of a given environment, while psychologists elaborated theories of mind that emphasized bodily susceptibility to material stimuli. In this intellectual climate, vitalism gained traction among those who feared that modern institutions promoted the ready-made, the habitual, and the reflexive at the expense of originality, creativity, and dynamism. But vitalism did more than simply diagnose the political and spiritual consequences of materialist science; it provided a solution to the problem of reflex by redefining life, agency, and intuition in ways that promised to revivify a social order that demanded automaticity from citizens.

Bergson's critique of determinism, or what in *Creative Evolution* (1907) he called "radical mechanism," took many forms over the course of his career, spanning issues of psychological materialism and agency in *Time and Free Will* (1889), perception in *Matter and Memory* (1896), and species in *Creative*

Evolution (1907).⁵ He was broadly guided by a belief in the intellectual superficiality of materialist theory and its deleterious effects on people. In lieu of "the gigantic mechanism of causes and effects" promoted by Münsterberg and his peers, Bergson outlined a philosophy that championed the flux of experience and the virtues of intuition over the intellect. Central to this philosophy was a critical analysis of the intellectual habits of materialist science. Rather than see humans as developing and behaving spontaneously, the sciences freeze dynamic processes to understand them, "spatializing" phenomena. As a result of this method, the body is always treated by materialists as a static system and the foundation of an inherent human automatism. For Bergson, the body, like all organic life, develops and behaves according to laws that cannot be known in advance. Life entails a "continual change of aspect" and "the irreversibility of the order of phenomena," meaning that we can neither deduce the origins nor the future of vital phenomena.⁶ Yet, everywhere Bergson looked he saw reigning intellectual paradigms treating life as a static object rather than one immersed in the unforeseeable flow of time. In *Creative Evolution* he cast a critical eye on evolutionary theory, which, he asserted, sees the growth of species as a static, material process. He writes, "It may perhaps be said that the form [of the species] could be foreseen if we could know, in all their details, the conditions under which it will be produced."⁷ In reality, however, science cannot see all of these conditions because the most important ones are perpetually coming into being. Life develops creatively and unpredictably, according to Bergson.⁸ The conditions of evolution, he explains, "are built up into it [the form of an organism] and are part and parcel of its being; they are peculiar to that phase of its history in which life finds itself at the moment of producing the form."⁹ Evolutionary theory is just one of many sciences that Bergson accused of "spatializing" temporal processes. Fields like psychology, for example, turn the intensive world of mind into an extensive object of analysis. For Bergson, life "is no more made of physico-chemical elements than a curve is composed of straight lines."¹⁰

This critique of materialism, it should be noted, was not an effort to undermine the validity of the sciences. Grounded in his own extensive training in physics and mathematics, Bergson affirmed the empirical tradition while asserting the rights of a vitalist one. As Mary Ann Gillies writes, Bergson "hoped to find a way of wedding the two and thereby allowing philosophy, and other intellectual endeavours, to mirror what the ordinary individual's common sense said: that the world consists of physical and spiritual aspects that necessarily work in consort to define human beings and their existence."[11] But even when Bergson affirmed the empirical tradition, his critique centered on its intellectual entailments—the "scientific habits" of thought that creep into every facet of modern life. These habits, he insists, invite us to view ourselves as part of "the vortex of things" rather than as a manifestation of the living universe.[12] Materialism lures us into the logic of cause and effect, such that the human is reduced to a mere "machine that works automatically," which "is no longer life" at all, but rather "an automatism."[13] T. E. Hulme stated the philosophical entailments even more forcefully. In his essay "Notes on Bergson," Hulme comments: "If you accept the mechanistic view of the world, not only does all freedom disappear from the material world, but also from the organic. The world is pictured as a mass of atoms and molecules, which are supposed to carry out unceasingly movements of every kind. The matter of which our bodies are composed is subject to the same laws as the matter outside. The motion of every atom of your brain is, then, subject to the same laws of motion as those which govern all matter."[14] Any "candid examination of one's own mind" demonstrates that such theories have "an irresistible hold over" us, Hulme writes; we are "compelled to submit" to a framework that vacates all volition, creativity, and dynamism. The things that most distinguish us as humans—consciousness and free will—are rendered meaningless. "Consciousness, then, does nothing; it makes no difference," Hulme writes.[15] To adopt the materialist perspective is not, as Münsterberg might have thought, to master consciousness and the physical world that constitutes it. Instead, such a perspective asserts that all consciousness and every action we take is a product of our materiality; even our values, the ostensible bedrock of the self, are little more than the contingencies of material forces. We are, in short, nothing more than what we have been conditioned to be—human automata obeying the demands of the material world. This, of course, is precisely the argument that John Watson would begin to make just prior to the First World War, and which would become a central conceit of the politics of reflex. Vitalist philosophers like Bergson understood the appeal of these "scientific habits" and worried over the consequences that materialist doctrine would have on the culture at large.

Part of Bergson's appeal to audiences was his ability to bring this high-level critique of materialism to bear on everyday life, particularly what he called "the easy automatism of acquired habits."[16] His philosophy harmonized with major critical currents within the culture of modernism, positioning him as *the* major philosopher of the era. In England alone, "Bergsonism" became an "epidemic," as T. S. Eliot wrote in 1932.[17] Eliot had himself moved to Paris in 1910, "motivated in large part by his desire to hear Bergson's celebrated lectures in person," and "declared himself a Bergsonian" through the middle of the teens, as Omri Moses notes.[18] Eliot's interest in Bergson and vitalist philosophy was entirely representative of the moment. *Time and Free Will*, *Matter and Memory*, and *Creative Evolution* all appeared in English around 1910, occasioning an avalanche of popular and scholarly writing about vitalism, with some two hundred articles on Bergson appearing between 1909 and 1911, just as he would begin lecturing to large audiences in London and Oxford. By the second decade of the twentieth century, Bergson's name was well known to a vast swath of the literate public, with modernist writers counting among some of his most prominent supporters. Scholars have noted the influence of Bergson on dozens of modernists, including the likes of Gertrude Stein, G. B. Shaw, Woolf, Joyce, Dorothy Richardson, Joseph Conrad, Wallace Stevens, Faulkner, and Proust, among many others in the literary and artistic world.[19] For these writers and others, Bergson's appeal lay in his ability to diagnose the spiritual consequences of materialist thought, and to imagine ways of escaping them. In his ideas of memory, duration, and the plenitude of a dynamic self, Bergson offered a conceptual framework that acknowledged science's limitations in explaining life. These signature concepts had such a profound appeal during the period that they can plausibly explain an array of modernist formal and thematic preoccupations, including concerns with memory, time, and consciousness.[20]

Of particular importance to writers was Bergson's analysis of intuition and the intellect, a binary useful in theorizing the proper ambitions of modernist literature. Throughout his opus, Bergson criticized the sciences for their "spatializing" tendencies—the effort to reify the dynamic processes in order to understand them. But as early as *Time and Free Will*, Bergson began to suggest that such tendencies were not exclusively a problem of the sciences but rather endemic to the intellect itself. In the conclusion to *Time and Free Will*, he made this connection explicit. Arguing that consciousness is homogenous and not composed of discrete units, he suggests that our intellect is driven by a need to understand *durée* in spatial terms, separating "psychic states . . . from each other."[21] If analyzed by the intellect, these separations are codified and obstruct our agency: "Between our ideas, thus crystallized, and our external movements we shall witness permanent associations being formed; and little by little, as our consciousness thus imitates the process by which nervous matter procures reflex actions, automatism will cover over freedom."[22] The mind, in its efforts to understand the world, necessarily treats dynamic processes as though they were static. And as we grow accustomed to seeing the world in these rational, mechanical terms, we ourselves become automata. As Paul Douglass summarizes, "Intellect renders things static, and unintentionally abolishes freedom by reducing fluid experience to snapshots and the richness of memory to automatic responses."[23] The mind, long understood to be the seat of human freedom, was now reduced by Bergson to its very opposite, the defining feature of an age of automaticity. This analysis of the intellect would go on to become a major element within Bergson's evolving philosophy as well as one of its most complicated legacies in twentieth-century politics.

The diagnostic vocabulary of vitalism—particularly its emphasis on the automatism of the intellect—was undoubtedly crucial to the successes of Bergson's philosophy. But this critique demanded a reparative agenda, as well, one that would allow subjects to understand action in terms that resisted the emphasis laid on rational agency in the liberal tradition—an alternative Bergson found in intuition. If the intellect "replace[s] the stream of immediate experience with a network of stable and useful concepts," Sanford Schwartz explains, intuition "reverses the habitual tendency of the mind to simplify and in a sense distort reality, and enables us to apprehend the object as it really is."[24] By approaching an object intuitively rather than intellectually, we are, Bergson asserted, able to understand it as it is in time, rather than as a fixed, spatialized concept. Intuition is a form of knowledge that inverts how the mind "habitually thinks," allowing us to understand the *living* world.[25] In *Introduction to Metaphysics*, intuition is limited to a philosophical activity that offers modes of knowing that are different in kind than those of the sciences. But intuition also has the virtue of opening up forms of agency that rationality inhibits. As the intelligence spatializes, it channels us into the grooves of thought and action, whereas intuition enables spontaneity, invention, and freedom to create the new. Bergson's defense of intuition would become crucial to early modernists like Hulme, who understood this critique of the intellect as a starting place for a new theory of art. Though Hulme was drawn to Bergson's analysis of materialism, he was also struck by Bergson's suggestion that language, especially conceptual language, was a tool of the spatializing intelligence. Bergson writes that concepts "have the disadvantage of being in reality symbols substituted for the object they symbolize, and demand no effort on our part."²⁶ Conceptual language can thus never capture duration and flux, which is solely knowable through intuition. In *Creative Evolution*, he goes further, calling conceptual language an inhibition against agency itself: "Our freedom, in the very movements by which it is affirmed, creates the growing habits that will stifle it if it fails to renew itself by a constant effort. It is dogged by automatism. The most living thought becomes frigid in the formula that expresses it. The word turns against the idea."²⁷ Bergson suggests, then, that a new kind of language is necessary to generate intuition in a reader, one based not in *concepts* but in *images*.

For modernists, this idea was perhaps the most significant in all of Bergson's writing. Though, as Michael Levenson shows in *A Genealogy of Modernism* (1984), Hulme eventually rejected vitalism on the road to a new antihumanist aesthetic of abstraction, the power of the image to frustrate the automaticity of rational thought played an important role in his thinking during the early years of the English avant-garde.²⁸ As the founder of a literary salon called the Poets' Club, Hulme facilitated the spread of Bergson's ideas about language to poets like Ezra Pound, who would join the group a year later and integrate Bergsonian concepts into an emerging aesthetic of Imagism.²⁹ As Hulme argued, images play an important role in any genuine art because they frustrate habits of thought. In his posthumously published essay, "Bergson's Theory of Art" (1922), he explains, "Human perception gets crystalized out along certain lines . . . it has certain fixed habits, certain ways of seeing things, and is so unable to see things as they are."³⁰ By providing readers with images that are not easily reducible to conceptual clarity, poets might offer not just a glimpse of the world as it actually is in time, but catalyze intuition for readers. As Patrick McGuinness summarizes, for Hulme and Bergson alike "images—successive or juxtaposed—do not simply convey the writer's precise or fuzzy impressions, but provoke new and different ones in the reader. Successive images are coterminous with intuition: they induce intuitive acts, disrupt ordinary, lazy habits of thought."³¹

Such a theory of language might invite us to see Imagism as one possible intervention into the politics of reflex, but it is hardly unique in its ambitions since the image for Hulme and Bergson neatly mirrors Formalism's definition of defamiliarization. Just as Shklovsky defined art against the automatism of perception, Hulme and Bergson saw the artist as superior to the reified habits of thought endemic to mass culture.³² As Hulme writes, the artist is "a person who is emancipated from the very strong habits of the mind which make us see not individual things but stock types"—the person capable of rupturing "the mechanism of expression" as we traditionally experience it.[33] In Hulme, emphasis always falls on poetic language, whereas prose "is due to a faculty of the mind, something resembling reflex action in the body."[34] But poetry does not have an exclusive license on intuition. Indeed, it would be in prose, not poetry, that one of the most robust responses to the politics of reflex would appear. As we will see, D. H. Lawrence developed a vitalist perspective from his own critical analysis of mechanism and the institutions it enabled. Out of this critique emerged an aesthetic and political agenda that sought to intervene in the politics of reflex by sanctifying the body against the automaticity of the mind.

Lawrence and "Idealism," or the Mind as Machine

D. H. Lawrence cuts something of an odd figure within the history of vitalism's influence on modernist culture. While many writers proudly wore the vitalist badge, Lawrence tended to be cagey about influences; he was just as likely to deny the appeal of a given thinker on his work as he was to attack those whose work he knew little or nothing about. Lawrence had, in fact, encountered Bergson's work, though he dismissed *Laughter* as "a bit thin" in his letters, and he makes only passing reference to Bergson elsewhere in his work.[35] Though he could have encountered Hulme's account of Bergson in *The New Age* (a magazine to which he subscribed), it is most likely that his own thinking emerged in tandem with Bergson's critique of science, not in conversation with it. As Jeff Wallace has documented in *D. H. Lawrence, Science and the Posthuman*, Lawrence was an accomplished reader of scientific literature, including all of Darwin's work, Spencer's *First Principles* (1860), Huxley's *Man's Place in Nature* (1863), and James's *Pragmatism* (1907), as well as cutting-edge sciences of the period. These interests suggests that he was broadly "in tune with contemporary, post-Darwinian science in its critical interrogation of all aspects of the 'human,'" as Wallace writes.[36] This is to say nothing of Lawrence's interest in older scientific theories of the nervous system, such as Marshall Hall's work on the reflex arc, which very likely fueled his ideas of an embodied consciousness, as Christopher Heywood has suggested. Taken together, these readings informed a broad critique of contemporary science that mirrored vitalism's own. In the same way that Bergson diagnosed materialism's tendency to "spatialize" dynamic processes, rendering life a series of static reflexes, Lawrence lamented the inadequacy of contemporary science in describing vital matter. As he wrote in the introduction to *Fantasia of the Unconscious*, "Our science is a science of the dead world."[37] The problem for Lawrence was not simply that these paradigms might be wrong, but rather that they were the ideological core of modernity's tendency to routinize citizens. Much of Lawrence's own career was animated by a need to diagnose the spiritual and political perils inherent in materialist science and the culture it produced. And, like vitalist philosophy itself, his work proposed solutions to the politics of reflex, often by exploring ways of reenergizing intuition and the body in political life. Lawrence consistently drew from his readings of science a sense that knowledge that was not narrowly cognitive or intellectual could provide a way of mitigating the worst aspects of an increasingly automatic society.

Lawrence's vitalism proceeded from an elementary observation about the nature of life in the twentieth century. Throughout his essays, novels, and short fiction, he expressed an anxiety common among his contemporaries about the rising role of automaticity in modern life. Institutions loom large in Lawrence's work as forces for tamping down the spontaneity of individuals to create citizens with regularized, predictable reflexes. Ursula Brangwen's work as a schoolmistress (which serves as one of the few plot continuities between *The Rainbow* and *Women in Love*) provides a characteristic example. Initially, Ursula applies for work as a schoolmistress to gain independence from her family. However, she soon finds that the school that hires her is intent on transforming both pedagogue and students into the receptacles of static ideas. As Lawrence describes, the goal of the school is "the graceless task of compelling many children into one disciplined, mechanical set, reducing the whole set to an automatic state of obedience and attention, and then of commanding their acceptance of various pieces of knowledge. The first great task was to reduce sixty children to one state of mind, or being. This state must be produced automatically, through the will of the teacher, and the will of the whole school authority, imposed upon the will of the children."[38] Here, as often throughout Lawrence's fiction, concern resides not simply with the collective pressures of these institutions, but rather with the demand that students and teacher both become part of a "mechanical set." By requiring that the children be "reduce[d]" to a single thing through "their acceptance of various pieces of knowledge," the school produces students incapable of anything other than reflex behaviors. In other words, knowledge here is treated as the master script that programs children to behave according to socially desired patterns. Even Ursula, the teacher, feels the inescapable pull of the institution "within her like a dark weight, controlling her movement."[39] In *The Rainbow* and *Women in Love*, schools bear the symbolic weight of a generalized sense of routinization, and both novels might accurately be described as narratives about attempts to escape a social milieu that has become "a repetition of repetitions," as Lawrence writes in *Women in Love*.[40] The "boredom" of modern life in these pre-First World War novels is often tied to collectives that inhibit spontaneity by providing individuals with ready-made ideas. Education is one such force, but just one among many figures of collective reflex that populate Lawrence's novels. Equally problematic for Lawrence were institutions of industrial labor (represented by the barons of industry such as Gerald Crich in *Women in Love* and Clifford Chatterley in *Lady Chatterley's Lover*), the army (Arthur Morel in *Sons and Lovers* and the young Skrebensky in *The Rainbow*), and domesticity (Aaron in *Aaron's Rod* and the Gundrun sisters in *The Rainbow* and *Women in Love*). These novels prioritize the spontaneity of individuals by defining it against the automaticity engendered by modern institutions. Unsurprisingly, these institutions often purvey the orthodoxies of materialist science. In *The Rainbow*, for example, Ursula Brangwen equates the "ready-made" knowledge of higher education with its promotion of sciences that treat life as no more than "a complexity of physical and chemical activities."[41] Later, in *Kangaroo* (1923), Lawrence's narrator rails against materialist psychology for treating man as "an automaton working in certain automatic ways when you touch certain springs."[42] For Lawrence, such a mechanistic understanding of life always goes hand in glove with institutions that delimit freedom by promoting the reflexes of modern society at large.

Creating a literary aesthetic in opposition to materialist science and the political world it enabled was a driving motivation from the very earliest stages of Lawrence's career. Just a month before the outbreak of the First World War, Lawrence wrote to his friend and fellow writer, Edward Garnett, urging him, "You mustn't look in my novel for the old stable *ego* of the character. There is another *ego*, according to whose action the individual is unrecognizable, and pass through, as it were, allotropic states which it needs a deeper sense than any we've been used to exercise, to discover are states of the same single radically unchanged element."[43] Written just after the publication of *Sons and Lovers* (1913), this statement was read by early critics as an articulation of Lawrence's literary agenda, and it has remained a durable center of Lawrence criticism. Discussions of this letter, however, seldom note the broader scientific context that Lawrence was invoking in elaborating this new aesthetic. This is somewhat surprising given Lawrence's use of the highly technical word "allotropic," a word derived from nineteenth-century science to mean a "variation of physical properties without change of substance."⁴⁴ Looking at the letter from a wider vantage reveals that when Lawrence proclaimed a new theory of literary character, he was doing so in opposition to materialist accounts of organic life:

> When I read Marinetti—"the profound institutions of life added one to the other, word by word, according to their illogical conception, will give us the general lines of an intuitive physiology of matter"—I see something of what I am after. I translate him clumsily, and his Italian is obfuscated—and I don't care about physiology of matter—but somehow—that which is physic—non-human, in humanity, is more interesting to me than the old-fashioned human element—which causes one to conceive a character in a certain moral scheme and make him consistent. . . . Because what is interesting in the laugh of the woman is the same as the binding of the molecules of steel or their action in heat, it is the inhuman will, call it physiology, or like Marinetti—physiology of matter, that fascinates me. I don't so much care about what the woman *feels*—in the ordinary usage of the word. That presumes an *ego* to feel with. I only care about what the woman *is*— what she IS—inhumanly, physiologically, materially—according to the use of the word: but for me, what she *is* as a phenomenon (or as representing some greater, inhuman will), instead of what she feels according to the human conception. That is where the futurists are stupid. Instead of looking for the new human phenomenon, they will only look for the phenomena of the science of physics to be found in human beings.⁴⁵

As critics have often noted, Lawrence's emphasis on the dynamism of characters represents an important break with Victorian aesthetics that prioritized wholeness, durability, and consistency. What fired Lawrence's imagination, though, was not Victorian literature but a critical analysis of contemporary studies of reflex, or what he calls "the science of physics to be found in human beings." Against the backdrop of radical mechanism, many modernists affirmed the importance of an ego that wills itself beyond the strict forces of its material conditioning, one in which the individual *is* recognizable. This is the agenda pursued by Wyndham Lewis, as we will see in the next chapter. In Lawrence, however, the ego takes a back seat to an "inhuman will" that is deeper and more authentic. Against "the science of physics," Lawrence posits a physiological substratum of human life that is intransigent—a "physiology of matter" that does not obey the deterministic frameworks posited by materialist science.

Though his novels often register the conjunction of materialist theory and human automaticity, it is perhaps in two nonfiction books of the early 1920s that he offered the most sustained analysis of materialist science. *Psychoanalysis and the Unconscious* (1921) and *Fantasia of the Unconscious* (1922) are both, ostensibly, attacks on psychoanalytic practice, though scholars like Jennifer Spitzer have noted that Lawrence had strikingly little direct knowledge of Freud's work.[46] Amazingly, in these books Lawrence takes as a given that Freud was only the latest in a long series of reflex psychologists—that Freud was, in fact, a kind of behaviorist. From Lawrence's perspective, the problem with such psychologies is that they treat the self as rooted in the mechanistic body: "Science is wretched in its treatment of the human body as a sort of complex mechanism made up of numerous little machines working automatically in a rather unsatisfactory relation to one another. The body is the total machine; the various organs are the included machines; and the whole thing, given a start at birth, or at conception, trundles on by itself. . . . The life within us fails more and more, while we marvelously tinker at the engines."[47] Freud is, accordingly, reduced to a tinkerer who would unveil "the mechanism of the psyche" by decoding "the mechanistic organism of the body."[48] While it is obvious that these books reveal a misreading (or non-reading) of Freud, it is telling that Lawrence could so confidently assume the role of materialism in Freud's work. It suggests just how prevalent materialist accounts of the human subject were even after Freud's work had begun to be translated and to circulate to non-specialized readers. Moreover, Lawrence's analysis of psychology suggests an understanding of materialist science that mirrors the main preoccupations of vitalist discourse—both in its diagnostic vocabulary of automaticity, and its reparative emphasis on intuition, spontaneity, and the body.

Like vitalists, Lawrence understood psychology as emblematic of a much wider cultural tendency in which ideas gain priority over feeling, affect, and the vicissitudes of the body—a cultural tendency he termed "idealism." To live according to our ideas rather than our "passional" selves, Lawrence asserts, is to be in thrall to the ready-made habits we acquire through social conditioning. Because modern life places a supreme emphasis on the virtues of the static framework of the intellect, we remain locked into repetitions of the social, cultural, and political positions to which we are exposed. Spontaneity, which is inherent to life itself, deserts us. As he describes in *Fantasia of the Unconscious*, "The ideal mind, the brain, has become the vampire of modern life, sucking up the blood and the life. There is hardly an original thought or original utterance possible to us. All is sickly repetition of stale, stale ideas."[49] To obey the intellect rather than one's intuition is, as he says in "Democracy" (1919), to give oneself over to "materialism or automatism or mechanism of the self."[50] In this respect, Lawrence's analysis parallels vitalism's own criticism of the intellect, which Bergson had suggested is an impediment to agency. Whereas much early twentieth-century discourse around reflex describes automatism as the absence of thought, Lawrence and Bergson consistently see things in the opposite way. If thought is the province of the mechanical and the ready-made, the deep, genuine self is one that does *not* think; it acts according to drives that are fluid and dynamic. The conscious ego is in some sense, then, the enemy; it is what wills by thinking, spatializing the world, and robbing us of genuine spontaneity. For Lawrence, ideas and the intellect are forms of automatism that render life a series of premeditated, inauthentic repetitions. Guided by the logic of materialist cause and effect, modernity becomes, in the words of one narrator, mere "mechanical repetition of given motions—millions of times over and over again—according to the fixed ideal."[51] It is, in short, a world of "pure automatism."[52]

Lawrence's concern with the intellect as a form of automatism only hints at the shared terrain between his work and that of vitalist philosophers. At the center of both resides a new definition of agency that challenged received notions of will and intentionality. By prioritizing the body as materially indeterminate, both Bergson and Lawrence redefined agency in terms of corporeality rather than mentality, feeling rather than thought, and intuition rather than intellect. Throughout his writing, Lawrence elaborates a model of the human subject in which the body, rather than the ideal mind, functions as "the fountain of real motivity," and the source of human agency.[53] As Lawrence writes in a later essay, the body "contains all our radical knowledge, knowledge-non-ideal, non-mental, yet still knowledge, primary cognition, individual and potent."[54] As the source of our "primary cognition," the material body serves as the baseline of all human consciousness and the source of action. Volition rooted in the ego, on the other hand, is coded as itself a kind of automatism. In *Psychoanalysis and the Unconscious*, Lawrence refers to the intellect as "the dead end of life," explaining that thought "has all the mechanical force of the non-vital universe. It is a great dynamo of super-mechanical force. Given the *will* as accomplice, it can even arrogate its machine-motions and automatizations over the whole of life."[55] Just as the intellect in Bergson's work is the organ that spatializes, turning the dynamic processes of life into a thing and stymying our will, Lawrence insists on the importance of alternative modes of knowing and acting that are rooted in the body. Equipped with an embodied, non-mental awareness, individuals are capable of exceeding the narrow boundaries imposed on them through exposure to their environment.

In such a revision of materialist science, genuine agency is no longer legible as purposive action but is instead tied to the unconscious vicissitudes of the body. Lawrence sums up his position succinctly in *Fantasia of the Unconscious*: "We have really no will and no choice, in the first place. It is our soul which acts within us, day by day unfolding us according to our own nature."[56] Lawrence would go on in later works to define agency in terms of impersonal powers working within the individual—not conditioned reflex, but organic, embodied forces beyond the scope of an automatizing modernity. In his essay on Benjamin Franklin in *Studies in Classic American Literature* (1923), he explains: "What we *think* we do is not very important. We never really know what we are doing. Either we are materialistic instruments, like Benjamin [Franklin], or we move in the gesture of creation, from our deepest self, usually unconscious. We are only the actors, we are never wholly the authors of our own deeds or works. IT is the author, the unknown inside us or outside us. The best we can do is to try to hold ourselves in unison with the deeps which are inside us."[57] Such an explanation of agency surely cuts against the grain of a host of traditional understandings of human behavior and individual life. If, as Lawrence argues, there is an "IT" or an "unknown inside us" that is the source of all genuine action, the ego is at best an impediment to spontaneity—the surface that sublimates our environmental conditioning into sets of habitual, routinized actions.[58] According to this line of thinking, we are at our best, most authentic, and most free, when we are guided by a will that exceeds common human volitions, which issues from the material body rather than the egotistic mind, and which is so unlike common willpower that it strains the very concept.[59]

This idea was already implicit in Lawrence's famous 1914 letter to Edward Garnett in which he claimed to be inventing a new kind of literary character beyond "the old stable *ego* of the character." There Lawrence told Garnett that what interested him were not characters motivated in petty, mundane ways, but the effort to understand character "inhumanly, physiologically, materially." Beginning with *Sons and Lovers*, Lawrence attempted to define literary subjects that were physiological in a more primary way than materialist contemporaries like Pavlov and Watson would have allowed. His characters are "inhuman" in the sense that they locate genuine agency in material life rather than the unified conceptual schema of ideas called "personality." Lawrence's theory of characterization, then, is clearly more than just a rejection of literary convention; Lawrence premised his "allotropic" characters on a vitalist understanding of the human body, in which will and agency are expressed primarily through bodily being rather than the automatism of the mind. This understanding of life is manifest throughout his novels in the bodily experiences of characters. In *Sons and Lovers*, to take just one example, twentieth-century life is represented as a force that fundamentally desiccates human agency; such a life "takes hold of one, carries the body along, accomplishes one's history, and yet is not real, but leaves oneself as it were slurred over."[60] As Lawrence makes clear in the character of Paul Morel, however, agency can only be restored by letting go of ideas and agency rooted in the mind. *Sons and Lovers*, like much of Lawrence's fiction, suggests that "real" agency resides in the unwilled promptings of our primary, corporeal cognition. Paul realizes through the sensuous experience of the body that "to be alive, to be urgent and insistent—that was *not-to-be*."[61] In the sexual act, however, "he became, not a man with a mind, but a great instinct. His hands were like creatures, living; his limbs, his body, were all life and consciousness, . . . living in themselves."[62]

That such issues were a primary thematic concern of Lawrence's work is beyond doubt. An emphasis on the body, particularly sex, is perhaps *the* most characteristic Lawrentian gesture. The fundamental concern of Lawrence's fiction, however, is not with a truer representation of sex or even the characters who obey the "primary consciousness" of the body. The problem that drives his fiction is how to conceive of *relationships* that might solve the problems that radical mechanism entailed for society at large. Even when novels like *Sons and Lovers*, *The Rainbow*, and *Women in Love* largely refrain from engaging political problems explicitly, they are motivated by a desire to imagine social structures that are dynamic and that allow the spontaneity of individuals to bloom. This is a familiar problem within vitalist philosophy, particularly for Bergson's follower, Georges Sorel, who tasked himself with applying Bergson's thought to political life. For both Sorel and Lawrence, the power to escape the ready-made ideas of mass society would require political structures that themselves lacked the conceptual dogmas of traditional politics—structures capable of catalyzing the intuition of citizens. In *The Plumed Serpent*, Lawrence realized a vision for just such a vitalist polity.

The Vitalist Polity: Spontaneity, Sorel, and *The Plumed Serpent*

Taken on its own terms, vitalism might seem like a philosophy that is altogether incompatible with politics. Distrusting both collective reflexes and the individual intellect, vitalism left few political options available to those persuaded by its claims. As Judith Shklar explained, Bergson "was not primarily a social philosopher" and "much of his work explicitly excludes any consideration of the social world in an effort to reach intuitively the truths that lie in the inner being of man."[63] Similar observations have been made about Lawrence, whose distaste for collective institutions might mark him as wholly unconcerned with any sort of political response to the automatisms of modern life.[64] Yet, in the early twentieth century, a major part of the appeal of vitalist philosophy lay not just in its ability to trouble materialist doctrine but in its efforts to provide escape routes from the politics of reflex. Writers across the political spectrum and in diverse national contexts embraced categories like *durée* and intuition in the hope of distilling their latent political implications.[65] These vitalist terms appealed in equal measure to those on the left and the right. Critics on the right saw in Bergson a quasi-religious affirmation of the spirit against the hegemony of science, while those on the left saw vitalism as a call to discard traditional institutions as fetters on the flux of experience.[66] These political ideologies were knit together by a shared interest in how political movements might escape established structures of action, particularly those inscribed by the hierarchies of political parties. Joel Nickels has argued that as modernist writers weighed the overlap between the problem of individual reflex and "modernity's large-scale mechanisms of public contestation and collective life," they gravitated toward theories of collective spontaneity.[67] As we will see, this in part explains the appeal of vitalism to fascists, but it was equally at home among leftists who sought to contest the routines of centralization, administration, and hierarchy. Vitalism performed a key role in this history, introducing categories of spontaneity into the lexicon of political philosophy and opening new avenues for thinking about mass politics. For Rosa Luxemburg, V. I. Lenin, Antonio Gramsci, and Franz Fanon, for example, the spontaneity of the proletariat formed one of the primary mechanisms through which revolutionary change might be effected, and their work turns time and again to questions of how to situate spontaneity within a Marxist political tradition. This emphasis grew out of a French sociological concern with the unpredictability of the masses and Sorel's interest in intuitive action as a vehicle for revolutionary change.⁶⁸ While the politics of spontaneity are not always tied to vitalist thinking, many early twentieth-century political theorists embraced ideas that exalted the unforeseen and unreasoned manifestation of political will because they provided a way of imagining a society free of the reflexes of mass modernity.

In Lawrence's fiction, we encounter one of the most significant modernist commitments to spontaneity as a political project. In the body's material vitality, Lawrence saw the possibility of a collectivity that "has for its true goal the purest individualism, pure individual spontaneity," as he wrote in a 1919 essay.⁶⁹ This political project can be seen most clearly in his novel *The Plumed Serpent*, where the discourse of human automatism is explicitly marked as an ideology that stifles the dynamism of individual and collective life. Prioritizing vitalist categories of spontaneity and intuition, in *The Plumed Serpent* Lawrence imagined a social structure in which reflexes of thought and action would be supplanted by the "primary cognition" of the body. While many of Lawrence's earlier novels eschew collective politics in favor of personal relationships, the vitalist politics of *The Plumed Serpent* constitute a culmination of Lawrence's political thinking. Reading novels like *Women in Love* and *The Rainbow* through the lens of *The Plumed Serpent* reveals an enduring interest in alternative social structures that enable spontaneity and move subjects beyond the automaticity of twentieth-century life. The dominant problematic of Lawrence's literary practice, then, entails imagining collective structures that catalyze our passage through "allotropic" states without foreclosing individuality. And as we shall see, these political solutions to reflex depend at every junction on a vitalist understanding of aesthetics and intuition.

Among Lawrence's novels, *The Plumed Serpent* ranks among those least read and most reviled. The story of Kate Leslie, the widow of an Irish revolutionary, *The Plumed Serpent* traces her transition from a Western tourist in Mexico to an active participant in a religious and political renaissance, and her elevation into the Aztec pantheon as a goddess. This novel may seem like an odd place to locate Lawrence's vitalism since it has generally been treated as either a literary failure or a novel beneath contempt. In his otherwise laudatory book *D. H. Lawrence, Novelist* (1956), F. R. Leavis set the stage for much later criticism when he argued that Lawrence was simply out of his depth in dealing with political themes. Unlike Lawrence's novels of "personal engagement," *The Plumed Serpent* "cherishes the illusion that it grasps and presents more in the way of [a] positive 'answer' to the large issues raised than it actually does."[70] The result is "a bad book and a regrettable performance," one that appears "willed and mechanical" and "produces boredom."[71] For subsequent critics, *The Plumed Serpent* has represented a dark moment of political confusion just before Lawrence found his footing again in *Lady Chatterley's Lover* (1928). Recent critics have thus read *The Plumed Serpent* as a minor work in Lawrence's oeuvre, the limited importance of which lies in the way it imagines racial alterity.[72]

Consigning *The Plumed Serpent* to the margins of Lawrence's body of work, critics have failed to appreciate a novel that represents the fullest achievement of his political vision. In fact, Lawrence himself was convinced that the novel was by far his best. Two months after having begun the first draft in 1923, he reported to Adele Seltzer, "I like my new novel best of all—much."[73] From the start, though, Lawrence recognized that there was something different about this novel that gave it particular importance. As he was completing an entirely new draft of the novel two years later, Lawrence wrote to Curtis Brown, "It is different from my other books: and to me, the one that means most," a sentiment he was to repeat again and again before the novel's publication in 1926.[74] As he told Brown in a different letter, "I consider this my most important novel, so far."[75] In part, *The Plumed Serpent* departed from Lawrence's earlier novels by shifting attention away from the challenges of intersubjective life. As he had put it to Thomas Seltzer in the spring of 1923, "you may just hold up your hands with horror. No sex."[76] Strictly speaking, *The Plumed Serpent* is not devoid of sex; the romantic relationship between Kate Leslie and the military general Cipriano forms one of the primary plotlines of the novel in much the way that sexual relationships dominate *Women in Love* and *The Rainbow*. However, in *The Plumed Serpent* the question of love and sexuality is subordinated to a larger problem: imagining a way out of the political reflexes of modern life.

Where automatism obliquely informs the content of Lawrence's earlier novels, here the politics of reflex are central, necessitating a revolution along vitalist lines. Many of this novel's concerns with reflex map onto Lawrence's earlier anxieties about "idealism." For example, Owen Rhys, Kate Leslie's nephew, exemplifies a typically modern form of automatism. As an American tourist, Rhys is constantly in pursuit of "Life" with a capital *L*. As a result of his dogmatic adherence to this *idea* of life, not only does he spend much of his time enduring events and people that he finds revolting, but this desire for experience binds him to rote ways of inhabiting the world. As Kate describes him, misgivings about not having lived fully "would make him rush like mechanical steel filings to a magnet, towards any crowd in the street."[77] He is an example of what she later calls "American automatism."[78] This brand of idealism reflects a larger, geopolitical context in which American economic structures represent new stimuli in the conditioning of reflex. As capitalist institutions overtake native ones, Lawrence foresees the ascension of prescribed ways of doing and thinking typical of mass modernity. Late in the novel, as Kate experiences a reluctance to accept the native religious renaissance, Cipriano accuses her of being stuck in American habits of thought:

> You can only think with American thoughts. . . . Nearly all women are like that: even Mexican women of the Spanish-Mexican class. They are all thinking nothing but U.S.A. thoughts, because those are the ones that go with the way they dress their hair. . . . But you only think like this because you have had these thoughts put in your head, just as in Mexico you spend centavos and pesos, because that is the Mexican money you have put in your pocket. It's what they give you at the bank. So when you say you are free, you are not free. You are compelled all the time to be thinking U.S.A. thoughts—*compelled*, I must say. You have not as much choice as a slave. As the *peones* must eat tortillas, tortillas, tortillas, because there is nothing else, you must think these U.S.A. thoughts. . . . Every day you must eat those tortillas, tortillas.—Till you don't know how you would like something else.[79]

Here Lawrence suggests that thoughts are conditioned not simply by one's education but also by the seemingly innocuous details of everyday life. The reference to Mexican pesos conjures the broader context of economic modernization, in which foreign values supplant native modes of social practice, even as the form of currency remains the same. Fashion is here coded as a particularly modern debility and an index of culture creeping from north of the border, which works to condition behavior in new and determinate ways—a process of "Americanizing" the habits of the populace. "U.S.A. thoughts" are, in other words, not just "foreign" to a Mexican indigenous population; the influx of American styles and American goods enforces fundamentally new forms of social life by prioritizing material wealth as the ultimate end of life, and the ideal (rather than the spontaneous) as its mode of realization. America and the "Cult of the dollar" are linked to a culture of reflex, one that would pluck "at the created soul in a man, till at last it plucked out the growing germ, and left him a creature of mechanism and automatic reaction, with only one inspiration, the desire to pluck the quick out of every living, spontaneous creature."[80]

A different author might have found the solution to the politics of reflex in socialist revolution. As Kate Leslie surveys revolutionary forces in Mexico, however, she encounters a mirror image of the automatisms that she detects in her nephew. As the novel puts it, Mexican bolshevists are the natural products of "American" materialist desires.[81] They are "symbols in the great script of modern socialism."[82] This is not just because socialism is, at base, an economic inversion of capitalism. Instead, Lawrence casts it as yet another form of idealism. "Spinning a great lot of words, burying themselves inside the cocoons of words and ideas," socialists behave with "a collective insect-like will, to avoid the responsibility of achieving any more perfected being or identity."[83] Like capitalists, their attachment to ideas makes them essentially mechanical, and thereby devoid of contact with the spontaneity of life itself.

The question that Lawrence poses in this novel, then, is how to create political structures that might allow citizens to avoid the collective reflexes of capitalism and socialism. Such a society would be one in which the dogma of ideas and the drive toward social uniformity do not crush the embodied spontaneity of individuals. In the creep of a Western economic system and its echo, Kate Leslie sees boredom and repetition. She prays, "Give me the mystery and let the world live again for me! . . . And deliver me from man's automatism."[84] This deliverance she finds in Don Ramón's native religious renaissance, which attempts to build collective social structures that honor intuition and spontaneity.

In imagining such a society, Lawrence foregrounded the role that myth might play in catalyzing intuition—an agenda previously pursued by Sorel in his 1908 book, *Reflections on Violence*. Deeply drawn to Bergson's critique of mechanism, Sorel worked to extend Bergson's understanding of intuition into the political realm by theorizing its role in modern mass movements. Central to his project was the very same problem that dogged Lawrence— how to negotiate between the demands of collective and individual life by creating political structures that do not foreclose individual spontaneity. Sorel poses this question in terms of production, asking how to "conceive of the transformation of the men of today into the free producers of tomorrow working in workshops where there are no masters."[85] Like Bergson and Hulme, Sorel eschewed dogma as a crutch of the intellect, insisting instead on the virtues of intuition and spontaneity. And just as Bergson and Hulme emphasized "the image" as an important catalyst to intuition, Sorel stressed that in the political realm, myth performs an equally vital function. As he explained in the "Letter to Daniel Halévy" (1907), "men who are participating in great social movements always picture their coming action in the form of images of battle in which their cause is certain to triumph."[86] He explains that "myth" is not a matter of practical outcomes but of motivating "pictures" that sustain a movement. In his particular case—that of the proletarian revolution—Sorel posited the value of the general strike as an actuating myth, though myth may take shape as any body of images capable of stimulating the intuitions of the group. In myths are found "all the strongest inclinations of a people, of a party or of a class, inclinations which recur to the mind with the insistence of instincts in all the circumstances of life, and which give an aspect of complete reality to the hopes of immediate action upon which the reform of the will is founded."[87] Because myth speaks to people at the level of unconscious and unspeakable desires, it offers a motivating power beyond the predictable behaviors promoted by modern political life.[88] Myth thus serves as the key term in a properly vitalist political framework, capable of both actuating a revolutionary movement and maintaining the balance between collectivity and individuality in society.

By placing myth at the center of a political revolution in *The Plumed Serpent*, Lawrence attempted to imagine a social structure that would safeguard against the automatic and the ready-made in political life. Lawrence's turn to myth is not, I want to stress, akin to Eliot's "mythic method," a rearguard attempt to stanch the social transformations wrought by modernization through an appeal to order.[89] To the contrary, Lawrence found in myth a structural impediment to the very concept of "tradition" as espoused by modernists like Eliot. Myth works in this novel not as a way of forging a cohesive and unitary collective whose members share common modes of thinking, but as a method of structuring collectivity on the basis of individual spontaneity. Here the revolution led by Don Ramón, who claims to be the living incarnation of the Aztec god Quetzalcoatl, strives to create a new social structure free of the reflexes promoted by capitalism. Unlike the "ready-made" world of the United States and the industrial West, Ramón's movement promises to restore spontaneity to both individual and collective life—to jostle people "*awake*," to provide them with a social structure in which they can be perpetually "on the *qui vive*."[90] In the context of the novel, this entails a religious framework capable of reanimating embodied life as a social good and eliminating the automatisms typical of twentieth-century life.

Lawrence insisted in his nonfiction writing that what twentieth-century modernity lacked was precisely what myth enabled. As he explained in *Apocalypse* (1931), "We have lost almost entirely the great and intricately developed sensual awareness, or sense-awareness, and sense-knowledge, of the ancients. It was a great depth of knowledge arrived at direct, by instinct and intuition, as we say, not by reason. It was a knowledge based not on words but on images."[91] The connection here between "images" and myth is telling; in myth, Lawrence found a solution to problems articulated by vitalists like Sorel, Bergson, and Hulme—how to catalyze collective intuition without requiring the automatisms of thought endemic to mass life. The indigenous gods of *The Plumed Serpent* motivate the sense-awareness of revolutionaries, who pursue the open-ended goals of the movement without regard to religious dogma. These gods operate as the "images" or myths that catalyze the revolutionary movement and preempt the collapse of spontaneity into the "idealism" of a modern political order. As Lawrence noted in *Apocalypse*, the power of mythic images resides in their ability to make people know in terms of feeling rather than in terms of the intellect. Myth enables people "to achieve a consummation of a certain state of consciousness, to fulfill a certain state of feeling-awareness."[92] This kind of awareness, we have already seen, is central to vitalist thought, and is the very thing disabled by modern social structures, according to Lawrence. *The Plumed Serpent* is rife with attention to affective modes of political life, with ritualized hymns, dance, and drumming functioning as prominent examples. Even the gods themselves are figured as little more than a "fertility of sound" that intuitively resonate with the mass of Mexican peasants.[93] Instead of serving as a system of dogma that unites a people in a common *understanding*, as propaganda might, myth actuates a people according to a common *feeling*. The gods provide Lawrence's characters with the images necessary for self-overcoming and revolutionary change. In so doing, these images activate the "primary cognition" of the body that Lawrence had elaborated in his writings on Freud.[94]

As a vision of social life grounded in vitalist principles, *The Plumed Serpent* represents a high point in the literary life of vitalism. Even more strongly than Sorel's work, it offers a utopian vision of the world in which vitalist principles solve problems inherent in mass modernity's drive toward automaticity. But the vitalist currents that manifest in *The Plumed Serpent* are hardly an aberration from Lawrence's larger literary project. Indeed, the novel reflects elements of Lawrence's thought that are central to his earlier novels. While late novels like *The Plumed Serpent* pointedly thematize the virtues of intuition and spontaneity against automaticity, these concerns were already present in the formal agenda of novels like *Sons and Lovers, The Rainbow,* and *Women in Love.* Though we may tend to think of these novels as less formally experimental than some modernist works, these novels frequently frustrate realist conventions and the idealist impulse that sustains them by challenging readers to engage texts intuitively rather than intellectually. Anne Fernihough has made this point well, arguing that in his prose style Lawrence attempted to prevent the total interpretive claim of readers: "We are never allowed to feel that a final 'signified' has been reached."[95] What does one make, for example, of Will Brangwen's ecstasies in the "Cathedral" chapter of *The Rainbow*? Here Lawrence describes Will and Anna Brangwen's experience of a church. As they enter the building, the narration departs from a realist description to indulge in signature Lawrentian prose:

> Containing birth and death, potential with all the noise and transitation of life, the cathedral remained hushed, a great, involved seed, whereof the flower would be radiant life inconceivable, but whose beginning and whose end were the circle of silence. Spanned round with the rainbow, the jeweled gloom folded music upon silence, light upon darkness, fecundity upon death, as a seed folds leaf and silence upon the root and the flower, hushing up the secret of all between its parts, the death out of which it fell, the life into which it has dropped, the immortality it involves, and the death it will embrace again.[96]

This passage does not offer readers a logical translation of Will and Anna's experience into "realist" description. Instead, Lawrence produces a hypersensual prose that becomes virtually unmoored from any reference outside itself. The organic figure of a seed suggests an unfolding or blooming—but of what? Through his juxtaposition of contraries (music and silence, light and dark, birth and death) and the use of the obsolete word "transitation," Lawrence pushes the image of the seed beyond the ordinary language of literary description, as if the passage were itself caught in the process of life. We are asked to sympathetically *feel* Will Brangwen's sublime experience but not allowed to *know* it. By withholding a more "realist" representation, many of Lawrence's novels attempt to produce for readers an experience in which thought gives way to feeling, and mind gives way to body. Form, in effect, is here deployed to disrupt the reader's reliance on the habits of mind over the primary cognition of the body.

It should come as no coincidence that vitalist philosophy employs a nearly identical formal strategy. For Bergson and Sorel, the efficacy of vitalist critique depended on a strategic rejection of conceptual language. This entailed forging a different—we might even say, modernist—form of philosophical discourse in which rational appeal is supplanted by what can only be called "aesthetics."[97] Sorel, for example, argued that a fully formed philosophy could only lead to the very kinds of dogmatism it was intended to obviate, and he therefore employed a formal strategy that he called "*diremption*," a term that literally means "a tearing asunder." Sorel argued that true political dynamism depends on an aesthetic of partial knowledge or incompletion. He explains in *Reflections on Violence*, "Ordinary language could not produce [spontaneous revolution] in any very certain manner; appeal must be made to collections of images, which, *taken together and through intuition alone*, before any considered analyses are made, are capable of evoking the mass of sentiments which correspond to the different manifestations of the war undertaken by socialism against modern society."[98] Here again, images are endowed with the power to catalyze intuition and frustrate the automaticity of thought. For Sorel, this argument was a direct consequence of Bergson's theory of "integral knowledge," which holds that explicit analysis stymies individual and collective motivations by becoming a matter of thought rather than feeling—what Lawrence would have called "idealism." Hulme's writing on Bergson and aesthetics makes much the same case, as we have already seen. But whereas for Hulme the poetic image evokes genuine experience for the reader, in Sorel and Lawrence this aesthetic strategy has clear political implications. Aesthetic diremption becomes in their analysis the motive power of collective spontaneity—an affective experience that inhibits the reification of desires into so many ready-mades of political action.

This investment in affect and intuition is something that we can clearly see in Lawrence's attempt to imagine a political solution equal to the automatizing nature of twentieth-century modernity in *The Plumed Serpent*. But it is also one that we can see throughout his work as a whole. Novels like *The Rainbow* and *Women in Love* attempt to represent the flux of individuals in their "allotropic" states without reducing these interactions to a series of static events or calling upon the reader's intellect alone. As Sorel argues, art "flourishes best on mystery, half shades and indeterminate outlines; the more speech is methodical and perfect, the more likely is it to eliminate everything that distinguishes a masterpiece; it reduces the masterpiece to the proportions of an academic product."[99] This sentiment is central to Lawrence's novels, and it holds roughly the same status in his political framework as it does in Sorel's. Such models of intuitive or "passional" knowledge form the backbone of Lawrence's responses to an automatizing modernity and emerge as explicit elements of a political project in novels like *Kangaroo* and *The Plumed Serpent*.

Hulme was adamant that poetry was the proper vehicle of a vitalist literature, not prose. By dealing in images, poetry divests us of our habits of perception and the ready-made categories provided by language. The familiar is made strange so that we might see the world as it really is; the stone is made stony, as Shklovsky would say. For Lawrence, on the other hand, the novel had resources that allowed for more than just defamiliarization along these vitalist lines. Poetry can shake off the shackles of language, but the novel trains its energies on life itself. This means not just showing characters that overcome the reflexes endemic to their environment but offering a picture of society that is itself dynamic. As he wrote in "Morality and the Novel" (1925), "The novel is a perfect medium for revealing to us the changing rainbow of our living relationships. The novel can help us to live, as nothing else can: no didactic Scripture, anyhow."[100] Lawrence was intent on developing a vitalist aesthetic attentive to the realities of mass modernity, and he consistently pitted the novel form against the ideology of automatism as elaborated in the sciences. In "Why the Novel Matters" (1925), he writes, "To the scientist, I am dead. He puts under the microscope a bit of dead me, and calls it me."[101] But the novel breaks this spell because it can "make the whole man-alive tremble."[102] What is made strange in Lawrence is not language but life—the ever-changing world, individual organisms in their dynamism, and the systems we build in order to survive. By showing us an image of these things in their material vibrancy, Lawrence attempts to prompt a response from readers in opposition to the determinisms of mass life—a response that is spontaneous, individual, and true.

Vitalist Legacies: A Philosophy of Blood?

Bergson died of pneumonia in January of 1941. It is believed that he contracted his fatal illness after "having stood for hours in line with other Parisian Jews registering with the Nazi government."[103] Though he had long since given up active Jewish practice, a rising wave of anti-Semitism in the interwar period had influenced him to not only abstain from converting to Catholicism (as he considered doing) but to renounce many of the honors bestowed upon him in protest of the Vichy government. Bergson's death and religious background represent a glaring historical irony. By the onset of the Second World War, vitalism—once a veritable craze among both the intelligentsia and the public—had become passé in many philosophical and literary circles. But as vitalism's appeal waned in some quarters, it gained new adherents in the fascist movement. Fascists found in vitalism a political philosophy that seemed to affirm a mistrust of rationalism while providing a basis for social cohesion rooted in new ideas of organicism and myth.[104] Out of Bergson's philosophy of freedom emerged a politics of control, one that would later embrace some of the strongest forms of conditioned reflex.

Vitalism represents one of the most extreme forms of political thinking to emerge from the politics of reflex; it promised a radical rewriting of accepted philosophical and political realities. Though the political consequences of vitalism were largely latent in Bergson, his critique of materialist science entailed a wholesale reevaluation of some of the most sacrosanct values of the Enlightenment. The virtues of the intellect and the power of the ego to resist the inertia of matter were swept away in favor of intuition, instinct, and the spontaneous flow of unpremeditated action. As a result of vitalism's attempt to rethink basic social structures, it found a ready audience across the political spectrum, not just among those swayed by race-thinking and the promise of national rebirth.[105] But because it also challenged the supremacy of the agential, rational self, it appealed especially to those at odds with the liberal democratic tradition.

Lawrence's vitalism broadly coheres to this pattern. As a result of his emphasis on spontaneity, the primary cognition of the body, and intuition, he was to find himself at the mercy of critics who lived to read him in the light of historical cataclysm. Looking back at Lawrence's work in 1946, the British writer V. S. Pritchett would argue that "Lawrence's teachings are interesting because they are a compendium of what a whole generation wanted to feel, until Hitler arose, just after Lawrence's death, and they saw where the dark unconsciousness was leading them."[106] In *Portraits from Memory* (1956), Bertrand Russell went even further, asserting that Lawrence's "philosophy of 'blood' " "led straight to Auschwitz."[107]

These arguments are not baseless; Lawrence's emphasis on the body often draws on the imagery of blood, and his late novels are fascinated by charismatic leaders who revivify the body as a site of political dynamism.[108] While these leaders often serve as Lawrence's mouthpieces in espousing a vitalist politics, vanguard figures like Kangaroo or Cipriano in *The Plumed Serpent* also flirt with political modes that are striking in their authoritarian tone. In *Kangaroo*, for example, the titular character promotes "the joy of obedience and the sacred responsibility of authority."[109] This is notable when we remember that Lawrence earlier associated "obedience" with automatism, as in Ursula Brangwen's rebellion against schools in *The Rainbow*. And while Lawrence had expressed tremendous enthusiasm for *The Plumed Serpent* in his letters, there is some evidence that he came to regret framing the narrative around a charismatic leader. In 1928, he responded to Witter Bynner's criticism of the novel, admitting, "The hero is obsolete, and the leader of men is a back number. After all, at the back of the hero is the militant ideal: and the militant ideal, or the ideal militant, seems to me also a cold egg."[110] Syndicalists like Sorel had seen in vitalism a way of making a political world free from masters and the doctrinal scripts of parties, but in Lawrence's hands the appeal to intuition and images had seemed to demand a visionary leader. That Lawrence would later link this central element of the novel to "the ideal" he spent so much of his career repudiating suggests just how difficult it ultimately was for vitalism to resolve the problem inherent in the politics of reflex.

The appeal of vitalism to reactionary politics is not specific to Lawrence, of course; vitalism served as an ideological way station for many on the road to more extreme political views. Influenced by Action Française, Hulme moved from being one of Bergson's chief expositors in the Anglophone world to celebrating the virtues of abstract art centered on "dogma" and the rejection of "human perfectibility," as Michael Levenson has noted.[111] There are many ways to account for the proximity between vitalism and early twentieth-century reactionary politics, but one cannot deny that vitalism's efforts to redefine agency complicated its larger political agenda. If "real" agency flows from the instinctual body rather than from the rational mind, as vitalists believed, it is virtually impossible to distinguish intuitive behaviors from those that we have merely been conditioned to regard as intuitive. In such a framework, there is little meaningful difference between the mob that behaves automatically and the vitalist masses who have sloughed off the fetters of rationality. Even though vitalism was, fundamentally, in favor of the freedoms afforded by the Enlightenment, its skepticism about the powers of rational agency cut against some of the most fundamental values of a liberal political order. For those looking to tear down that order, vitalism was unmistakably seductive. In this sense, vitalist efforts to solve the problems raised by the politics of reflex may have been worse than the problems themselves.

But aligning vitalism or Lawrence with fascism might also be seen as a facile attempt to assimilate what is strange to what is familiar. Vitalism cut across political ideologies because it offered a genuinely new approach to problems of twentieth-century life. We are on firmer ground assessing vitalism and its appeal to modernists like Lawrence by remembering the shared anxieties about science and politics that animated them both. F. R. Leavis, who felt that Lawrence's political thought was misguided, noted in 1932 that Lawrence was best assessed in contrast to the science of reflex. The great virtue of Lawrence's novels was that they actively worked to combat the routinization of life through the passive work of conditioning, a process he saw everywhere at work in modern culture. Leavis writes, "As for Lawrence's extravagances about 'ideas,' 'mind-knowledge,' science and education, we shall be fairer to him if we juxtapose them with [Watson's behaviorism]. . . . Juxtaposed with this scientific horse-sense of Dr. John B. Watson, Lawrence's wildest extravagances appear less extravagant. Dr. Watson . . . represent[s] in a pronounced form certain tendencies that are general in the West. And the pronounced form brings home to us that Lawrence had excuses for his prophetic passion."[112] Leavis's juxtaposition of Lawrence with Watson is an apposite one. Rather than see in his "extravagances" an ideology of control, Leavis sees a contest between competing visions of humanity. He recognized the virtues of a writer motivated by opposition to a culture of reflex that was "general in the West"—one in which materialist science was rapidly impoverishing the richness of experience by devaluing individuality and agency. Lawrence, at the very least, "has done much to make this more widely and more keenly realised than before," Leavis asserts. Whether we believe that Lawrence's work was genuinely capable of catalyzing intuition and the primary cognition of the body, it cannot be doubted that he saw such faculties as important to building a better world, one free of the reflexes endemic to mass modernity.

Vitalism, for all its appeal in the early part of the twentieth century, is just one field within the larger politics of reflex, and one with manifest limitations. While Bergson and his followers attempted to craft a philosophy that might restore power to ordinary people, it did little to overthrow the world that mechanistic science was bringing into being. Indeed, philosophers like Bergson largely accepted the basic premises of materialist science while rejecting its mode of inquiry. As intellectuals were debating vitalism and mechanism, experts continued to draw upon the insights of materialism in a variety of political, commercial, and intellectual realms. As Bergson's star fell after the First World War, a whole new set of institutions and disciplines were emerging that took seriously Pavlovian and behaviorist models of reflex to create a more "rational" world. This world was not to be the utopian one of the vitalist vision but one in which our desires and behaviors would be more finely adjusted by our environments than ever before.

3 Public Reflex
Wyndham Lewis, Public Relations, and the Invisible Government

When we think of the historical period of literary modernism, we often remember it as an era that promised unprecedented individual and collective freedoms, including women's suffrage, the independence of colonized nations, new sexual subjectivities, and the like. But this same period also saw the rise of institutions and branches of knowledge that threatened to erode the promises of modernity. For those who saw humans as born free but everywhere reduced to machines, vitalism offered intellectual and spiritual uplift. It seemed to demonstrate that it is the nature of living things to behave and grow unpredictably, and that social structures that inhibit spontaneity were to be overthrown. In this sense, the philosophy of Bergson is one of the most important discourses to emerge from the politics of reflex, leaving a crucial mark on the literary politics of the day. As we have seen, vitalism expressed a widespread cultural and political attitude, one that affirmed the essential freedom of humans from their material conditioning. And yet, for the many successes of the gospel of spontaneity, it is arguably the *rejection* of Bergson that would have a more pronounced impact on the literary culture of the early century.

By the time he began serving as an artilleryman on the Western Front, T. E. Hulme, once the primary champion of Bergson in England, had come to reject the philosophical project of vitalism. Amid the literal blasts of the First World War, Hulme conceived and published a collection of short essays that diagnosed a lacuna at the heart of Bergson's work. While vitalists treat the distinction between gross matter and life as the most fundamental of philosophical categories, Hulme came to feel that such a philosophical system failed to address the much more essential chasm between human life and the divine. Even the most vital of living phenomena, he explains, never approach the absolute value of divinity, which is itself not reducible to vitalist categories: "It is necessary to realise that there is an absolute, and not a relative, difference between humanism (which we can take to be the highest expression of the vital), and the religious spirit. The *divine* is not *life* at its intensest. It contains in a way an almost *anti-vital* element; quite different of course from the non-vital characters of the outside physical region."[1] Unlike the vast majority of Hulme's writings, which treated ideas and dogma as accessory to automaticity, these anti-humanist essays imply that some kinds of dogmas are necessary. For modernists like Eliot, who emerged from the war certain of the need to redeem the modern world through a renewed religiosity, this line of thinking would prove tremendously influential. But the critique of vitalism would also appeal to those enmeshed in the politics of reflex who were weary of the ideological entailments of vitalism.

One writer particularly close to these debates was Wyndham Lewis. Lewis might have seemed a natural ally of the vitalist project. Central to his writing, particularly during the interwar period, was a keen awareness of the place of reflex within contemporary science and politics. During this period—what Hugh Kenner called Lewis's "automaton phase"—emerging scientific orthodoxies about reflex appear as evidence of a historic moment that was culturally bankrupt and politically cowed.[2] In both fiction and non-fiction, Lewis worked to penetrate those political and cultural transformations of the early twentieth century that worked, as he wrote in *Time and Western Man*, to "thrust most people into prescribed tracks" of thought and action.[3] The language of reflex and automatism is never far from Lewis's mind, whether in discussion of modern philosophy, aesthetics, or science. Yet, the adage "the enemy of my enemy is my friend" never applied to Lewis, least of all when it came to vitalism. While he shared with vitalists a critique of materialist science, he was brutal about the failures of the vitalist project as a whole.[4] In *The Art of Being Ruled* (1926), he called Sorel "the key to all contemporary political thought" and characterized Bergson as "the great organizer of disintegration in the modern world," the man most responsible for "the enslaving of the intelligent to the affective nature."[5] For Lewis, vitalism represented the worst kind of faux liberation; the efforts of writers like Lawrence to transcend the politics of reflex resulted, he averred, not in the true volition of the creative individual but the "transform[ation] [of] the living into the machine."[6] In vitalism's disregard for cognition in favor of intuition, he saw a political project whose shortcomings were painfully obvious. As he would write of Lawrence's fiction, the "important thing" in his work is its "insistence upon *mindlessness* as an essential quality of what is admirable."[7] Against vitalists like Lawrence, Lewis asserted the virtues of the rational mind: "I would rather have an ounce of human 'consciousness' than a universe full of 'abdominal' afflatus and hot, unconscious, 'soulless,' mystical throbbing," he concluded in reference to Lawrence.[8] Vitalism was quite typical of modernist culture at large in his estimation since it merely reproduced the very same political problems it had set out to solve. Bergson found good company in Lewis's writings beside modernists like Joyce, Woolf, and Stein, whose aesthetic strategies not only appear indebted to vitalist values of *durée*, but whose writing failed to adequately address the habituating forces of mass life. For Lewis, their "revolutionary" approach to literary form encodes the worst kinds of cultural cliché and sham individualism. Their attempts to imagine aesthetic solutions adequate to the politics of reflex simply reproduced its worst elements, just as vitalists had done. "Whenever we get a good thing, its shadow comes with it, its *ape* and familiar," Lewis wrote in *The Art of Being Ruled*.[9]

Vitalism was for Lewis the most representative phenomenon of a culture that celebrated the reflexive and mechanical at the expense of the creative individual. But try as he might to blame Sorel and Bergson for the ills of the period, Lewis ultimately regarded them less as the agents of mass cultural decay than as its most telling symptoms. The transformation of the living into the machine required a more potent enemy than the vitalists presented, a true puppeteer to pull the strings. This chapter looks at an institution that was, in key ways, the historical source of Lewis's anxieties. As democratic countries coped with the social and economic transformations of the interwar period, they increasingly returned to the tactics of propaganda developed during the First World War. Rebranded by American experts as "public opinion" or "public relations," this emerging industry represents one of the strongest institutions within the politics of reflex—indeed, a kind of ideological antithesis to vitalism itself. Buoyed by the findings of crowd psychologists and the behaviorist perspective that we are all "organic machine[s]," public relations experts rejected the vitalist emphasis on the material indetermination of human life.[10] Instead, they worked to deploy the new technologies of the mass media to corral human reflex in the service of their clients.

This chapter focuses on Lewis's writings of the 1920s and 1930s, which examined the political and aesthetic consequences of a changing media ecology, one that gave experts the ability to condition reflexes and manufacture consent. For Lewis, the use of propaganda techniques within democracies represented the ultimate swindle of mass culture—an effort to inhibit the world-changing powers of individuals through the technologies of the mass media. Lewis's writing of this period mirrors discussions already underway in England and the United States about the uses of propaganda in a democracy. As cultural commentators and an emerging generation of PR experts understood, the new techniques of public relations threatened to undercut liberal ideals of agency, individualism, and the value of a free press at the same time that they promised to solve some of the most pressing issues of mass democracy. As I will show, the new values of reflex celebrated by the public relations industry manifest in Lewis's work in his attention to the hidden, secret, or covert "manipulators" of public opinion—what the American PR expert Edward Bernays called the "invisible government."[11] By placing the invisible government at the center of his massively ambitious literary and critical project, Lewis offered an acute diagnosis of the problems that the politics of reflex posed to both modernist culture and the political structures of mass modernity.

Public Reflex in Peacetime

Among the many forms of utopianism that animated late nineteenth-century Europe was a faith in the power of the press to usher in an era of mass democracy. In *Degeneration* (1892), Max Nordau caricatured a fin-de-siècle optimism that a mass media would radically expand the political horizons of the newly enfranchised masses:

> The humblest village inhabitant has to-day a wider geographical horizon, more numerous and complex intellectual interests, than the prime minister of a petty, or even a second-rate state a century ago. If he do but read his paper, let it be the most innocent provincial rag, he takes part, certainly not by active interference and influence, but by a continuous and receptive curiosity, in the thousand events which take place in all parts of the globe, and he interests himself simultaneously in the issue of a revolution in Chili, in a bush-war in East Africa, a massacre in North China, a famine in Russia, a street-row in Spain, and an international exhibition in North America.[12]

Nordau here satirized a sentiment, common at the turn of the century, that in leveling access to information, modernization acted as an antiseptic on the narrow prejudices and provincialisms of common people. The circulation of British newspapers to a million readers in 1850 exploded to over 10.6 million by the interwar period, allowing an ever more literate populace the ability to satisfy their "continuous and receptive curiosity" and transcend the limitations of knowledge imposed by geography.[13] The laying of underground cables by the British Empire, the growth of commercial and postal infrastructures, and a boom in the diversity and number of newspapers all helped transform the information ecology of the nineteenth century into a modern, mass enterprise with radically democratizing potential.

But the modernization of the print media—and the later growth of media forms like cinema and the wireless—also opened the door to new forms of political control antithetical to the hopes of fin-de-siècle Europe. Already by the end of the nineteenth century, the French sociologist Gabriel Tarde lamented that as newspapers offered to "nationalize . . . and even internationalize, the public mind," they threatened to speed the dissemination of opinion without elevating reason.[14] This problem would only grow more acute in the opening decades of the century; with the complete mobilization of both military and civilian forces in the First World War, belligerent nations were forced, for the first time in history, to consider the importance of civilian morale. Active efforts were made by most governments to not only gauge the public's attitudes toward the ongoing conflict but to shape them using new technologies of communication and an expanding print press. As British "press barons" like Lords Beaverbrook and Northcliffe were tapped to oversee the newly formed Ministry of Information and the Department of Enemy Propaganda, respectively, the organized control and dissemination of information became an object of study in its own right. And though the conclusion of hostilities saw the demobilization of such bureaus, the war had decidedly changed the political significance of the new "mass media."[15] While Nordau's contemporaries could see a democratizing force, veterans of propaganda efforts on both sides of the conflict entered the interwar period aware of the power of information in shaping electorates and armed with new techniques for doing so. Codified in the interwar period as "public relations," professional efforts to control and manipulate an information milieu would prove as valuable in peacetime as in wartime, becoming an enduring fixture of the twentieth century and one of the most important institutions within the politics of reflex.

Despite the demobilization of England's wartime propaganda efforts, commentators on both sides of the Atlantic were quick to see the potential of such techniques in the interwar period. In *Propaganda Technique in the World War* (1927), the American political scientist Harold Lasswell predicted that a newly professionalized industry of shaping public opinion would continue to expand in peacetime: "It is to be expected that governments will rely increasingly upon the professional propagandists for advice and aid," he opined.[16] Lasswell's prophecy was, if anything, slightly behind the times. In England, corporate interests had already begun efforts to actively shape public opinion before the onset of the war. According to David Miller and William Dinan, by 1911 British financier Dudley Docker "was organising corporate propaganda outfits known as 'Business Leagues' under the slogan 'pro patria imperium in imperio'—For our country; a government within a government."[17] These leagues would go on to form part of a much wider network of efforts to promote a free enterprise agenda during the decidedly pro-labor decade of the 1920s. Such efforts to mobilize public opinion were cognate with larger attempts by government to employ the mass media and the techniques of public relations. Charles Higham, an expert in corporate propaganda in the United Kingdom and one of two people knighted after the war for pioneering work in propaganda, explained that corporate techniques of publicity could easily be used to orchestrate political consent during peacetime. Arguing that the twentieth century would be an epoch defined by emotion rather than reason, he advocated for a "science" of sculpting public opinion.[18] In his 1920 book, *Looking Forward: Mass Education through Publicity*, he argued that "there is no good habit or lofty idea that could not be inculcated in a People in a few short years if the right methods were used."[19] Through a scientifically minded state publicity bureau, "We can create a new outlook . . . we can move human energy in any direction by organized and public persuasion."[20] The desire to "educate" citizens through a science of mass persuasion was in part driven by commercial exigencies of the interwar period, but Higham was also attentive to the utility of such a science to government itself. He appropriately dedicated *Looking Forward* to David Lloyd George, whose coalition government took an active interest in the use of propaganda during peacetime. In spite of widespread misgivings about the use of such techniques in peacetime, within the volatile environment of the 1920s propaganda techniques—now recast as "publicity," "education," or "public relations"—were in high demand in both the public and private sphere. As Mariel Grant notes, "During the inter-war years the use of publicity [in England] underwent considerable expansion" and "publicity" became "a legitimate function of government departments."[21] The nineteenth-century ideal of the state as a disinterested institution capable of standing apart from politics gave way to a state that was not only involved in the everyday life of citizens but that actively worked to shape the perceptions of citizens. Richard S. Lambert, founding editor of the BBC journal *The Listener*, explained in 1938 that while there is "no central agency for government propaganda in Britain . . . gradually there has sprung up piecemeal a large number of separate departmental or semi-official propagandist agencies which, though unco-ordinated, cover much the same ground as would be covered by a modern Ministry of Information."[22]

That England came to rely on techniques of mass persuasion is in part a consequence of the new infrastructures of communication and technologies for propagating information. But the emergence of a public relations industry also depended on shifting understandings of human psychology, especially those that prioritized reflex and the power of milieu over the rational agency of citizens. Scholars have often linked the rise of public relations to a growing recognition of the power of the unconscious, particularly as it manifested in Freudian psychology. Priscilla Wald, for example, has grounded the work of the American PR pioneer Edward Bernays in psychoanalysis, noting that as Freud's nephew, "Bernays was exceptionally familiar with his uncle's formulations" and that they "informed his most basic sense" of how to manipulate the public.[23] Michael North has likewise argued that, in establishing the role of the unconscious in ordinary life, Freud's work provided an intellectual foundation for public relations as a whole. "Psychoanalysis," he argues, "taught its adherents, among many other things, that perception is not spontaneous and voluntary but conditioned and that bias is therefore not incidental but intrinsic to human consciousness."[24] However tempting it is to place public relations within a history of psychoanalysis, models of the unconscious that emphasized bodily conditioning were hardly Freudian in nature. As Douglas Mao notes, Freud's evolving conception of the unconscious stood in tension with older models that stressed the "conspicuous physical interactions between individual and environment that seemed to occur in the absence of conscious decision."[25] While Freudian categories would by midcentury underwrite important elements of the American public relations industry, in the 1920s the first generation of PR experts were as likely to critique Freud as to celebrate him.[26]

In lieu of Freud's system of complexes and psychological structures, early PR experts drew upon the empirical tradition of Watson, Pavlov, and their predecessors in conceiving a mode of politics in which conditioned reflex was the key to promoting products and policies. Like Watson, who understood behavior as the product of bodily contact with a given milieu, public relations explored the idea that citizens vote and consume based not on rational deliberation but on the ways they have been conditioned. Efforts to manipulate public reflexes were always grounded in an understanding of public opinion as both empirically knowable and malleable. In this sense, public relations experts worked within a behaviorist paradigm; images, language, and information encountered within the mass media were, for PR experts, material stimuli that could be manipulated in order to condition reflexes—thus, in Watson's words, opening "the behavior of the human being as a whole . . . to objective control."[27] Like behaviorists, PR experts regularly used the language of physical reflexes to describe the cognitive habits they hoped to instill in the populace. In *Crystallizing Public Opinion* (1923), Edward Bernays stated the link directly: "Mental habits create stereotypes just as physical habits create certain definite reflex actions. . . . They are determined by the outward stimuli to which the individual has been subject as well as by the content of his mind."[28] The task of the public relations expert was thus, Bernays averred, "to discover what the stimuli are to which public opinion responds most readily."[29] In *The Phantom Public* (1925), Walter Lippmann rooted mass democracy in conditioned reflex, arguing that "the number of mice and monkeys known to have been deceived in laboratories is surpassed only by the hopeful citizens of a democracy."[30] Because "man's reflexes are, as the psychologists say, conditioned . . . he responds quite readily to a glass egg, a decoy duck, a stuffed shirt or a political platform."[31]

In interwar England, professional efforts to manipulate public opinion along behaviorist lines raised considerable concern among the public. According to Jacquie L'Etang, as institutions for mobilizing public sentiment expanded, many citizens voiced the opinion that "such activities were not entirely appropriate for a democratic country and, in particular, that they were somehow 'un-English.'"[32] The idea that efforts to covertly shape public opinion were undemocratic was justly earned. Even when conducted in the service of democratic ends, public relations challenged pieties about the role of individual agency, rationality, and the press within a liberal political order. Walter Lippmann, a founding editor of *The New Republic* and a leading figure in America's wartime propaganda efforts, turned his attention in the interwar period to elucidating the political dangers for democracy implicit in the collusion of science, politics, and the media. In his 1922 book, *Public Opinion*, he offered a critical analysis of how this new mass media threatened to exacerbate tendencies already implicit in human susceptibility. Our political attitudes and behavior, he argued, always take shape within circumscribed conditions rather than the total universe of possible information. While we like to think that the mass media gives us access to the real world at large, in truth we are susceptible to the much more limited milieu we inhabit—what he called "pseudo-environments." These pseudo-environments always present a challenge to citizens because they incapacitate disinterested, rational choice by imposing "stereotypes" of thought on citizens. Because we inhabit pseudo-environments, he explains, "We are told about the world before we see it. We imagine most things before we experience them. And those preconceptions . . . govern deeply the whole process of perception."[33] For Lippmann, our political behaviors depend to a large degree on how we have been conditioned by our milieu, which means that collective perceptions are always freighted in preestablished ways; between "man and his environment" a "pseudo-environment" is always at work, and "to that pseudo-environment his behavior is a response."[34]

British citizens might reasonably have expected that the mass media would solve such problems. After all, ready access to information from every corner of the globe should have shattered the cognitive stereotypes enforced by one's pseudo-environment. But visions of the press as a force for exploding the cognitive boundaries imposed by geography were increasingly treated as a fantasy native to the nineteenth century. As British author and politician Norman Angell wrote in his 1922 book *The Press and the Organisation of Society*, "It is one of the disillusionments of a purely political democracy that the 'free Press' . . . has become one of the worst obstacles to the development of a capacity for real self-government, perhaps the worst of all the menaces to modern democracy."[35] Lippmann's experience during the war had suggested that for all the promises of the modern mass media, it could not deliver to readers an unbiased perspective of the real situation of the modern world. Rather than eliminating pseudo-environments, public relations and the new mass media intensified stereotypes of thought, inhibiting apprehension of "the real environment."[36] Citing Pavlov, Lippmann suggests that "the whole structure of human culture is in one respect an elaboration of the stimuli and responses of which the original emotional capacities remain a fairly fixed center. No doubt the quality of emotion has changed in the course of history, but with nothing like the speed, or elaboration, that has characterized the conditioning of it."[37]

For writers of the modernist generation, public relations and this new information ecology raised important issues about the nature of political modernity and the role of literature within it. In some ways, PR and modernism can be thought of as occupying shared intellectual terrain. According to Michael North, literary modernism and modern public relations emerged "in close association with one another" because the modernist emphasis on the unconscious mirrored public relations' own effort to put the unconscious to practical use.[38] Even more centrally, the notion of a public unconscious promoted by early PR experts proved a key determinant of modernist aesthetics and politics. The idea that humans were inherently susceptible to conditioning by the environment they inhabited suggested, among other things, that art and literature were not autonomous from the political realm, and that they necessarily participated in conditioning the public. For Mark Wollaeger, this realization endowed modernism with deep anxieties about its role in the new information ecology, effectively aligning modernism and PR as political opposites. As he understands it, modernism worked to manage "flows of information that exceed human comprehension" through new aesthetic forms, such as "lyric immediacy and modernist mythologies."[39] Wollaeger's argument provocatively suggests a mirroring between modernism and public relations; even as modernists rejected the politics of reflex instantiated by public relations, they nevertheless elaborated new aesthetic forms with which to manage the new mass media and the precarious place of the individual within it.

In the next chapter, we will encounter a modernist in Rebecca West who participated in the politics of reflex, not by rejecting automatic behaviors but by rooting the endurance of national traditions in Pavlovian models of reflex. Here, however, I want to suggest that it is the work of Wyndham Lewis, perhaps more than any other modernist, that grapples with the manipulation of reflex through the techniques developed by PR specialists. Lewis saw the dependence of democracies on covert modes of conditioning reflex as evidence of hypocrisy at the heart of liberal politics. As wartime political techniques were being retooled in the interwar period, Lewis produced a wide-ranging body of fiction and nonfiction that took aim at the anti-individualist currents in contemporary political life. Like Lippmann, who underscored the impediments to apprehending the "real environment" within mass modernity, Lewis framed much of his interwar work as an effort to uncover "the real" and pierce the ideological veil perpetrated by those that would treat the human as "essentially a repeating-machine, a habit-machine."[40] Yet Lewis largely eschewed the "solutions" proposed by fellow modernists—including the forms identified by Wollaeger—as unconsciously replicating the politics of reflex they meant to critique. As we will see, the political techniques pioneered in fields like public relations raised anxieties for Lewis about the autonomy of individuals and our ability to access an unmediated reality, questions that left deep marks on his work during the 1920s and 1930s.

The Educationalist State and the Invisible Government

Following the dissolution of the Vorticist movement after the First World War, Lewis embarked on a massively ambitious, multigeneric criticism of the political, scientific and artistic ideologies of the twentieth century, producing well over a dozen works of fiction and nonfiction.[41] From the beginning of his career, he had been attuned to the new discourses of embodiment of the early twentieth century, including those of both vitalists and their adversaries. His short stories, collected as *The Wild Body* (1928), and the Vorticist manifesto *The Caliph's Design* (1919) drew on the physiological language of automatism to treat the body as a conduit for the inner life. But it was not until the interwar period that Lewis placed the political ramifications of reflex at the center of his work. In the fiction and nonfiction he produced between the world wars, contemporary scientific debates about embodiment, particularly the work of Pavlov and Watson, occupy a central place. Lewis repeatedly turned his ire on behaviorism—that "extreme gospel of the Machine Age"—including in his 1932 novel *Snooty Baronet*, which is narrated by a British disciple of Watson.[42] While he regarded behaviorism as intellectually pernicious, Lewis was broadly convinced of its claims and weary of its use as a political tool.

The idea that bodies are susceptible to the welter of stimuli in their environment, and thus manipulable, became the foundation of Lewis's sprawling analysis of mass modernity throughout the interwar period. In his nonfiction work, particularly *The Art of Being Ruled* and *Time and Western Man*, Lewis's concern with automatic behaviors cathects on the role of the mass media to condition the reflexes of the populace, and the power of trained experts in working the levers of power. While these texts pursue distinct arguments, they make a remarkable pair because they cohere around a shared understanding of the role of unseen agents in manipulating political and cultural life. For Lewis, as I will show, the ability of these hidden manipulators to pull the strings of culture and politics depends to a very large degree on the scientific and technological horizons of the early century, including behaviorism's emphasis on human automatism. But these texts also extend this analysis of the mass media to a critique of liberal democracy itself. In this, Lewis's work shared with public relations a sense that classical theories of democracy, with their emphasis on individual, rational agency, were incompatible with what science had shown about human behavior. But unlike some PR experts, Lewis did not see mass conditioning as an answer to the problems of liberal democracy; indeed, much of the energy in these nonfiction texts is trained on diagnosing the political and cultural peril that these new institutions posed. While PR experts often write about the virtues of rule by invisible, unelected experts, Lewis saw such institutions as an affront to those individuals capable of genuine creativity.

Though these nonfiction texts broadly survey the cultural landscape, Lewis was particularly struck by what he saw as a secret alliance between the science of reflex and mass politics. In his 1926 book *The Art of Being Ruled*, he argues that liberal, democratic governments had effectively appropriated the lessons of the behavioral sciences and that "politics and science are today commutative."[43] One of Lewis's primary claims is that political institutions utilize the science of reflex in order to tamp down individuality in favor of social stability, uniformity, and docility. This happens not through the overt application of force or disciplinary control but through the creation of an ideological milieu that conditions the behavioral and cognitive reflexes of the populace. In Lewis's account, twentieth-century modernity had vastly simplified this process, both because science had provided the blueprint for how the human body registers the stimuli of experience, and because technology had greatly expanded the tools at the command of the state. Like public relations experts themselves, Lewis saw the new mass media as a way of conditioning citizens to the political, aesthetic, and social values of the unseen agents who stood behind such mechanisms, a process he ironically called "education." As he explained, "the machinery of education, of the press, cinema, [and] wireless" creates a "social environment" that tends to diminish people's genuine individuality in favor of social orthodoxy.[44] This "education" "provides [people] with a system of habits which agree with their neighbor's habits, and from this coma they seldom wake."[45] Being "ruled" in *The Art of Being Ruled* thus entails nothing more than simply existing within an ideological environment—"soaking in certain beliefs and conventions"—and unconsciously reproducing the stereotypes of thought it provides.[46]

Of course such environments have always existed, but Lewis's argument is that the organized creation of these environments constituted an entirely new approach to political life, one that dramatically skewed democratic values of individuality. In "our educationalist era," he writes in *The Art of Being Ruled*, "education plays, and will continue to play, a much more important part in government than physical and exterior force. Force is a passing and precarious thing, whereas to get inside a person's mind and change his very personality is the effective way of reducing him and making him yours."[47] Like D. H. Lawrence, who feared the "idealist" strand within modern institutional structures, Lewis regarded the state's ability to condition thought and action as an immediate threat to the creative potentiality of the individual. Lewis clearly had formal schooling in mind, but "education" here includes any form of stimuli intended to condition the habits of a citizenry, particularly those in the new mass media.[48] Unlike Charles Higham, whose *Looking Forward* used "education" and "persuasion" as synonyms for a new, enlightened form of government, Lewis regarded such a politics as a malignant and ubiquitous facet of mass modernity. "What we call conventionally the *capitalist* state," he concludes, "is as truly *an educationalist state*."[49]

As we have already seen, Lewis was far from the only writer of the era to fret about the power of milieu. But his work is marked by a particularly strong sense that the "education" to which citizens were subject depended on a small, unseen cabal of "manipulators" pulling the levers of power, as he suggested in *Time and Western Man*.[50] This idea saturates Lewis's writing of the period; as a result, scholars like David Trotter and Andrew Gaedtke have seen in Lewis a brand of paranoia common to modernist experience.[51] To write off Lewis as simply paranoid, however, is to miss how an emerging class of British media experts themselves saw the new mass media. For pioneers in radio and cinema, among other fields, the power to manipulate public opinion and "educate" citizens was a source of great optimism. While media experts were, in some cases, anxious about the antidemocratic significance of mass education, they were also optimistic about their own ability to solve the problems Lewis identified with the "educationalist state."

One cultural field whose political thinking was shaped by these concerns was the British Documentary Film Movement. Lewis had classed cinema among the institutions that made up "the machinery of education," and it is easy to see why. The British Documentary Film Movement took root in the interwar period in lockstep with public relations, and directly took up its political agenda. Founded in the 1920s by John Grierson, the Documentary Film Movement grew out of an understanding of media's power to condition the reflexes of citizens, a political project Grierson explicitly linked to the thinking of Lippmann.[52] "Many of us after 1918," he writes, "were impressed by the pessimism that had settled on Liberal theory. We noted the conclusion of such men as Walter Lippmann, that because the citizen, under modern conditions, could not know everything about everything all the time, democratic citizenship was therefore impossible."[53] Documentary film, as he understood it, was an attempt to "solve the problem" of mass democracy by using "the new wide-reaching instruments of radio and cinema as necessary instruments in both the practice of government and the enjoyment of citizenship."[54] Grierson was initially tasked by the Empire Marketing Board (EMB) with promoting the products of the British Empire and selling the idea of the empire itself. Headed by noted public relations expert Stephen Tallents, the EMB looked to the new mass media, as Grierson wrote in *Cinema Quarterly*, "to change the connotation of the word 'Empire'" by bringing it "into common imagination."[55] In a spate of films about the products of the British Empire—such as the tea of Ceylon (*Song of Ceylon*), North Sea herring (*Drifters*), and New Zealand butter (*Solid Sunshine*)—Grierson worked to propagate an image of the empire as a site of cultural modernity and technological sophistication.[56]

While Grierson understood that cinematic propaganda could be an impediment to democracy, he largely agreed with public relations experts who argued that propaganda was essential to making democracy function. "Instead of propaganda being less necessary in a democracy," Grierson argued, "it is more necessary" because it allows the state to advance a common agenda rather than contend with a morass of individuals.[57] Making democracy work thus entailed largely forgoing an older ideal of democratic society, which prioritized the rational agency of citizens. Instead, he understood cinema as a way of conditioning viewers—what, in an address to the National Union of Teachers, he described as "stimuli to behaviour."[58] The problem of mass democracy, Grierson concluded, was not that citizens are susceptible to the pseudo-environments in which they are situated, as Lippmann had argued; it is that these pseudo-environments are precarious and would require proper manipulation if England and its empire were to survive the challenges of mass enfranchisement.

Straddling the private and public realm, the British Documentary Film Movement drew on the technological means of the mass media to propagate political reflexes and manage the unruliness of public opinion in an era of mass democracy. But the anxieties and optimism that animate Grierson's thinking—and fueled Lewis's so-called paranoia—were also manifest in discourse around radio technology. For the leading figures within British broadcasting, the wireless represented a way of stimulating public rationality as well as a dangerously antidemocratic force of mass education. The director-general of the BBC, John Reith, promoted the wireless as a method to create, in his words, "an informed and reasoned public opinion as an essential part of the political process in mass democratic society."[59] While radio offered a means of mass education that promised to unify the electorate, even the most ardent evangelists of the wireless, including Reith, noted that such visions stood in tension with the apparatus's very pervasiveness. As Debra Rae Cohen notes, Reith was often accused of being a kind of dictator, shaping public opinion through the ubiquitous but invisible force of the radio. Unlike the cinema, whose institutional backing within existing political channels was limited, the BBC was granted a royal charter, which endowed the new medium with the imprimatur of the state.[60] Many contemporary observers thus distrusted the wireless as an antidemocratic institution, whose "monoglossic power" was "seemingly impossible to ignore, rival, or subvert."[61] The tension between the wireless as a democratizing force and an essentially authoritarian one motivated many editorials in the BBC journal, *The Listener*, which acknowledged "the danger of mechanizing thoughts through broadcasting" and hoped to promote active forms of listening.[62]

Like John Grierson, Reith resolved the antidemocratic implications of the medium by insisting on the necessity of wireless within a democracy rather than by eschewing its monopolistic power. Reith seems to have been aware of the contradictions implicit within the new media; promoting democracy meant, in effect, saturating the milieu of citizens in a way that made the pseudo-environment more powerful rather than less. But the wireless raised another issue within interwar criticisms of the mass media, namely the role of unseen, vested interests in the creation of public opinion. Part of the danger of the radio, contemporary commentators observed, was the sense that content was not only being absorbed wholesale by listeners, but that it was often shaped by hidden powers. In *Broadcast over Britain* (1924), Reith's celebration of the unifying character of radio turns on a slightly sinister figure common to public relations and interwar media discourse: invisibility. The wireless, Reith notes, "ignores the puny and often artificial barriers which have estranged men from their fellows. It will soon take continents in its stride, outstripping the winds; the divisions of oceans, mountain ranges, and deserts will be passed unheeded. It will cast a girdle round the earth with bands that are all the stronger because invisible."[63] According to Cohen, this moment in the history of the medium was rife with anxieties about the "nonappearance" of orchestrating figures like Reith and the invisible presence of wireless communications.[64] For interwar modernists like Lewis, the democratizing potential of the medium tended to collapse in to its opposite; as Cohen writes, "Accessibility becomes inescapability; education, indoctrination; radio's phatic power an almost Marinettian destructive force; and its peculiar intimacy, intrusion, seduction, violation."[65]

If Lewis's analysis of the "educationalist state" appears to turn on a paranoid sense of mass manipulation, these sentiments were rooted in a rapidly changing media ecology and what he called "the hypnotism of cinema, wireless, and press."[66] The problem for Lewis was not simply that men like Reith and Grierson could condition the reflexes of citizens, but that they could do so from a position of invisibility. *Time and Western Man* and *The Art of Being Ruled* repeatedly denounce "the mechanical pressure of public opinion" and its creation through regimes of publicity, advertisement, and public relations.[67] In these texts, Lewis wanted to illuminate the efforts of these invisible figures "imposing [their] values upon the impressionable material of life."[68] As he wrote in the introduction to *Time and Western Man*, every person has a choice: "Either he must be prepared to sink to the level of chronic tutelage and slavery, dependent for all he is to live by upon a world of ideas, and its manipulators, about which he knows nothing: or he must get hold as best he can of the abstract principles involved in the very 'intellectual' machinery set up to control and change him."[69] But while Lewis was sensitive to the emergence of public relations and the power of the mass media to "educate" citizens, he was not on firm ground in identifying the figures orchestrating public opinion. His efforts to anatomize the conditioning forces of mass society come up, again and again, against a vision of social relations manipulated by absent or invisible agents whose interests, tactics, and means are, by definition, unknowable.

The existence of such hidden manipulators became a hugely important aspect of Lewis's thought, configuring some of the main formal features of his interwar work. As we will see, Lewis's novels often cohere around the unseen agents that operate the marionettes and automata that populate them. But the work of such manipulators left its own marks on his nonfiction as well, challenging Lewis to discern their traces and the "hidden liaisons" between the educationalist state and modernist cultures of various stripes.[70] If Lewis could not represent a will at work in mass culture, he could at least demonstrate the "hidden cable" that united the most salient features of the culture created by the educationalist state.[71]

It is worth noting that Lewis's obsession with the "hidden" forces in culture and politics found an echo in the thinking of public relations experts themselves. Edward Bernays's work proves valuable in this connection. A pioneer of "public relations"—a term that he coined—Bernays, like Lippmann, had gained much of his insight into the power of media through his work as a propagandist during the First World War. In his 1928 book, *Propaganda*, Bernays suggests that individual agency is radically determined by the environment citizens inhabit, and that these political environments are the deliberate creation of powerful interests within society. In the opening lines of the book, Bernays suggests, without irony, that democracy actually *depends* on such control. He writes, "The conscious and intelligent manipulation of the organized habits and opinions of the masses is an important element in democratic society. Those who manipulate this unseen mechanism of society constitute an invisible government which is the true ruling power of our country."[72] Bernays's account of public perception coheres around the same physiological paradigm that Lewis and Lippmann employ—that of conditioned reflex and habits. But Bernays adds an important element to Lippmann's analysis of mass society in his candid attribution of influence to powerful men who control public opinion from behind the scenes. The modern media apparatus, he suggests, simultaneously benefits and occludes the interests of powerful men. This group can dictate "almost every act of our daily lives," Bernays claims, and yet never enter the consciousness of those they manipulate.[73]

While Lippmann had regarded the birth of this media apparatus as a radical affront on the operation of democracy, in Bernays's analysis the "invisible government" is a necessary element of civil society. Just as Grierson celebrated documentary's ability to propagate collective values and thus make democracy work, Bernays argued that in an increasingly complex society the everyday citizen cannot be expected to make up his or her mind about esoteric matters, like economics, without the guidance of an expertly manipulated pseudo-environment. But in foregrounding the manipulation of habit as the foundation of mass democracy, Bernays laid bare the undemocratic nature of modern political life. Mass modernity is not, his analysis suggests, a structure in which the electorate approaches a perfect democratic ideal through access to the real environment; it depends, instead, on mechanisms for corralling and enforcing the goals of the invisible government. To be educated—to be a member of the educationalist state—is not to be enlightened but to be habituated. As Bernays explicitly puts it: "Instead of a mind, universal literacy has given [the citizen] rubber stamps inked with advertising slogans, with editorials, with published scientific data, with the trivialities of the tabloids and the platitudes of history, but quite innocent of individual thought. Each man's rubber stamps are the duplicates of millions of others, so that when those millions are exposed to the same stimuli, all received identical imprints."[74] In Bernays's account, it is precisely the stereotypes provided by an environment that make democracy work—even if "democracy" now means something like rule by a small, unelected and unseen cabal, and political choice most closely resembles the salivation of Pavlov's dog.

If for Bernays this new media apparatus could appear as the culmination of liberal democratic practice, for Lippmann and Lewis the mass media underscored just how mistaken the original theorists of democracy had been about the nature of political will. These early theorists mistakenly assumed that the art of government is a natural endowment within all minds, Lippmann argued. "What counted [for civic participation] was a good heart, a reasoning mind, a balanced judgment," not a consideration of how facts were acquired.[75] The democrat, Lippmann says, "is hypnotized by the belief that the great thing is to express the will of the people, first because expression is the highest interest of man, and second because the will is instinctively good."[76] However, in the era of the new mass media, the will of the common citizen could no longer appear as authentically individual, much less a uniquely privileged vantage from which to apprehend the real. As Michael North has argued, "public opinion" became "synonymous with prejudice and stereotype . . . a web of partially articulated presuppositions, received ideas, beliefs, and prejudices from which there is essentially no appeal, because there is no space outside from which they might be perceived."[77] The result for Lippmann, as for Lewis, was an unprecedented assault on the nature of the individual self. "The private self is already thoroughly public, but in a negative sense now that the public has lost its aura of impartiality," North explains.[78] In this political context, will could appear as nothing less than the product of one's conditioning. Thus, for Lippmann, the democratic fetish for expressing the collective political will is folly of the greatest sort. He explains:

> Under the impact of propaganda, not necessarily in the sinister meaning of the word alone, the old constants of our thinking have become variables. It is no longer possible, for example, to believe in the original dogma of democracy; that

the knowledge needed for the management of human affairs comes up spontaneously from the human heart. Where we act on that theory we expose ourselves to self-deception, and to *forms of persuasion that we cannot verify*. It has been demonstrated that we cannot rely upon intuition, conscience, or the accidents of casual opinion if we are to deal with the world beyond our reach.[79]

Lippmann readily acknowledged that immersion within the new media ecology of the interwar period necessarily entailed an inability to account for the forms of persuasion silently conditioning citizens. As a result, not only could individual opinions not be distinguished from those engineered by the likes of Bernays, but the engineers of public opinion would themselves remain beyond the apprehension of common, democratic subjects.[80]

Throughout the 1920s and early 1930s, Lewis worked within the very political paradigm outlined by Bernays and Lippmann. For Lewis, the inability to know where our opinions come from threatened to undermine the operation of democracy by curtailing individuality itself. In *The Art of Being Ruled*, he offers a prolonged attack on the essentially democratic faith in "the *will of the greatest number*," or what, citing a then current phrase within discussions about the popular press, he calls "the dogma of *What the Public Wants*."[81] Like Lippmann and Bernays, Lewis's analysis extends from a reading of twentieth-century modernity in which will itself had become little less than the product of social and political conditioning. As he writes in *The Art of Being Ruled*, "nothing that can properly be called *will* exists," for "in speaking of 'the Public' we must speak of that sad product of publicity that we see around us."[82] Here as elsewhere, "publicity" connotes not commercial advertisement but the political techniques of mass democracy—a reliance on "suggestion, persuasion, and 'education'" for political ends.[83]

This new political paradigm—rule by an invisible government—constituted for Lewis a staggering rebuke of the premises of democratic practice. Founded on an ideological commitment to the will of the greatest number and the logic of the common man, liberalism appears helplessly backward in the era of mass manipulation—ready to hail any political decision, no matter how scripted by public relations experts, as the genuine expression of rational individuals. As Lewis saw it, democracy is not a free system; it is a system of habit in which "the vote of the free citizen is a farce."[84] Newspapers, the cinema, and the wireless come to symbolize the vast communication network through which citizens are physiologically conditioned to vote in prescribed ways. In *The Art of Being Ruled* he writes, "At a word (or when sufficiently heated by a week's newspaper-suggestion), at the pressing of a button, all these hallucinated automata, with their technician-trained minds and bodies" can be mobilized toward specific ends—ends not "willed" in the usual sense of the word.[85] Ultimately, this transformation of political life derives from what Lewis had termed the "commutative" nature of science and politics in the modern era, one which, in Lippmann's view, constituted *the* crisis of modernity. As Lippmann explains in *Public Opinion*, "As a result of psychological research, coupled with the modern means of communication, the practice of democracy has turned a corner. A revolution is taking place, infinitely more significant than any shifting of economic power."[86]

For Lewis, this revolution constituted a repudiation of the traditionally democratic emphasis placed on individualism. Because our choices are always formed in relation to stimuli and agents we cannot see, Lewis averred, the very notion of individual autonomy has been poisoned. The result was that much that passes for individualism is in fact the flux of our conditioning circumstances. Fashion is exemplary of this shift. In *Propaganda*, Bernays outlines the process by which the "individual" choice of clothing is conscripted by a set of agents that are never visible to the consumer. He explains, "A man buying a suit of clothes imagines that he is choosing, according to his taste and his personality."[87] "In reality," however, "he may be obeying the orders of an anonymous gentleman tailor in London" whose decisions percolate through a system of social relations, affecting customs even on the frontiers of the fashionable world. Importantly, this mode of transforming behavior works not according to an older advertising paradigm in which repetition creates an association in the consumer's mind; instead, the public relations specialist strategically saturates the milieu of the consumer so that ideas will come to him *as if they were his own*.[88] In this way, what appears at first sight as an expression of individual volition—the choice of clothes—appears on further analysis to disclose a process of manipulation.[89] In Lewis's nonfiction, fashion became a functional metaphor for describing the work of the invisible government. As he puts the matter in *The Art of Being Ruled*, "The ideas of a time are like the clothes of a season: they are as arbitrary, as much imposed by some superior will which is seldom explicit."[90] In the long run, Lewis argues, such a situation is bound to transform the nature of individuality itself since we are perpetually invited to hold "a kind of fashionable attitude to [our] own beliefs," which are forever changing with the needs of the invisible government.[91] As he explains in the opening chapter of *Time and Western Man*, life "regulated by the clock of fashion" necessarily demotes the individual to a mere "containing frame" for the stimuli we erroneously call "'personality.'"[92] "Personality" was a term fraught with contradiction. John Watson had defined personality as "the totality or sum of my habit systems, my conditionings," and the rising cachet of the term within advertising and practical psychology emptied it of virtually all meaning for Lewis.[93] As Heather Arvidson has written, personality was for Lewis but a "hypnotic token that means the reverse of what it purports."[94] Personality, in short, was a sham concept meant only to conceal the work of others in constructing the attitudes and behaviors of the populace. Much of modernism's insistent individualism, then, appeared to him as little else than an ideological celebration of others' ability to covertly condition us. Personality is but "a pattern imposed . . . by means of education," a refuge for the weak, he wrote.[95]

Even as *The Art of Being Ruled* and *Time and Western Man* attempt to provide a diagnostic methodology for discerning the invisible agents at work within the educationalist state, the diabolic hypnotists of mass society remained hidden even from Lewis. Instead of exposing the powerful interests behind the apparatuses of mass suggestion, Lewis attempted to apprehend the *symptoms* of a political system that dissolved the genuinely democratic values of individuality, rationality, and agency, in favor of reflex and political passivity. By unmasking the anti-individualist tendencies lurking underneath the most varied phenomena of the modernist world—from philosophy and science, to literature and history—his nonfiction casts an antiseptic light on the shadowy world of mass manipulation.[96] Lewis hoped that so doing would make England more suitable to a genuinely revolutionary form of art. "The rôle of the creative artist," he explained in *Time and Western Man*, "is not merely to be a medium for ideas supplied him wholesale from elsewhere, which he incarnates automatically in a technique which (alone) it is his business to perfect."[97] The genuine individual—the real artist—needed to root out the values of the educationalist state and "take steps to keep these ideas out, except such as he may require for his work."[98] Lewis made no attempt to keep these ideas out of his contemporaneous creative endeavors. Indeed, at the same time that he was elaborating a critique of the educationalist state and rule by the invisible government in his nonfiction, he was forging a new literary project in which the effects of the invisible government—if not its agents—loom large.

The Pseudo-Environment Prevails: Invisibility and *The Childermass*

Composed at the very moment that the propaganda networks of the First World War were being redeployed in peacetime and rebranded as "public relations," Wyndham Lewis's nonfiction forcefully testifies to the new power of reflex with twentieth-century political life. As I have suggested above, texts like *The Art of Being Ruled* and *Time and Western Man* stress the problems inherent in a political system governed not by overt rulers but by what Bernays called the "invisible government." For Lewis, it is the very invisibility of these governors that ensures that the masses will imagine themselves individuals, each unique in the same way, and that automatism will masquerade as agency. The problems raised by such covert conditioning determine to a large extent the nature of Lewis's nonfiction, which documents mass manipulation not by thrusting the invisible into the light, but by elucidating the ideological thread that runs through diverse aspects of mass culture. In his 1929 nonfiction book, *Paleface*, Lewis referred to this method as a "system" that might allow readers to detect the "attitudes of mind imposed upon the Many . . . by political experts."[99] Yet, even as his nonfiction offered a thoroughgoing diagnosis of how the politics of reflex changed the cultural landscape, he was careful to insist throughout that it was in the realm of aesthetics, rather than cultural critique, that solutions to the problems of mass manipulation would be found. As he wrote in *The Art of Being Ruled*, it is "along aesthetic lines that the solution of this problem should be sought rather than along moral (or police) lines, or humanitarian ones."[100] In his 1928 novel, *The Childermass*, Lewis would respond to new forms of political reflex by dramatizing for readers the operations of the invisible government.

Among the strangest texts of literary modernism, *The Childermass* represents Lewis's first effort to put into practice the political principles elucidated in *The Art of Being Ruled* and *Time and Western Man*. Begun as early as 1921 and constituting the first part of his "Human Age" trilogy (completed in 1955 with *Malign Fiesta* and *Monstre Gai*), *The Childermass* tells the story of two recently deceased men, Satters and Pullman, as they learn how to navigate purgatory. Lewis almost entirely forgoes the kind of dramatic structure that characterizes his other novels; instead, the narrative consists of only two elements—Satters and Pullman's travels through the physical landscape, and a debate they witness between political factions within the afterlife. In this last section of the novel, a character named the Bailiff, ostensibly a representative of Heaven, debates the nature of the Absolute with a faction of the dead, represented most centrally by Hyperides. Their debate ends as one character asks, "Who is to be *real*—this hyperbolical puppet [the Bailiff] or we?"[101]

The final question of the novel invokes a problem that unites *The Childermass* and the politics of reflex instantiated by public relations. As Lippmann explained, the use of propaganda techniques in peacetime interposed a politically freighted pseudo-environment between individuals and the real environment. Mark Wollaeger has argued that in the context of a mass media, the deliberate manipulation of pseudo-environments had a "derealizing effect," one that "contributed to the modernist investment in authenticity" and an "increasingly urgent fantasy of unmediated connection to the real."[102] A desire to apprehend "the real"—including the operations of hidden manipulators—certainly characterizes Lewis's work between the wars. As we have seen, much of his nonfiction attempts to differentiate between the false world of cultural and political ready-mades, and a "reality" that exists beyond them. As he wrote in *Time and Western Man*, he wanted to locate the forces that existed "*beyond the influence and reach of the individual's active and naturally imitative, but unreliable, mind.*"[103] Part of the challenge Lewis confronted in his nonfiction was the very non-appearance of the invisible government behind efforts to habituate citizens. As a result, both *The Art of Being Ruled* and *Time and Western Man* attempt to diagnose the "hidden liaisons" between cultural fields. This inability to identify the invisible government would become a structural feature of *The Childermass*, though in a different way. Centered on a main character that never appears—namely, God—this novel dramatizes for readers the political consequences of rule by an invisible government and the de-realizing effects of the pseudo-environment.

As many commentators have noted, *The Childermass* mocks many of the ideological trends diagnosed in Lewis's nonfiction. The philosophy of Bergson, Einstein's relativity, Watson's behaviorism, Spengler's theory of history, and literary modernism broadly: these all appear in the novel as objects of Lewis's contempt. In this sense, *The Childermass* works as a satirical anatomy of the various political, artistic, and scientific trends that Lewis saw as antagonistic to genuine individuality. Yet the *Childermass* is not "simply *The Art of Being Ruled* dramatized," as Hugh Kenner once posited.[104] Where Lewis's nonfiction offers itself up as a "system" for identifying anti-individualist values in mass culture, *The Childermass* works to inhibit the reader's ability to synthesize the forces conditioning characters. Extended sections that mimic the likes of Gertrude Stein and James Joyce vie with characters and scenes built according to a vast—but largely esoteric—allegorical architecture. By withholding the information necessary to understand the nature of the satire, Lewis maps the experiences of Satters and Pullman on to the real historical context of modernism's pseudo-environments—circumscribed realms of experience that inhibit knowledge of the real. To put it another way: *The Childermass* is a novel that seems to present a panoramic critique of twentieth-century modernity even as it forces the reader to confront the limits of knowledge that such a context imposes upon citizens.

This sense of limitation is accomplished in part through the genre of the afterworld narrative that Lewis adopted in *The Childermass*. But unlike traditional afterworld narratives, such as *The Divine Comedy*, *The Childermass* employs an unusual conceit: the purgatory Satters and Pullman inhabit is a *material* afterlife. As embodied souls, they physically traverse the afterworld, susceptible to all the same forms of conditioned reflex that characterize terrestrial life. Discarding the self-evident rules governing the physical universe, Lewis constructs an alternate universe that more closely adheres to the protocols of fantasy or science fiction than realism. This design allowed Lewis to stage a spectacularly hypostatized form of the subjective flux he saw as key to the educationalist state. For example, in the first chapter, "Outside Heaven," we meet Pullman. Before he is introduced by name, his observation of wild ducks in flight occasions a physical metamorphosis. Through the mere act of looking, he becomes "the man-sparrow, who multiplies precise movements, an organism which in place of speech has evolved a peripatetic system of response to a dead environment. It has wandered beside this Styx, a lost automaton rather than a lost soul."[105] Lewis hints that Pullman is the very image of a behaviorist subject, visibly manifesting his subjection to his environment; his capacity for thought and speech is replaced by reflexes and what Watson termed "word-habit."[106] Like a Pullman railroad car, his course is strictly determined. He is not a will so much as an automaton whose actions are the direct consequence of his environment. As Pullman later tells Satters, they are "behaviourist machines" damned to "a static millennium of suffering for purposes of purification."[107]

The environment to which these automata respond is not, however, simply physical. Throughout *The Childermass*, Lewis depicts characters reflexively responding to their social environment, variously aping the behavior of others and shape-shifting to fulfill specific social roles. Lewis's main characters are locked into a routine of stimulus-response, in which even their thoughts move in what the novel describes as a "silent rhythm, according to the system of habit set in motion by their meeting."[108] Silent though this rhythm may be, it constitutes one of the major dramas of the novel; as Pullman and Satters make their way through purgatory and toward the court of the Bailiff, they find themselves repeatedly transformed into a host of literary and cinematic types depending on their social context. To take just the example of Pullman, he is physically metamorphosed into a lady, the principal of a school, a school chum, a governess, a hero, a nurse, a spy, a suitor for Satters's hand, a mother, a father, a geologist, a "gelded herd-dog," an undergraduate, and a dozen other roles.[109] These transformations are occasioned by the immediate needs of the moment—namely what kind of "self" Pullman needs to be to get Satters to the Bailiff's court. Locked into a dyadic relationship, Satters and Pullman become a series of clichés as they act out set pieces and predetermined "motifs."[110] As in Lewis's later novel about behaviorism, *Snooty Baronet* (1932), the interaction between characters is as important as the physical environment itself; the roles they adopt function as a primary form of stimuli, conditioning reflex and determining action in ways that are not willed. In *The Childermass* the physical and social environments conspire to undermine the stable ego of characters—to, as Satters repeatedly says, make them "poseur[s]."[111]

We can see the function of environmental conditioning in this narrative partly as a satirical attack on the ideological trends that Lewis identified in his nonfiction. By conceiving of the afterlife in physical terms, Lewis may seem to literalize—and thus mock—the vitalist emphasis on the endless flux of self that was favored by the likes of Sorel, Bergson, and Lawrence. But we might just as well call this the logic of public relations, which had posited an idea of the subject that is transient to the point of illegibility. Within Lewis's novel, the specific causes and meanings of this subjective flux remain elusive, even when openly discussed by the Bailiff and his adversaries in the second half of the novel. In fact, only once we get beyond these moments of metamorphosis do we learn that the goal of this afterworld is to winnow out the real individuals from the conformists. As the Bailiff puts it, "To be oneself is after all the main concern of life."[112] Fredric Jameson has summarized the essential drama of the novel as "something like a search for the ego"—a kind of Dantesque pursuit of individuality rather than the soul's search for God.[113]

However, being oneself in this context means something very specific for the Bailiff. According to Pullman, the Bailiff "wants us all to *feel* as much as we conveniently can . . . on no account entirely to lose our capacity for acute and disagreeable sensation—also agreeable."[114] Indeed, as they will later learn, the Bailiff's idea of the self is entirely one based on the physical substance of the human body. As he explains it, "The more highly developed the individual . . . clearly the more the exterior world is a part of him: the more sensitive he is to stimulus, the more of the world he registers and includes, and so forth and so forth."[115] It is these "individuals," the most susceptible to stimuli, that will find their way into Heaven, the Bailiff claims. This mania for sensation certainly links the Bailiff with Lewis's disdain for vitalists like Bergson and Lawrence, as well as public relations and behaviorism. However, to read *The Childermass* through any of the specific targets blasted in Lewis's nonfiction is to misconstrue the broader agenda of this text. Even as Lewis makes periodic reference to such figures, *The Childermass* largely refuses to frame any particular agent as the source of the automatisms present in the novel. Instead, it sees the new emphasis on reflex as itself the problem. When the Bailiff claims, "There is no *you* apart from what you perceive: your senses and you with them *are* all that you habitually see and touch," we are not confronted with the dogma of Bergson, Watson, or Bernays so much as an orthodox statement of how the politics of reflex had refigured categories of agency and individuality.[116] The physical irregularities of Lewis's purgatory allow him to stress this political reality, not in relation to the specific political position that may result, but by conceptualizing human and literary character in a new way. In *The Childermass*, character is revealed as transitory, determinable, and devoid of depth—a human character that, as Lewis had suggested in *The Caliph's Design*, *is* the environment that surrounds it.[117]

However true an account this may be of the organizing logic of *The Childermass*, this analysis does not answer the question of why Lewis insisted on setting this narrative in an afterworld as opposed to, say, a dream. As I have suggested, the difficulty inherent in *The Childermass* lies in Lewis's refusal to provide a clear map of the various artistic, philosophical, and political tendencies it satirizes. If this novel is about the emphasis placed on reflex as a form of politics, the question debated by the Bailiff and Hyperides—who or what determines the rules of purgatory?—becomes more than just a metaphysical question about God, the Absolute, or the real; it is also a question about who or what determines the values promulgated in political life. Although the Bailiff presents himself as a representative of Heaven and an engineer "in human plastics," Lewis suggests throughout that he is in fact an impostor who is himself being manipulated by an invisible government.[118] Hyperides and his associates accuse him of being a fake, rejecting the Bailiff's authority over them, addressing him always as "puppet." The Bailiff's legitimacy matters a great deal to any reading of the text, for it is his failure to authoritatively explain the unusual phenomena of purgatory or the requirements of entrance into Heaven that undermines the reader's ability to definitively understand the nature of the trials undergone by Satters and Pullman. That is to say, the characters, like the reader, cannot fully make sense of the social system of this purgatory. As David Ayers explains, "The tirades of Lewis's Bailiff in *The Childermass* represent nothing less than an attempt to establish a totality of meaning where no actual meaning exists."[119] It is for this reason that the novel ends as inconclusively as it does: "Who is to be *real*?" Just as *The Apes of God* swirls around the vortex of an agent that never appears in the character of Pierpoint, the absence of God in *The Childermass* mirrors a Bernaysian invisible government, strategically inhibiting anything like a full account of what is real and what is false, what is depth and what is surface, what is authentic and what is automatic. The pseudo-environment prevails.

The non-appearance of a deity who exercises power over the bodies that populate purgatory has a dramatically de-realizing effect for characters and readers, a quality of the novel that inheres in the stylistic registers of Lewis's prose. Lewis insisted throughout his writing that the proper aesthetic category for catalyzing awareness of the new political realities of the twentieth century was what he variously called the visual, the exterior, or the surface.[120] Lewis geared his aesthetic toward depictions of a society in which individuals were driven by the most immediate and superficial forms of cultural and political stimuli. Like Satters and Pullman in *The Childermass*, the human forms that populate Lewis's novels are one-dimensional in ways that are characteristic of much modernist painting, but those human forms go out of their way to dramatize the political and social peril inherent in their one-dimensionality. As Lewis explained in *The Art of Being Ruled*, the surface is nothing other than the body that had been incorporated into the political tactics of a properly modern political sphere: "All the meaning of life is of a superficial sort, of course: there is no meaning except on the surface. It is physiologically the latest, the ectodermic, and most *exterior* material of our body that is responsible for our intellectual life."[121] In this context, "the surface" refers to the way in which political principles become physiologically embodied—"ectodermic," visible on the very surface of the body. In the same way that Watson saw human consciousness as a black box of little scientific import, Lewis's aesthetic is fundamentally geared toward the observable. But where behaviorism's "hard vision" animated an eager class of political elites, in Lewis the surface is intended to provoke "a radical uncertainty over ontological differences between the human and the machine, the living and the dead, and self and world," as Andrew Gaedtke has argued.[122] In the indistinction between people and things, Lewis stages the problems that arise in society where individual depth gives way to the superficiality of reflex, habit, and the cognitive clichés of mass society.

In this sense, Lewis's novelistic work proves to be an interesting riposte to Georg Lukács's critique of literary modernism. In Lukács's account, modernist formalism failed to present readers with an easily synthesizable vision of "the overall objective social context," a totality that might allow them to understand the historical dimension of political struggle.[123] In "Realism and the Balance" (1938) he explains, "If literature is a particular form by means of which objective reality is reflected, then it becomes of crucial importance for it to grasp that reality as it truly is, and not merely to confine itself to reproducing whatever manifests itself immediately and on the surface."[124] That Lukács employs the figural language of surface and depth, of course, conjures Lewis's own insistence on the political potential inherent in an aesthetic of the surface. While Lukács and Lewis certainly shared a critical attitude toward certain iterations of modernist literary practice, Lewis's work offers itself up as a strong challenge to the very accessibility of "the real" within the modernist context.[125] For if, as he suggested in *The Art of Being Ruled* and *Time and Western Man*, modern subjects are structurally inhibited from apprehending the real forces that influence their thought and action—if modern social relations are so constituted that we cannot apprehend the sources of the ideas we embody—then fiction's job is to represent this idea in its most superficial and automatic character.

Superficiality manifests itself in two contrary registers of *The Childermass*. On the one hand, the prose of this novel might be seen as an attempt to foreground the stereotypes that Lippmann identified as the products of mass society. As Jameson has noted, one of the central features of *The Chil-*

dermass is Lewis's emphasis on stylistic cliché. As he reads it, the novel "draws heavily and centrally on the warehouse of cultural and mass cultural cliché, on the junk materials of industrial capitalism, with its degraded commodity art, its mechanical reproduceability, its serial alienation of language, in short, with . . . that systematized network of cultural code and representation which preexists, speaks, and produces the individual subject by means of the ruse of a belief in individuality itself."[126] In Jameson's reading, Lewis's knowing appropriation of stylistic clichés produces "a kind of perceptual freshness" for readers.[127] However, while Lewis's prose often satirizes mass cultural cliché, it does not always allow the reader to hold such ready-mades at an ironic distance. As Paul Edwards argues, *The Childermass* is replete with a language of specialization that stymies any reader's efforts to fully map the world of the novel. As he writes, "That culture [that supplies Lewis with stylistic cliché] is not simply second-hand and fragmented in the sense of having been subjected to mechanical replication, it is actually replete with specialised discourses beyond the cultural horizon of most readers. . . . This culture is atomised beyond the capacity of any one person to reintegrate it."[128] So, at the level of style we get both at once—the familiar world of cliché, in which the expressions and postures of Lewis's characters reflect the ready protocols of mass society, *and* a language of specialization that gestures toward modes of experience the reader is unlikely to recognize. This stylistic duality points to a duality of the work as a whole in its efforts to dramatize the pseudo-environment. While *The Childermass* can seem to work as an anatomy of modern industrial life—one that pillories the work of Bergsonian *durée*, behaviorism, fascism and democracy, cinema, the ultra-wealthy, fashion, and a host of other targets—this jumble of cultural trends figures a world of social relationships at the same time that it exhausts any reader's ability to effectively assimilate the critique being offered.

For readers, the tension between depth and surface, between the pseudo-environment and the real, produces a curious affective experience, since the novel points toward political conditions that must—but cannot—be known. As Jameson has pointed out in relation to Lewis, in literary naturalism readers are given the ability to project themselves "into such alien experience as those of the worker or the prostitute, the beggar or the criminal" even as it "comfortably reassures the reader as to his or her fundamental difference."[129] In *The Childermass*, Lewis effectively does the opposite. Because the reader is denied a definitive understanding of the Bailiff, the meaning of the transformations undergone by the characters, or the Punch-and-Judy drama generally, we cannot easily dissociate ourselves from the physiological susceptibility that governs Satters, Pullman, and the legions of embodied souls. Readers are, in short, invited to feel lost in the welter of stimuli, to sense the personal debility promulgated by a system that inhibits knowledge of a real environment. Such has been the experience of generations of readers, including I. A. Richards, who noted the peculiar affective dimension of Lewis's novel: "I think everyone who has tried to write or talk about *The Childermass* has found himself in the same hole—the very deep and dubious hole Wyndham Lewis so craftily keeps us in. We don't know—to an agonizing degree we are not allowed to know—what it is all about. That very ignorance may be, of course, what it is all about."[130] This book is not, then, "a Rabelaisian fictional anatomy of post-war Britain," or an account of the ideological currents that animate it.[131] In place of Lukácian realism, *The Childermass* attempts to catalyze for readers an awareness of their place within a modern regime of ideological reflex, one that effectively institutes a blockage in efforts to map the social body. It narrates how an invisible government, by virtue of its invisibility, generates a phantasmagoria of ideology. In this sense, the aesthetic of the surface is the aesthetic of a social sphere in which reflex becomes *the* form of politics.

Reflex Redux

It would be difficult to overstate the accomplishments of public relations. The successes of advertising in an emerging consumer society and the propaganda machines of the First World War allowed PR to become a major, enduring institution across the twentieth century. Turning the empirical lessons of physiologists and psychologists toward pragmatic political ends, public relations experts were able to manufacture consent for a variety of political projects for which political will was otherwise absent. In this sense, the picture of society as highly susceptible to mass conditioning was to a large degree substantiated. The manifest ability of experts to influence the behaviors of great numbers of people without their knowledge allowed public relations to become the province not of a small elite, but an industry firmly established within the institutional structures of mass modernity. Yet, the early publications of PR experts reflect a certainty about their own abilities that was largely speculative. Painting a picture of the masses as endlessly susceptible to the conditioning work of the mass media, public relations imagined its own ability to dictate "almost every aspect of our daily lives," as Bernays argued in 1947.[132] In *Propaganda*, published almost twenty years earlier, he had argued for PR's unlimited power: "In almost every act of our daily lives, whether in the sphere of politics or business, in our social conduct or our ethical thinking, we are dominated by the relatively small number of persons . . . who understand the mental processes and social patterns of the masses. It is they who pull the wires which control the public mind, who harness old social forces and contrive new ways to bind and guide the world."[133] Claims about the extensiveness of public relations and its ability to "bind and guide the world" through the manipulation of "everyday life" manifest throughout the writings of early experts like Bernays and would become influential on a rising generation of public relations specialists. As Stuart Ewen has noted, the ambitions of public relations extended well beyond the commercial and political projects of mass society to include "fashioning and projecting credible renditions of reality itself."[134] These ambitions represent, at best, a utopic vision of mass society, in which the habits and reflexes of the populace could be integrated and managed to ensure the smooth functioning of economic and political life. At worst, claims about PR's extensive powers were themselves a form of advertisement—propaganda for an industry still working to gain credibility and dispel the antidemocratic associations it carried into the interwar period.[135] The vision, shared by midcentury behaviorists like B. F. Skinner, of a world more finely calibrated through regimes of conditioning was just that—a vision. In reality, while behavioral research continued to develop the political and social consequences of Watson's original program, the total mapping of the human machine required experimental knowledge not yet available. But the rhetorical power of such a program remained strong. As we will see in the next chapter, the idea of a complete control over the reflexes of the populace would, by the 1930s, become yoked to fascism and its purportedly "Pavlovian" approach to politics, even as several modernists saw in Pavlov's theories an answer to fascism.

As a strong form of the politics of reflex, PR nevertheless concretized a host of modernist anxieties about the autonomy and agency of individuals within an increasingly mediated society. In Lewis's engagement with the mass media, we can perhaps discern a link to the fascist politics that came to characterize some of his labors in the 1930s. After all, the idea that a small cabal of unelected people is secretly dictating the widest variety of social and political phenomena is a trademark of anti-Semitic paranoia, particularly as it manifested in *The Protocols of the Elders of Zion*. My sense, however, is that the appeal of fascism to Lewis rests much less on anti-Semitism than it does on a sense of liberalism's misplaced faith in the agency of ordinary people. In *Hitler* (1931), Lewis describes the class-riven society of capitalist modernity, arguing that it requires a "colourless, featureless, automaton... Nothing but a mind *without backgrounds*, without any spiritual depth, a flat mirror for propaganda, a parrot-soul to give back the catchwords, an ego *without reflection*."[136] Mass modernity, in short, is a system whose one goal is to produce predictable behaviors. The virtue of fascism seemed to be not that its citizens were freer, but that political control in such a system was overt. Fascist citizens might be automata, but at least they were not deluded into celebrating a nonexistent freedom.

It should be remembered that Lewis's vision of citizens as behaviorist marionettes was never total; while he denounced the conspiracies of control and the mass conditioning that PR represented, he retained a belief in the ability of humans to transcend these forces. For all the vitriol Lewis expends in denouncing the "creatures of habit," he was never able to shake his own early interest in the vitalist principles elaborated by Bergson. The susceptibility of bodies to their environments presented a real challenge to entrenched theories of democratic practice for Lewis. But it is a mistake to suppose that the vision of human life on display in his interwar work—with its inherent corruptibility and brute materiality—constituted an unflagging anti-humanism.[137] If we mistake the automaton as Lewis's model citizen, his entire criticism of modernity becomes an exercise in futility—possibly itself the product of mass manipulation. While works like *The Art of Being Ruled*, *Time and Western Man*, and *The Childermass* present an image of the world as dominated by conditioning forces whose origins cannot be known, it should not be forgotten that these books were written as attempts to combat the reflexive nature of interwar life, not simply to describe it. In a 1922 essay, Lewis explicitly called for an art that would at once alert us to our material susceptibility and help deliver us from the automatisms of the world: "The art impulse reposes upon a conviction that the state of limitation of the human being is more desirable than the state of the automaton; or a feeling of the gain and significance residing in this human fallibility for us. To feel that our consciousness is bound up with this non-mechanical phenomenon of life; that, although helpless in the face of the material world, we are in some way superior to and independent of it; and that our mechanical imperfection is a symbol of that."[138] Lewis's interwar work is bound, on one side, by faith in the "non-mechanical phenomenon" of life, and, on the other, by a realization that the claims of behaviorists and PR experts rested on essential truths. Industries like public relations were largely successful in exploiting the material susceptibility of citizens and consumers in the service of a more automatic society. But the existence of modernist art was a telling reminder that individuals could, with effort, escape the clichés and reflexes of modernity. By the 1930s, Lewis would argue that art's job was not simply to stand as a "symbol" for the materialist bind, but to help the denizens of mass society confront their materiality. As he would put it in his 1934 book, *Men without Art*, art helps us "recognize our animal limitations—our enormous physical and intellectual handicaps."[139] When Lewis says that we need to "*humanize* ourselves," he underscored the need for an art that simultaneously recognizes the force of conditioned reflex *and* helps us overcome the merely material world, with its attendant clichés of thought and action.[140] Like Russian Formalism, which celebrated art's ability to rupture the "automatisms of perception," Lewis's work places a primary stress on the material constraints on human life and the political consequences of ignoring them.

That the efforts of invisible governments could be overturned, contested, and made visible is the very promise of Lewis's art. In this sense, while *The Childermass* forcefully suggests the political and cultural peril of modernity's pseudo-environments, it militates for a self that transcends these conditions—a self that does not metamorphose with every passing novelty. *The Childermass* asks us to flatly reject the Bailiff's insistence throughout the text that "the mind *is* the body."[141] For if any kind of solidity exists in the modern world, it is to be found in a self that is individual, one that is capable of divesting itself of the reflexes promulgated by environment. Like Lewis's recurrent methodological injunction to locate the hidden liaisons and shared fatalisms at work across cultural fields—to, as he put it in *Paleface*, locate the centralized "syllabus of patterns" and "automatic processes" by which modern life is governed—*The Childermass* bespeaks an essentially optimistic faith in the indeterminacy of a life.[142] These methods speak, moreover, to his effort to craft a properly modernist art whose consequences would be shattering—an art capable of making contact with real, physical bodies.

4 Pavlovian Nationalism
Rebecca West's Reflex Communities

By any measure, public relations has been one of the most successful institutions to emerge from the modernist era. Though PR was still very much in its infancy as Lewis was blasting it as rule by an invisible government, by the start of the Second World War it had already become well established within commercial and political practice in the United States and Europe. By the 1950s, one could increasingly speak not just of the practice of public relations but of an entire "public relations industry." Buoyed by a postwar consumer society, particularly in the United States, this industry was firmly entrenched in the public consciousness by the middle decades of the century, when Vance Packard would assail the political and cultural effects of PR in his book, *The Hidden Persuaders* (1957). There, Packard continued in the vein of Lewis's earlier critique, arguing that "hidden" experts depend on techniques designed to influence and manipulate "the patterns of our everyday lives," typically "beneath our level of awareness."[1] Despite Packard's warning about efforts "to channel our unthinking habits, our purchasing decisions, and our thought processes by the use of insights gleaned from psychiatry and the social sciences," the industry's development continued apace.[2] Almost a hundred years after Edward Bernays coined the term "public relations," it is estimated that global revenues for the industry now top $15 billion annually, a figure that shows no signs of slowing.[3]

The rapid institutionalization of PR in the early twentieth century testifies to just how successful its underlying theories of political reflex were. It is no coincidence, then, that as PR fortified its place in Western life, behaviorism was simultaneously becoming entrenched in the scientific agenda of the twentieth century. Indeed, we might describe public relations and behaviorism as secret sharers in the politics of reflex. Even as some of the more sensational claims of John Watson's work met with skepticism, in the centers of higher learning behaviorism was gaining adherents that largely accepted its foundational premises. New institutional investments solidified the financial base for behaviorist research in the 1920s, while Watson helped create a wide, popular audience for behaviorist principles, penning influential articles in *The New Yorker*, *The New York Times*, and *Harpers Monthly* under the moniker of "Mr. Behaviourist."[4] Behaviorism would also receive a boost from Bertrand Russell, whose 1927 book *Philosophy* offered readers a glowing account of behaviorism and would find an ideal reader in B. F. Skinner, who would go on to pioneer new directions in behaviorist research after the Second World War.

The coterminous rise of PR and behaviorism speaks to a shared endeavor—an understanding of human susceptibility and the role of reflex within political life. Perhaps the most telling detail in their entwined history is the fate of Watson himself, who left Johns Hopkins in 1922 for a job with the J. Walter Thompson advertising agency. Much like Edward Bernays, Watson put the lessons of science to work in the field of public relations, helping to pioneer market research. Among other things, he showed that consumer loyalties are much more firmly grounded in their associations with a given brand name than in products themselves. By using the empirical methods of behaviorism to understand such associations and condition new ones, Watson became a successful ad man, taking on accounts with Maxwell House Coffee, Pebeco Toothpaste, Johnson's Baby Powder, and Pond's Cold Cream, among others. By 1924, he was made one of J. Walter Thompson's four vice presidents.[5]

Given the immense successes that PR and behaviorism enjoyed, it is something of a surprise to consider the fate of Ivan Pavlov. For contemporary commentators, the similarities between Pavlov's and Watson's thinking were clear. Wyndham Lewis classed Pavlov among "Testers" like Watson and Robert Yerkes in *Time and Western Man*, and I. A. Richards, in his 1925 review of *Behaviorism*, noted that the methodology invented by Watson, with its emphases on "observable responses" to stimuli, "derive[s] very largely from Pavlov's conditioned reflex methods."[6] Though not exact mirror images of each other, the differences between Pavlov's and Watson's thinking were largely a matter of nuance, with behaviorism proving far more audacious and rhetorically bombastic.[7] Despite the similarity between the two, however, the reputation of Pavlov would generally fare worse over the decades as "conditioned reflexes" and the figure of the salivating dog became a shorthand for the worst, most automatic forms of political behavior. For Cold War cultural critics, Pavlov represented a fundamental challenge to Western models of rationality and individual autonomy believed to underpin democratic practice. In an era shaped by the repressive politics of fascism, the language of Pavlovian reflex served as a useful way of understanding the popularity and success of totalitarian governments. At the same time, however, this image of political conditioning was paralleled by a positive emphasis on reflex's role in national cohesion. By the 1930s, modernist writers were appropriating Pavlov's work to imagine the nation as a site of shared reflexes rather than as a community bound by a shared story or common set of beliefs. In short, Pavlov's work was appropriated to substantiate two competing visions of nationhood—the dream of a national tradition rooted in an organic milieu, and a dystopian nightmare of totalitarian control.

This chapter unfolds the place of Pavlov's research in a disciplinary moment when reflex was gaining political currency and explores the political tensions engendered by his work. One writer who understood these tensions particularly well was Rebecca West. As an author of suffragist tracts, realist and fantasy novels, travelogues, literary criticism, and an immense body of journalism, West was in her day seen as a one-of-a-kind writer whose skills were bounded by neither genre nor subject. She was, as *Time* magazine wrote in 1947, "indisputably the world's No. 1 woman writer."[8] Her life traversed almost every corner of literary modernism and the political world that shaped it, extending well beyond the confines of female suffrage and the radicalism of the teens to include a virulent and often conservative critique of Nazism and Soviet Communism.[9] The same writer who in the mid-1920s befriended Emma Goldman and contributed an introduction to her *My Disillusionment in Russia* (1925) had by the 1950s come to feel passionately aligned with the cause of anti-communism. Given this background, it should come as no surprise that West's work represents one of the most sustained inquiries into the politics of reflex in the modernist era. Encountering Pavlov's ideas following the translation of *Conditioned Reflexes* in 1927, West was fascinated by the implications reflex had for aesthetics and politics. While contemporaries like Lewis and Lawrence were overwhelmingly opposed to the automatic in its many guises, West worked to understand how reflex could be both a positive and a negative force in a rapidly changing world. Classing Pavlov among her modernist peers, including Joyce and Proust, West hailed the work of the Russian physiologist as a true innovation with immediate implications for politics and literature. Yet, even as she celebrated Pavlov's findings for England and literary modernism, she shared the anxiety of many about the use of laboratory techniques on the public.

In West's 1941 nonfiction work, *Black Lamb and Grey Falcon*, these competing ideas of conditioned reflex grounded her analysis of nationalism. As this chapter will show, her work emphasizes the embodied, conditioned reflexes of a population as the site of national particularity. In this way, it is representative of a broader modernist affirmation of English cultural tradition that emerged with the crises of the Second World War and the ongoing decline of the British Empire. The language of physiological embodiment allowed these modernists to understand the nation as a community united by a shared space—a milieu—that endowed citizens with those uncognized modes of thought and action that Watson and others called "habit." At the same time, however, West was sensitive to the dark side of reflex for which Pavlov would soon become infamous—the application of conditioned reflex by repressive regimes. These contrary notions of the nation as a reflex community, I suggest, underpin West's work, particularly in *Black Lamb*, where they serve as a rationale for her defense of nationalism. In focusing on West's strategic deployment of Pavlov in this text, this chapter illuminates the allure and peril that Pavlov held for modernists more generally, as well as the difficulties they faced in negotiating the political tensions of conditioned reflex.

Pavlovian Politics

Very little of Ivan Pavlov's biography portends the considerable notoriety that would soon attach itself to "conditioned reflexes." Like many of his professional contemporaries in Russia, Pavlov was deeply enmeshed in debates about materialism. Influenced by nineteenth-century studies of reflex by the Russian scientist Ivan Sechenov, Pavlov benefited from readily available translations of English scientists like Darwin and Herbert Spencer. George H. Lewes's *Physiology of Common Life* (1859), in particular, was foundational for his scientific interests; encountering the book as a young man, Pavlov was fascinated by Lewes's studies of food, hunger, and digestion, concerns that would drive his own research interests and push him to refine experimental methods for testing materialist doctrine. In his early career, Pavlov devoted his labors to understanding how it is that the body knows which kinds of chemicals to secrete and in what proportions to allow food to move through the digestive tract. His innovation was to study the digestive system of animals intact, rather than through surgical methods. Unlike vivisectionists, Pavlov believed that a surgical approach that minimized the duress of animals would yield a more accurate understanding of the normal processes undergone in digestion. To do so, he invented a technique for creating fistulas that would allow researchers to feed dogs but retrieve the food just after it entered the esophagus, as well as a technique for extracting, measuring, and quantifying gastric fluids. This research became the basis of *Work of the Principal Digestive Glands* (1897), for which he was awarded the Nobel Prize in Medicine in 1904.

In and of itself, Pavlov's early work represented an important advance in research methods, but it lacked any of the political resonance that would soon be attached to his work. Following this early period of research, however, Pavlov's interests turned from digestion to a different phenomenon, one that become the central issue of early twentieth-century materialist sciences, like behaviorism. As Robert Boakes explains, in the course of his research Pavlov and his assistants became aware of the fact that "a dog would secrete gastric juice as a response, not just to the presence of food in its mouth, but also to the sight of food; or, for that matter, to the sight of anyone who regularly came to feed him."[10] Pavlov initially regarded this reaction as a "psychic secretion," reasoning that no physical stimuli had caused it. But by 1900, he came to think that such a psychological phenomenon might be explained in physiological terms. In his 1927 book, *Conditioned Reflexes*, he offered a synthesis of the experiments and findings that came of this hypothesis. Measuring and manipulating the defensive and alimentary responses of dogs to a variety of stimuli—including, most famously, dogs' salivary production at the sound of a metronome—Pavlov and his technicians attempted to empirically map the mechanisms by which bodily habits are learned and to chart the complex networks that form between these "conditioned" responses. According to Pavlov's view, such reflexes were not the product of "psychical" processes, but of material sensations. Though an individual acquires an infinitely complex accretion of these reflexes over the course of a lifetime, Pavlov hoped to illuminate the rules that dictate the way reflexes are acquired at a cognitive level, or how new neural "paths" were laid down in nerve centers. As he explained in *Conditioned Reflexes*, "We recognize them in ourselves and in other people or animals under such names as 'education,' 'habits,' and 'training'; and all of these are really nothing more than the results of an establishment of new nervous connections during the post-natal existence of the organism."[11]

Appearing at a pivotal moment when materialist science and introspective psychologies stood in increasingly direct tension, Pavlov's work aspired to offer an empirical understanding of cognition that appealed to a populace still largely wary of Freud and psychoanalysis. Crucially, *Conditioned Reflexes* offered an experimental model of how thought and action could be shaped by stimuli *even when* the organism did not consciously apprehend such stimuli. In so doing, his work substantiated earlier physiological models of the psyche, including the idea of "unconscious cerebration" posited by William Carpenter in *Principles of Mental Physiology* (1877). In demonstrating the passive operation of stimuli on a "rigidly determined" mind, Pavlov both anticipated the methods and assumptions of Watson's behaviorism and offered a materialist rebuke to vitalism.[12] The vital energy hypothesized by the likes of Bergson was, as Pavlov asserted before a British audience, not only "unnecessary" to the physiologist, but "injurious to his work, vainly limiting his courage and the depth of his analysis."[13] For Pavlov, thought and action were ultimately grounded in determinate, material forces. All organisms, he explained, are "definite circumscribed material system[s]" that respond in a dynamic but determinate manner to the stimuli of their environments.[14] This sentiment was to find a very close echo in Watson, who shared Pavlov's sense that "psychological phenomena have to be described and explained in physiological terms or else they cannot be understood."[15] The job of the physiologist, Pavlov argued, was to unlock the rules and mechanisms through which these purely material systems work—to understand how the mind assimilates information in its environment and acquires the behavioral and cognitive reflexes essential to its survival.

For Pavlov's nonspecialized readers, the consequences of conditioned reflexes for the political realm far outstripped any implications they might have for the study of psychology. If both thought and action are essentially determined by the stealth stimuli of our environment, the ability to manipulate and condition reflexes represented tremendous political and social power. As Pavlov's English-language translator, G. V. Anrep, summarized, "The phenomena of education and the adjustment of the individual within the environment, in fact, his whole social existence, depend on these learnt or conditioned reflexes."[16] Even though Pavlov, a dissident in revolutionary Russia, was generally circumspect about the political applications of his theories, he remained convinced that the study of conditioned reflex would yield scientific management over human affairs. Already in 1906, when he gave the Thomas Huxley Memorial Lecture at Charing Cross Hospital in London, Pavlov asserted that physiology would soon provide "the actual solution" to "those questions which hitherto have vexed and perplexed humanity."[17] "Mankind," he promised, "will possess incalculable advantages and extraordinary control over human behaviour when the scientific investigator will be able to subject his fellow men to the same external analysis as he would employ for any natural object, and when the human mind will contemplate itself not from within but from without."[18] As Pavlov's fame grew along with his research support in Russia, he indulged the theoretical possibility that the study of conditioned reflexes would, in time, open into a wider social realm than his own rudimentary work had allowed. As he explained in the preface to the Russian edition of *Lectures on Conditioned Reflexes* (1928), "I am deeply and irrevocably convinced that along this path will be found the final triumph of the human mind over its uttermost and supreme problem—the knowledge of the mechanism and laws of human nature. Only thus may come a full, true and permanent happiness."[19]

The image of a "full, true and permanent happiness" achieved through scientific means: for many of Pavlov's first readers, it was this image that came to dominate the reception of his work. In Lewis, as we have already seen, Pavlov stands as one among a multitude of professionals who would inhibit the expression of individual creativity through mass cultural conditioning. Aldous Huxley, in an even more anxious mode, rooted the dystopian society of *Brave New World* (1932) in Pavlovian physiology; social control, in Huxley's novel, is enforced through a rationalized regime of psycho-physical conditioning. The citizens of Huxley's novel are perfectly—and monstrously— adjusted to the needs of society, impelled by a desire for unanimity "which their conditioning had so ineradicably implanted in them."[20] Such conditioning aims to manage strife among unlike sectors of the modern economy, but it also aspires to realize the supreme fantasy of Bernays's public relations: "adapting future demand to future industrial supply."[21]

With Huxley, we can already see the lines upon which Pavlov's legacy would calcify after the Second World War—the scientist as social engineer. While in the 1930s, "conditioned reflex" and the image of the salivating dog suggested the political techniques of strong, centralized states and what Althusser later called the "ideological state apparatus," it was not until the postwar period that the link between Pavlov's research and totalitarianism took on an axiomatic quality. This was particularly the case as Western audiences came to associate Pavlov with a Soviet government eager to claim his research as "official" Russian science. In fact, however, Pavlov was notably unsympathetic toward the Soviet revolution and the authoritarian forms it took after Lenin's death. As a product of czarist Russia, he was intensely nationalistic and never learned to read in any language other than Russian. But by the 1920s, he had become an international celebrity, prompting Lenin to grant him special treatment from the local soviet. As Boakes explains, "compatibility between Pavlov's science and Lenin's philosophy, together with the desire to demonstrate to the rest of the world that the work of a prominent scientist could flourish within a communist society, made Pavlov's own political outlook of little import."[22] Huxley noted this irony in *Brave New World Revisited* (1958), writing, "In politics Pavlov seems to have been an old-fashioned liberal. But, by a strange irony of fate, his researches and the theories he based upon them have called into existence a great army of fanatics dedicated heart and soul, reflex and nervous system, to the destruction of old-fashioned liberalism, wherever it can be found."[23] For most Cold War commentators, these political incongruities mattered little; the mere proximity of Pavlov's thought to Soviet realpolitik suggested that conditioned reflex was inherently nefarious.

Whatever Pavlov's own politics, his work would become inextricable from authoritarianism by 1950, when the American journalist and anti-communist crusader Edward Hunter coined a term for the political use of conditioned reflex: "brainwashing." According to writers like Hunter and the Dutch psychologist Joost Meerloo, the singular quality uniting all totalitarianisms was not a shared ideology but a common set of political practices. Just as Pavlov had succeeded in replacing arbitrary stimuli (light or sound) for another (food) to produce automatic reactions in dogs (salivation), totalitarian governments endowed cultural signifiers (images, keywords, names) with surcharged political significance through regimes of conditioning. Regarding a Soviet film about Pavlov, Hunter explains: "Conditioned reflexes could conceivably be produced to make this youth react like the dog that rolled over at its trainer's signal. Only instead of a light, the Kremlin could use words as signals—any words would do—*imperialism, learning, running dog of the imperialists, people, friend of the people, big brother,* without any relationship to their actual meaning. The Kremlin's plan was to make these reflexes instinctive."[24] For Hunter, the politics of conditioned reflex were legible in communist techniques of clinical "reeducation" and "thought control," but were already evident in the "brainwashing" of German citizens under Nazi rule.[25] According to Meerloo, such techniques were the logical outgrowth of a mass society that relied on centralized techniques of conditioning reflex, whether in authoritarian or democratic societies. As he explained in his 1956 book, *The Rape of the Mind*, "Cultural routinization and habit formation by local rules and myths make of everybody a partial automaton. National and racial prejudices are acted out unwittingly. Group hatred often bursts out almost automatically when triggered by slogans and catchwords."[26] But, Meerloo insisted, "in a totalitarian world, this narrow disciplinarian conditioning is done more 'perfectly' and more *ad absurdum*."[27]

There is good reason to regard the link between Pavlov and totalitarian "brainwashing" as a spurious one. In the context of the Cold War, the invention of the term "brainwashing" to describe the political tactics of foes old and new had a kind of ideological appeal, one that, as Kathleen Taylor notes, allowed some Western nations "to avoid confronting the idea . . . that they themselves were capable of great evil."[28] "Brainwashing" held particular appeal for American citizens, Scott Selisker notes, since it allowed them to "imagine that the citizens of totalitarian states had been somehow conditioned, such that they became masses of human automatons, will-less and therefore less than human."[29] With this term, Hunter effectively created a potent propaganda tool—a keyword that marshaled deeply felt anxieties about the limits of rationality and agency within a modern political sphere increasingly dependent upon the effects of social conditioning. But even as "brainwashing" emerged as central to anti-communist propaganda, cognate approaches to reflex were informing postwar analyses of Nazism. Hannah Arendt, in her monumental study *Origins of Totalitarianism* (1951), regarded Nazi policies as a clear instantiation of Pavlov's research. "Pavlov's dog, the human specimen reduced to the most elementary reactions, the bundle of reactions that can always be liquidated and replaced by other bundles of reactions that behave in exactly the same way, is the model 'citizen' of a totalitarian state," she wrote.[30] From Arendt's perspective in the early 1950s, the entirety of Nazi Germany was structured to delimit the range of thoughts available to the social body, and thus the modes of resistance among individual citizens. The picture that emerges from her study is that of a mechanized system—the banality of evil not as administrative murder, simply, but as a political system intent on inhibiting individual agency through conditioned reflex. The world of Nazism, she writes, is "a world of conditioned reflexes, of marionettes without the slightest trace of spontaneity."[31] The year after Arendt's book was published, "Pavlovian" entered the lexicon to denote the absence of independent agency, qualities seen as typical of citizenship in repressive regimes.

By the postwar period, Nazism had become paradigmatic of the politics of reflex—a community bound less by organic customs than by government-sponsored conditioning, what Robert Jay Lifton later termed "milieu control."[32] But in 1927, when *Conditioned Reflexes* was new to Western audiences, the connection that commentators like Huxley and Arendt would draw between conditioned reflex and totalitarianism was still an evolving one. As the example of Huxley demonstrates, modernists were quick to understand the implications of such research for mass politics. But not all modernists responded to Pavlov's theories with outright anxiety. In fact, for some, conditioned reflex appeared as a potentially progressive force amid the turbulence of the interwar moment. H. G. Wells, for example, considered Pavlov's research so socially significant that he declared his allegiance to scientific materialism over the politics of fellow socialist George Bernard Shaw.[33] Writing in a 1927 article in the *New York Times*, Wells weighed the relative merits of Shaw and Pavlov: "If 'A' is drowning on one side of a pier and 'B' is equally drowning on the other, and you have one lifebelt and cannot otherwise help, to which of the two would you like to throw it? Which would I save, Pavloff or Shaw? . . . I was manifestly obliged to ask myself, 'What is the good of Shaw?' And what is the good of Pavloff? Pavloff is a star which lights the world, shining above a vista hitherto unexplored. Why should I hesitate with my lifebelt for one moment?"[34] Wells's desire to "save" Pavlov rather than Shaw reflects a political environment in which physiological science could still stand as a utopian force. Not only had Pavlov not yet acquired the stigma that would later be associated with his work, but for politically minded artists like Wells, advances in physiological research augured new political tactics that promised to trump the modest ambitions of Shaw.[35] When the American publisher Liveright released *Lectures on Conditioned Reflexes* in 1928, Wells's encomium appeared on the dust jacket just below a blurb from Watson.

But Wells's celebration of Pavlov only hints at the wider discourse of Pavlovian conditioning in the interwar era. If after the war Nazism came to be regarded as a community bound only by conditioned reflex, the 1920s and 1930s represent a time when reflex could still offer a positive ideal of collective belonging, one suitable even to democratic countries. For Rebecca West, Pavlov's ideas came to inform her evolving thought on the social function of art, the political perils of twentieth-century life, and the perpetuation of national culture.

Nation and Necessity

Well before Pavlov's book found its way to West's hands, milieu had already announced itself as a prime concern in her work. In her debut novel, *The Return of the Soldier* (1918), much of the drama of the text concerns the effects of physical space on individual psyches. As Douglas Mao has noted, "The relation between fine surroundings and fine souls" is "an inescapably central theme" of West's novel, making it a drama of environmental conditioning avant la lettre.[36] This concern retained an important place in other novels, as well; her 1929 novel, *Harriet Hume: A London Fantasy*, for example, employs a fantastic conceit that underscores the strictly determined behavior of the tale's antagonist and the role of London in conditioning behavior. These novels reflect an intuition about the cultural and moral import of milieu, but such issues rarely take on the sustained emphasis that they would attain in her later work. It would not be until 1928, when she encountered Pavlov's *Conditioned Reflexes*, that her understanding of conditioning found an intellectual architecture—and with it, a way of understanding the politics of reflex. For decades thereafter, conditioned reflex would occupy a central place in her fiction and nonfiction.

Ten years after publishing *The Return of the Soldier*, and almost a decade before she began the travels she would document in *Black Lamb and Grey Falcon*, West published a book-length aesthetic treatise that attempted to answer a simple question: From what human necessity does art spring? In *The Strange Necessity* (1928), she suggested that the answer to this question was not to be found in any philosophical statement about human nature but rather in scientific knowledge about those reflexive behaviors innate to all organisms. In seven chapters, West explores the compulsion to create—this "strange necessity"—by studying a number of novelists, including modernists like James Joyce and Marcel Proust. While these writers occupy a prominent position within West's personal canon, it is the scientist Pavlov who emerges as the analytic engine of the treatise and who would ground her understanding of the relationship between physiology and art. In affirming Pavlov's research, West discovered a solution to some of the pressing problems of national identity confronted by interwar modernists.

In this first-person narrative essay, West documents first encountering Pavlov's work after leaving the Casino at Monte Carlo. Whereas the Casino represents an aesthetic and intellectual void, in Pavlov West detects a victory of the mind over the chaos of incomprehension, "as superb an attempt to learn something as ever was made."[37] In many ways this portrait of the scientist as a dedicated and selfless truth seeker echoes Wells's affirmation of Pavlov. But West went a step further by appropriating the physiological paradigm of behavior outlined in his lectures as a way of understanding the origins and effects of literature. Central to this Pavlovian theory of art is the notion of an "investigatory reflex," the automatic impulse of organisms to orient themselves in their environment. In his lectures Pavlov explained that when lab technicians introduced new stimuli into a controlled environment, his test subjects would immediately investigate them. West asserts that this instinctive desire to understand and map one's environment is hardwired into the biological makeup of the organisms as a kind of "cellular memory."[38] Reading art in these physiological terms, she suggests that literature, music, and painting stem from these "demands ingrained in the flesh," an animal need to investigate and experiment that the arts and sciences share alike.[39] "It can easily be understood why an artist creates works of art," she explains.[40] The desire to live requires that "from man's earliest moments" he is compelled to "to know what it [life] is all about."[41] Echoing Zola's argument in "The Experimental Novel" (1880), West asserts that literature is a unique form of experimentation through which we can understand the effect of environment on the human organism. Literature, in this analysis, performs the same kinds of empirical modeling as the sciences. But whereas science can tell us only of outward behaviors, West asserts, literature "has some technique for expressing the emotion of the subjects of its experiments."[42] Art is thus "science only more scientific."[43]

This facet of West's aesthetic theory draws only slightly on Pavlov's study of conditioned reflex. But her inquiry quickly modulates from questions of artistic creation to the conditioning force of art itself. Creativity is for West a strange necessity not just because it allows individuals to understand their environment, but because art and literature are themselves aspects of that environment. A truly great work of literature, she argues, "overflows the confines of the mind and becomes an important physical event," conditioning the reflexes of readers and allowing them to adapt themselves to their environment.[44] This Pavlovian perspective on culture was to have far-reaching implications for West's politics and prove foundational for her understanding of the nation as a physiological entity.

One of the key implications of *Conditioned Reflexes* in West's reading is that the human body plays a direct role in establishing those forms of likeness that we recognize as a national community. She suggests that humans are endowed with two forms of consciousness—what she terms "mind-consciousness" and "body-consciousness." "Mind-consciousness," she argues, is our intellectual and conscious capacity to imagine the minds of other human beings.[45] Yet for West, it is the quality of embodiment, rather than any rational, conscious thought, that allows for collectivity. Our bodies, she argues, are perpetually storing away "latent information" in our environments, allowing us to establish the sympathetic bounds of community with others. Through the ongoing conditioning of bodies, she explains, we naturally acquire a sense of likeness that allows us "to penetrate imaginatively into the experience of others."[46] Acknowledging that we are, like Pavlov's dogs, rigorously conditioned by our environment, West suggests that the bonds of community are based on a shared milieu, not on any racial characteristic. Thus, as she reasons, even a bishop can form a community with the man who beats his wife because they share a common physiological experience; the bishop, while incapable of beating his own wife, can have "the active power of empathy" that will allow him to "imagine also that the same stimuli are being applied to him[self]."[47]

The idea that communities cohere around shared reflexes and habits would prove fundamental for West's later understanding of the nation in *Black Lamb and Grey Falcon*. Already in *The Strange Necessity* her emphasis on a shared, bodily susceptibility to stimuli was unmistakably nationalist in nature. In a chapter that largely foreshadows the political philosophy of *Black Lamb*, West argues that exile presents one of the greatest "psychic disadvantages" of the modern world because it threatens to divest citizens of the conditioning environment appropriate to a moral and artistic existence.[48] Groups such as the Anglo-Indian and the Anglo-Irish represent communities whose physical alienation from the space of the nation prevents them from acquiring necessary embodied traditions and cognitive habits. West considers the fate of Italian Americans through the example of Al Capone: "What is this process which links the individual to the universal if he stay with his people, which leave the individual solitary and desolate if he be an exile? I can conceive it most clearly when I think of Scarface Capone. There is a man who is superbly in possession of the present, who is destitute of the past. It must demand power amounting to genius to perform the analyses and syntheses of his own personal experience necessary to establish him as king of the Chicago bootlegging gangs."[49] West's suggestion is that Capone's lawlessness is a direct result of the failures of a national conditioning environment. Never, she says, would immigrants like Capone have lived such violent lives if they had stayed in their home countries: "In a thousand million ways their country would have taught [lawful living] to them, from the day they were born."[50] In West's theory, environment imprints citizens with values and a sense of historicity not through rules but through the multitude of cultural forms that need not be explicitly articulated; the citizen's immersion in a complex network of cultural and social practices conditions him to behave in socially coherent ways and exhibit cognitive habits derived from previous generations. West's point is that there is no need for the overt training of Pavlov's laboratory since every aspect of social life does the work of conditioning reflex. As she would explain in a 1935 essay titled "The Necessity and Grandeur of the International Ideal," national belonging is one of the "truths which we learn almost without exercise of thought, by immediate perception."[51] The nation, she writes, can "help [a man] to live as no other can, because it can give him a tradition which is appropriate to him, which springs from the experience of men of his own blood contending with the same environment."[52]

The relationship between tradition and a national environment fascinated West for many years, influencing her novel *The Thinking Reed* (1935), her biography *St. Augustine* (1933), as well as her analyses of Nazism in *Black Lamb and Grey Falcon* (1941) and wartime sedition in *The Meaning of Treason* (1949).[53] The figure of the exile was, as we will see, of particular importance within West's politics since she saw exile communities as symptomatic of a modernizing world that dissociated citizens from the conditioning of a national community. Characters like Capone become representatives in West's work of those unmoored from history and tradition, and thus susceptible to the allure of fascistic violence. In her appropriation of Pavlov, West effectively discovered a way of conceptualizing the nation without appealing to those qualities of citizenship that would come to represent fascist ideology, namely racial identity or biological inheritance. In a 1928 article in the *Daily Express* entitled "Environment Matters Most," West explicitly argued against "Mendelian laws of inheritance," explaining that "where mind and character are concerned, heredity seems to be so controlled by environment that it is no use taking it into account."[54] Given Pavlov's place within critiques of totalitarianism, West's use of *Conditioned Reflexes* in substantiating her aesthetic and political ideas can seem somewhat surprising. However, her thinking mirrored the concerns of numerous modernists eager to define "tradition" in terms of collective habits and embodied memory.

Perhaps the best example of this turn toward national embodiment can be found in T. S. Eliot. In "Tradition and the Individual Talent" (1919), Eliot famously theorized the ongoing reorganization of tradition by individual artists, arguing that literature constitutes a privileged site of historical endurance that the poet must negotiate. In this widely rehearsed formulation of "tradition," stress falls on the written text as a privileged site of historical knowledge and cultural endurance; through engagement with the words and ideas of past generations, the individual artist gains knowledge of a collective history and is thus able to forge new literary forms within an evolving canon. In privileging literary artifacts in this way, Eliot employed what sociologist Paul Connerton refers to as an "inscriptive" theory of cultural memory by suggesting that cultural values are transmitted through what is written.[55] But recent commentators have argued that while Eliot's essay links tradition to canon formation, it also contains a latent emphasis on embodied memory as an important site of cultural tradition. Jeremy Braddock, for example, has argued that for Eliot, archives reach "beyond literature" to include "the embodied practices that were the subject of the anthropological writings he was then avidly reading," such as Frazer's *The Golden Bough*. "Eliot's thesis," writes Braddock, prioritizes "communal, or 'real' memory, in which the tradition is experienced not only intellectually but *affectively*."[56] However, if the relationship between embodied knowledge and tradition was only latent in Eliot's 1919 essay, by the 1930s he would, like West, stress the importance of collective habits and corporeal processes in sustaining a national community.

In the Page-Barbour Lectures delivered at the University of Virginia in 1933 and subsequently published as *After Strange Gods* (1934), Eliot returned to his theory of tradition. Minimizing his earlier emphasis on inscription, Eliot now defines tradition as a specifically national category that includes "all those habitual actions, baits and customs, from the most significant religious rite to our conventional way of greeting a stranger, which represent the blood kinship of 'the same people living in the same place.'"[57] Customs shared collectively—whether they be highly ritualized "religious rite[s]" or mundane ways of "greeting a stranger"—became for Eliot important sites of cultural particularity and historicity. In the lectures, Eliot uses this theory to substantiate a decidedly racist theory of national belonging.[58] This position stands in sharp contrast to West, who celebrated cultural endurance while rejecting race and "Mendelian laws of inheritance." Yet Eliot's shift in thinking reflects a larger trend in interwar approaches to tradition in several ways. First, by defining "tradition" as a collective and corporeal process, rather than one dependent on the hermeneutic process of textual interpretation, Eliot asserted that the perpetuation of a national culture did not require the hard work of a literary education. Referencing Leopold Bloom's definition of a nation in *Ulysses*, Eliot argued that the fact of living in the shared space of the nation is sufficient to bring individuals into contact with collective memory.[59] Second, and more importantly, Eliot's theory suggested that iterative bodily performances were themselves conduits of a shared sense of *value*. Tradition is, he writes, "a way of feeling and acting" in common that "characterises a group throughout generations."[60] Such feelings are far more durable than the content of inscribed artifacts because they are collective, "unconscious" and "habitual."[61] Like "taboo," tradition acquired through a common corporeal experience works through us without the need of our conscious mind; indeed, we become conscious of such forms of tradition only when they falter—"only after they have begun to fall into desuetude, as we are aware of the leaves of a tree when the autumn wind begins to blow them off when they have separately ceased to be vital."[62] In revising tradition along these lines, Eliot shifted his focus from the inscriptive practices of individual artists to the embodied experience of the community as a whole. Through the bodily experience of living in a shared milieu, both physical and literary, communal values are transmitted and reinforced in members of the community.

Unlike many later theorists of nationalism, such as Benedict Anderson, who emphasized the imaginative work of discourse in binding the nation together, Eliot and West regarded the material body as a conduit for the transmission of national identity—of tradition. This emphasis on reflexes, habits, and behaviors over shared ideals is, as Jed Esty has noted, typical of interwar shifts in approaches to national belonging. In *A Shrinking Island* (2003), Esty argues that the demographic and political crises of the 1920s and 1930s endowed British writers with anxieties about definitions of the national community dependent upon a collective imagination. He argues that as Britons confronted the rising threat of fascism and the coterminous decline of the British Empire, writers and thinkers of diverse political orientations "proposed to define national community in terms of the cohesion of shared habits (immemorial Englishness) rather than the cohesion of shared goals (imperial Britishness)."[63] This renewed emphasis on "shared habits," he asserts, manifested in a quest for "local authenticity, of folk consciousness, of chthonic identity," which came to dominate the cultural life of England in the period.⁶⁴ In writers like Eliot and West, we can witness the evolution of ideas about the nation—a turn not toward the local, per se, but a new investment in habits enforced by the physical environment. As the historical pressures of the interwar moment forced writers to conceptualize England anew, the physical space of the nation and the embodied traditions of its inhabitants vouchsafed the endurance of cultural particularity without the need to draw on tropes of biological or genetic homogeneity.⁶⁵

Within this context, Pavlov's research on the acquisition of reflexes offered a valuable conceptual framework for understanding the reproduction of cultural values that Eliot had termed "tradition." For West, the idea of conditioned reflex provided a way of conceiving of the nation as a unity of shared stimuli in which art and literature had a central role to play. But Pavlov's theories were not without their limits, even for West. In the years following *The Strange Necessity*, she would continue to draw on ideas of conditioned reflex in various political contexts.⁶⁶ But as fascism consolidated in Europe in the 1930s, the work of Pavlov began to attach itself ever more powerfully to authoritarianism. In *Black Lamb and Grey Falcon*, West would navigate between her own commitment to Pavlov and the association of his work with Nazism. Deploying two competing ideas of the nation as a reflex community, *Black Lamb* would simultaneously defend nationalism as a physiological necessity and cast Nazism as a dangerous instantiation of Pavlovian conditioning.

Reflex Communities I: Fascist Gramophones

Written amid and responding to the political crises of the 1930s, *Black Lamb and Grey Falcon* bears witness to changing public sentiments about Pavlov and the politics of reflex. As another world war became ever more likely, the discourse of conditioned reflex gained traction among British writers as a critical vocabulary for understanding the attributes of fascism. Yet Pavlov's emphasis on the conditioning power of milieu also remained a viable framework for those intent on resanctifying the values of national belonging. With the ongoing retrenchment of the British Empire and the threat of a newly expansionist Germany, writers like West could think of the nation as both the site of necessary, chthonic conditioning *and* a distinctly modern disease of regimentation. *Black Lamb* deploys both notions of conditioned reflex. Drawing upon the language of habit and conditioned reflex at every turn, West's text exemplifies the competing uses to which Pavlov's theories were increasingly put in the 1930s. In *Black Lamb*, conditioned reflex serves as a framework for understanding the endurance of cultural particularity as well as the dangers of rule through milieu control. *Black Lamb*, in short, exhibits the political value and peril of conditioned reflex at a time when such reflexes were coming under suspicion.

The magnum opus of a long and distinguished literary life, *Black Lamb* is a notoriously difficult book to classify. As a history of Yugoslavia, travelogue, portrait of interwar Europe, and exposition of West's own political philosophy, *Black Lamb* is, as Christopher Hitchens has said, "at least four fine books."[67] Lightly fictionalizing three trips West made to Yugoslavia between 1936 and 1938, *Black Lamb* offers an extended meditation on the history and culture of the Balkans, a region West (rightly) feared would soon come under the domination of fascism. Indeed, by the time *Black Lamb* was published in 1941, Yugoslavia had been invaded by Hungarian, Italian, and German forces, with the various regions of the multiethnic state parceled out to the Axis powers. West's melancholy dedication to the book reads, simply: "TO ALL MY FRIENDS IN YUGOSLAVIA WHO ARE NOW ALL DEAD OR ENSLAVED."[68]

West's interest in the region stemmed not from any particular interest in Balkan culture but from the outsized role it seemed to have played in modern European history. In the book's introduction, she details how, recovering from a surgery in 1934, she learned that King Alexander I of Yugoslavia had been assassinated during a visit to France. Sensing that this event could catalyze a new European war (much as the assassination of Archduke Franz Ferdinand had), West recounts everything she knew at that time about Yugoslavia. Upon reflection, she realizes that Yugoslavia had witnessed a shocking amount of political violence, making it a flash point for international conflict. West decides to remedy her ignorance of Yugoslavia, reasoning that "there proceeds steadily from that place a stream of events which are a source of danger to me, which indeed for four years threatened my safety and during that time deprived me for ever of many benefits."[69]

Though framed as a highly personal experience, West's text is less the record of her own travels than a prolonged analysis of the political lessons offered by Yugoslav culture and history. In a moment of rapid change and imminent conflict, West could read Yugoslavia as both a rough analogue for England's own political situation and one that militated for a new approach to foreign affairs, particularly empire. In the book's epilogue, West surveys the centuries of bloodshed for which "the Balkans" had, even then, become synonymous, and places much of the blame on the shoulders of

Western imperialism. As a pawn in various imperial schemes across the ages—Ottoman, Austro-Hungarian, and a rising German empire—Yugoslavia became for West emblematic of a continent perpetually threatened by its own political rapacity. Marina MacKay has called *Black Lamb* "a 1200-page essay on imperialism and its legacies in the Balkans," which "details what a history of occupation has done to the [region] by way of showing what it might mean for Britain to lose the war."[70] West's argument against imperialism—including the British Empire—pivots on a compensatory affirmation of national identity and the values of nationalism. Arguing against pacifist currents in England, including those of Bloomsbury intellectuals, West castigates the British left for espousing the belief "that nationalism is always antidemocratic and aggressive, and that internationalism is always liberal and pacific."[71] Yugoslavia becomes, in effect, a kind of test case for the fate of Europe, with West cajoling her readers to wake England from the "cataleptic quiet" of fascist appeasement.[72] *Black Lamb* thus makes a case for the active and continued role of England in European politics—indeed, of the grandeur of national identity—at the very moment when the sun was setting on the largest empire in the history of the world.

The nationalist and anti-imperial thrust of *Black Lamb* has been the center of most critical appraisals of West's book since the 1990s, when a flurry of interest in Yugoslavia led to its renewed popularity.[73] Of particular interest to scholars has been West's use of modernist literary techniques in advancing this agenda. With its unusual blend of genres and its assemblage of literary and philosophical fragments, *Black Lamb* is "manifestly a work of literature," as Geoff Dyer has written, one that fits into a number of recognizable literary tropes, including, most notably, the epic. Originally published in two volumes totaling about half a million words (close to twelve hundred pages in recent editions), *Black Lamb* is in many senses a nationalist epic for the modernist age. Bernard Schweizer, for example, has classed *Black Lamb* as an epic that, rather than "legitimize the authoritative historical narrative of the imperial winners," excoriates domination, including empire and "gender-based injustice."[74] MacKay, borrowing T. S. Eliot's term, has argued that *Black Lamb* employs a highly politicized version of Joyce's "mythical method" in an effort to "rehabilitate nationality."[75]

Missing from recent analyses has been an awareness of the political import of reflex in West's most audacious work. Throughout *Black Lamb and Grey Falcon*, West frames her analysis of national communities in the same physiological terms she employed in *The Strange Necessity*, a fact that offers to clarify (and even correct) some recent analyses of *Black Lamb*. MacKay's reading, in particular, suggests that *Black Lamb* delimits a vision of national identity grounded in the *discursive* creation of the nation. "Demonstrable historical truth is not the issue" for West, MacKay argues; "what counts is that a population becomes a group in conceiving of its present as part of a long shared story."[76] In MacKay's analysis, *Black Lamb* champions "myth against materialism" by "unpacking for the first time myth's nation-making origins and implications."[77] This emphasis on the nation as an imagined community misses West's lifelong emphasis on the materiality of experience—on the physical interaction between bodies and culture, the perpetuation of communal values through iterative acts, and the conditioning power of a national environment. For West, stories matter, but only as part of a wider set of cultural stimuli that endow citizens with a hierarchy of values and the ability to synthesize their experience. Much of *Black Lamb* can be understood as an overt effort to read the particular historical problems of England through the materiality of Yugoslav national identity.

Black Lamb and Grey Falcon continues West's project of understanding the nation as a reflex community. Working within the physiological framework of nationalism elaborated in *The Strange Necessity* but deploying new popular opinion about the Pavlovian character of authoritarianism, *Black Lamb* negotiates competing valences of conditioned reflex. On the one hand, West affirms her earlier emphasis on national identity as a necessary and sacred product of one's environment, a form of embodied likeness produced through the conditioning of "tradition." Yugoslavia—and England, by extension—emerges as a reflex community rooted in the conditioning of a common environment and the habits formed over the *longue durée*. At the same time, West deploys the rhetoric of Pavlovian habituation in her depiction of fascists, in many ways anticipating the discourse of "brainwashing" that would emerge from postwar analyses of totalitarianism. Germans appear in *Black Lamb* in a form that would become a cliché of twentieth-century political discourse—that of political automata.

West frames *Black Lamb* as a tale of physiological communities early in the text. A prologue and opening chapter present a first-person account that characterizes fascism as a malady of physiological conditioning. In many ways, these opening sections of *Black Lamb* recapitulate the political terms at the heart of *The Strange Necessity*. There West attempted to understand exile as a form of environmental deprivation; dispossessed of a national conditioning environment, emigrants like Al Capone lack a guiding, embodied sense of tradition and are thus prone to violence. In *Black Lamb*, West repurposes this language of environmental conditioning to understand the case of the anarchist Luigi Luccheni. In the prologue West recalls the death of Empress Elizabeth, the wife of Franz Joseph I, who had been stabbed by Luccheni in 1898. The narrative of Elizabeth and Luccheni is emblematic for West since, to her mind, it presages much of the mass politics of the age to come. West explains the actions of Luccheni, like those of Capone, as the product of poor environmental conditioning. "Many people," she asserts, "are unable to say what they mean only because they have not been given an adequate vocabulary by their environment."[78] Devoid of this "vocabulary," people like Luccheni turn to violence as a form of expression. According to West, such behavior is the natural consequence of modernization, which wrests masses of people from the conditioning environment of the nation. Luccheni was, she explains, "an Italian born in Paris of parents forced to emigrate by their poverty and trodden down into an alien criminal class: that is to say, he belonged to an urban population for which the existing forms of government made no provision, which wandered often workless and always traditionless, without power to control its destiny."[79] Deprived of the embodied traditions of the nation, Luccheni is rendered a passive subject of history—unable to control his destiny and condemned to the incomprehension of violent action. Where West differs from her earlier analysis is in the new stress she puts on the political form that such exile takes. If emigration is what promotes Capone's violence as an individual actor in *The Strange Necessity*, in *Black Lamb* Luccheni's emigration prefigures fascism as a whole.

West only hints at the physiological foundations of fascism in the prologue of *Black Lamb*. In the first chapter, she depicts a train journey to Yugoslavia in which she encounters a group of German tourists on their way to the Adriatic coast, a popular spot for German tourists. Here she offers a blunt profile of fascism that emphasizes its dependence on Pavlovian reflex. West reports that she initially enjoyed her fellow travelers, taking delight in their conversation and forthright satisfaction with the scenery. But this initial sense of good cheer gives way to feelings of unease as West begins to notice the group's angst about food, money, and other mundane details of the trip. Although these travelers are clearly not members of the Nazi Party, West notes they suffer a mindless and debilitating anxiety when faced with the prospect of staying in Yugoslav hotel rooms and eating Yugoslav food. The predominant impression West has of these German tourists is not just that of an unconscious sense of German superiority, but rather their utter inability to act as agents. "The necessity for making a decision" about where to stay causes one of the travelers "real anguish," West reports.[80] What first appears as an anxiety about traveling hides a deeper political problem: life in Nazi Germany has effectively annulled their ability to make decisions. West concludes that Nazism has trained these citizens to think in predetermined ways and to be indecisive in general, "incapable of making decisions or enforcing a condition where they could make them."[81] In light of this discovery, it is telling that one traveler is en route to Dalmatia seeking a cure for "a nervous disorder affecting the stomach which made him unable to make decisions."[82] West's emphasis on German indecisiveness is not a judgment against the individual travelers but a critical appraisal of the way Nazism has conditioned them. As a result of their national environment, they are "utterly incompetent in the conduct of a simple journey."[83]

West's analysis of these travelers' behavior insinuates a failure of milieu, much like that of Luccheni and Capone, but without direct reference to the physiological categories she favored in *The Strange Necessity*. But as their journey reaches its destination, West stresses the physiological reflexes of her traveling companions:

> Their businesses were, I am sure, most efficiently conducted. But this only meant that since the Industrial Revolution capitalism has grooved society with a number of deep slots along which most human beings can roll smoothly to a fixed destination. When a man takes charge of a factory the factory takes charge of him, if he opens an office it falls into a place in a network that extends over the whole world and so long as he obeys the general trend he will not meet any obvious disaster; but he may be unable to meet the calls that daily life outside this specialist area makes on judgment and initiative. These people fell into that category. Their helplessness was the greater because they had plainly a special talent for obedience. In the routine level of commerce and industry they must have known a success which must have made their failure in all other phases of their being embittering and strange. Now that capitalism was passing into a decadent phase and many of the grooves along which they had rolled so happily were worn down to nothing, they were broken and beaten, and their ability to choose the broad outlines of their lives, to make political decisions, was now less than it had been originally. It was inevitable that the children of such muddlers . . . would support any system which offered them new opportunities for profitable obedience, which would pattern society with new grooves in place of the old, and would never be

warned by any instinct for competence and self-preservation if that system was leading to universal disaster. I tried to tell myself that these people in the carriage were not of importance, and were not typical, but I knew that I lied. These were exactly like all Aryan Germans I had ever known; and there were sixty millions of them in the middle of Europe.[84]

In this, the culminating moment of the introduction of *Black Lamb*, West invokes the physiological theory of nationalism she first outlined in *The Strange Necessity* through her repeated use of the word "grooves." Physiological studies of behavior, from William Carpenter and T. H. Huxley, to Pavlov and Watson, regularly likened the human sensorium to the nascent recording technologies of the gramophone and the phonograph. Through such an analogy, the mind was said to be like a disc endowed with the "grooves" of reflex imprinted by one's milieu. William James, for example, insisted upon the physicality of the nervous system in his discussion of habit in *Principles of Psychology* (1890): "The whole plasticity of the brain sums itself up in two words when we call it an organ in which currents pouring in from the sense-organs make with extreme facility paths which do not easily disappear."[85] These habitual actions "by incessantly repeated presence and reproduction, will plough deep grooves in the nervous system."[86] By the time Pavlov used the terminology of cognitive grooves in *Conditioned Reflexes*, it had become an established trope among physiologists and even their critics.[87] In *Behaviorism*, Watson complained that "most of the psychologists talk, too, quite volubly about the formation of new pathways in the brain, as though there were a group of tiny servants of Vulcan there who run through the nervous system with hammer and chisel digging new trenches and deepening old ones."[88] Watson's griping signals not that such an analogy had become a contested model for describing environmental conditioning but rather that it had passed beyond the confines of professional scientific inquiry and into the discourse of laypeople, such as Rebecca West.

The physiological language of *Black Lamb* underscores West's evolving conception of the vexed relationship between economic modernization and the nation's capacity to condition citizens. What defines fascism for West is not that it fails to condition its citizens absolutely. Instead, she sees fascism as the attempt to manufacture new, facile traditions without regard to the organic practices of its citizens and the long, shared history of the nation. According to Patricia E. Chu, fascism is a kind of "irrational subject formation" for West because genuine "political allegiance is not something men make but rather something that makes men."[89] As West understood it in *Black Lamb*, fascism attempted to supply citizens with an ersatz substitute for the collective habits lost in the process of modernization; in the place of the old, embodied traditions and the hierarchy of values native to bounded national communities, fascism substitutes a new unanimity. Fascism gives its citizens "new opportunities for profitable obedience," patterning society "with new grooves in the place of the old."[90] In this sort of political regime, citizens are nothing but their cognitive grooves—automata incapable of thinking or doing in volitional ways. Such conditioning saps their agency instead of enabling it, endowing them with a kind of moral passivity.

As the passage above suggests, West understood industrial modernization as the driving force behind the cognitive determinism of fascism. The industrial revolution created "grooves" in two senses—first as a network of business relations, supply channels, and the infrastructure of modern commercial practice (including the train on which she meets the German travelers), and second as habits of thought that allow citizens to easily navigate the demands of everyday life. West returns to this argument throughout *Black Lamb*, arguing that fascism arose out of societies that were rapidly modernized, resulting in large urban populations "defrauded of their racial tradition."[91] Mass urbanization put people physically (and thus physiologically) out of touch with the everyday world of craft labor and folk knowledge, elements that stabilize communities and entrench individuals in communal manners of behavior. The destruction of peasantries thus created what, in the epilogue of *Black Lamb*, West calls a "mindless, traditionless, possessionless section of the urban proletariat" upon whose backs people like Mussolini and Hitler rose to power.[92] In Italy, she explains, the urban proletariat that sustains the Fascist Party is composed of a population of "peasants who had been industrialized for a generation or so without becoming cultured, had lost the tradition of its small states without acquiring a new national one."[93] Having lost corporeal knowledge of long-standing cultural traditions that would serve as ballast in a rapidly changing world, these peasants seek forms of identity and stability in what West calls the "magical rite of regimentation."[94] What the leaders of fascist governments offer their people, then, is a substitute for the habits and traditions forged over generations; in lieu of tradition, they provide the "grooves" along which West's traveling companions can glide through their lives. But for West, these habits are spurious and sterile because they lack foundation in a long history, a people rooted to the land and the embodied practices and values that such a history entails.

West's appeal to the figure of the gramophone was tied directly to an understanding of fascism that stressed its use of propaganda to condition reflex and thus short-circuit the agency of ordinary citizens.[95] Many of West's contemporaries employed the gramophone as a metaphor because it both literally instantiated technologies for conditioning reflex and figured the human automaton that such technologies produced. Wyndham Lewis, as we have already seen, anticipated this metaphor in his assertion that publicity and propaganda thrust citizens into "prescribed tracks." Virginia Woolf, in her 1938 book, *Three Guineas*, drew extensively on the image of the gramophone to describe the effects of "atmosphere" in conditioning the denizens of mass society. For Woolf, spectacle, advertisement, and publicity all act as stereotyping mechanisms, creating cognitive grooves that tend irremediably toward repressive ideologies—"the bark of the guns and the bray of the gramophones" working always in concert.[96] The contemporary text that most doggedly employs the imagery of the gramophone in this way is Orwell's *Coming Up for Air* (1939). Orwell punctuates his drama of everyday interwar life with attention to reflex as a constitutive feature of mass society. Throughout the novel, Orwell's protagonist, George Bowling, feels the coercive power of "atmosphere" in producing collective grooves of thought and action.[97] Though the nature of this "atmosphere" remains vague, near the novel's conclusion he articulates a sense that hidden manipulators are controlling him—"the people whom you've never seen but who rule your destiny all the same."[98] The work of such forces leaves a mark on the regularized behaviors that Bowling witnesses around him. For example, at a meeting of the Left Book Club, Bowling listens to a talk by an anti-fascist activist. After hearing a string of slogans about concentration camps, European civilization, and the need for British resistance, Bowling reflects, "You know the line of talk. These chaps can churn it out by the hour. Just like a gramophone. Turn the handle, press the button and it starts. Democracy, Fascism, Democracy."[99] Part of the appeal of the gramophone for modernists like Woolf, Orwell, and West resided in the fact that broadcasting technologies were themselves a novel means of orchestrating behaviors. As Walter Lippmann explained, mass communication means that everyone in the modern world "live[s] in grooves."[100] Orwell's protagonist attempts to avoid the automatisms he encounters in the atmosphere of London, but in his return to Lower Binfield, his childhood home, he discovers that a prewar world of personal agency no longer exists. The best indication of this is, perhaps, the presence of gramophones themselves. In place of the mom-and-pop industries he grew up with, Bowling finds Lower Binfield is now an industrial center that produces both military weaponry and gramophones.[101] The presence of gramophones here and throughout the novel testifies to modernism's indebtedness to physiological metaphors of behavioral reflex, and, like Woolf and West, yokes these concerns to a new media ecology capable of engendering such reflexes.

In West's thinking, fascism appears as a political system intent on perfectly mechanizing the reflexes of the populace without regard to a common history. Throughout *Black Lamb*, West likens fascism to the barest forms of cognitive reflex—what she calls, in reference to the Turks, "abandonment to the tropism of a militarist system."[102] In so doing, West transmutes the apolitical implications of physiological reflex to suggest a kind of cognitive and moral torpor within certain national communities. Like the caterpillars central to Jacques Loeb's theory of "animal tropisms," fascists are defined for West by an absolute and uncritical automatism—a dependence on political reflex that aligns them more with the amorality of insects than with the moral agency of humans. The Germans that West depicts in *Black Lamb* are "Pavlovian" in the senses that the term later acquired; conditioned by the strictly controlled milieu of fascism, they are driven by the cognitive grooves that later commentators would associate with "brainwashing." These citizens are thus "Pavlovian" without any of the life-affirming qualities of conditioned reflex West extolled in *The Strange Necessity*. But as we will see, the inherent human susceptibility to "atmosphere" was not necessarily a political detriment. Indeed, like many of her contemporaries, West presents a multifaceted understanding of the politics of reflex. What was needed was a literary form that would elevate the embodied traditions of the nation over the appeal to cheap tropisms.

Reflex Communities II: Embodied Traditions and the Nation

In framing her journey against the backdrop of Germany's particular forms of reflex, West can seem to advance a narrow idea of fascism, one very much of a kind with anti-German propaganda and postwar analyses of totalitarianism.[103] However, to class *Black Lamb* as another instance of wartime propaganda, easily equating conditioned reflex with fascism, is to misunderstand West's commitment to the nation as a physiological entity. While

Black Lamb and Grey Falcon partially inverts the value West attributed to Pavlov in *The Strange Necessity*, it simultaneously develops a competing, positive notion of national reflex and embodied traditions—a sense of reflex explicitly modeled in the Balkan cultures she documents. What intrigued West about Yugoslavia was that it seemed to present a version of nationalism that was grounded in collective reflexes without depending on the strict cognitive grooves that she sensed in the German travelers she met. West understood the national identity of Yugoslavia, like that of England, as rooted in common ways of doing and thinking that emerged as generations contended with a shared environment. As Douglas Mao notes, West uses the word "nationalism" "to name something we would more usually call 'culture.'"[104] As he explains, for West "nationalism" is quite often regarded as "a natural and essentially benign set of attitudes shared by people who live together."[105] Physical proximity thus serves as a privileged category through which she advances a positive theory of national belonging. In *Black Lamb and Grey Falcon*, Yugoslavia and England stand as communities bound by reflex and the guiding force of an organic tradition.

Integral to this idea is an investment in those forms of habit that emerged gradually over the *longue durée*. Whereas fascism compensated for the dislocations of modernization through the ex nihilo creation of new forms of collectivity, West locates genuine national belonging in the shared experience of a physical milieu across generations. Yugoslavia's claim to such a national ideal is founded on a history that spans almost one thousand years and whose roots West discovers in the living traditions of the region, including the ancient wounds of empire and sectarian conflict. The long history of the region endows the people West meets not only with a sense of historicity lacking in figures like Luccheni, but with a mutual, guiding sense of value—what Eliot had called "a way of feeling and acting" in common that "characterises a group throughout generations."[106] While the people West meets on her journey belong to distinct ethnic and religious communities, "they are all the same" to her because they share a "unity of origin," a common physical milieu that engenders in them a collective way of feeling.[107] Yugoslav culture, in its most ordinary and enduring forms, works to orient the thought and action of citizens, grounding them amid the turbulent tides of mass modernity.

For this reason, much of West's analysis in *Black Lamb* concerns not just the long history of Yugoslavia and its various regions, but the depiction of its material traditions. Brian Hall has noted that "a reader of any of West's work will immediately be struck by how often and lovingly she details the clothes, furniture, and objets d'art of her surroundings."[108] West's characteristic attention to material culture takes on an unmistakably political significance in *Black Lamb* as a way of understanding the embodied traditions of the nation. *Black Lamb* is, as Lene Hansen has pointed out, "packed with descriptions of architecture, music, houses, frescos, paintings, clothing, embroidery, and food and wine, recorded not simply as observations but as expressions of a culture's identity."[109] Such material practices and habits take center stage for West because they express collective identity *and* are the mechanisms necessary to its perpetuation—ways of conditioning the reflexes of the nation.

At a luncheon in the Bosnian town of Travnik, for example, West surveys the home of her hosts, locating a collective political fortitude in its material furnishings. She muses, "Built into this room, and inherent in every word and gesture of its owners, was a tradition more limited in its scope than the traditions of Vienna, Berlin, Paris, or London, but within its limits just as ancient and sure and competent. Whatever event these people met they could outface; the witness to that was their deep serenity."[110] This sentiment is quite typical of West's encounter with the material traditions of the people she meets on her journey. In local aesthetic customs of clothing and architecture, religious rituals, and the economic practices of craft labor, West discerns the manifestations of a collective political disposition as well as a way of reproducing it. "Tradition," in this sense, denotes a material process through which a political cast of mind (here, the ability to contest fascism) is forged. That such a tradition relies on bodily susceptibility to one's atmosphere is explicit in West's descriptions; as she later notes of a Macedonian woman, knowledge gained through connection with a given milieu is not narrowly cognitive in nature. Speaking of "the Byzantine tradition," she writes, "With our minds we all know what Byzantium was," a culture of architecture, painting, mosaics, metal-work, textiles, and calligraphy "unique in its nobility."[111] Yet, for most readers, such knowledge is not genuine knowledge: "All this we know with our minds, and with our minds only. But this woman knew it with all her being. . . . It was the medium in which she existed."[112] This woman "was Byzantine in all her ways, and in her substance" simply by virtue of existing within the milieu of a culture that had retained its identity amid the onslaught of modernization.[113]

Elsewhere West emphasizes the routines and rituals of daily life as ways of perpetuating autochthonous cultural identities. On the Dalmatian island of Korchula, for example, she encounters a fisherman working with his knife to improve his tackle, nets, and lobster pot. Witnessing the deftness with which he accomplishes his actions, West reflects, "He must have performed this action hundreds of times, yet his body was happy and elastic with interest, as if this were the first time. It was so with all things on this island."[114] The habitual actions of Yugoslavs appear in *Black Lamb* as both the embodiment of cultural value and the mechanism of its dissemination—a form of conditioning that is organically bound up with life in the national community. West cites Proust in the prologue of *Black Lamb*, noting that "if one goes on performing any action, however banal, long enough, it automatically becomes 'wonderful.'"[115] In Dalmatia, as throughout her travels, West documents such iterative behaviors, asserting the sacredness in the expression of national identity. By the book's end, the endurance of cultural particularity becomes the rallying cry against fascism. As she tells a Cardinal in Korchula, "'You have a way of living here that is special, that is particular to you, that must be defended at all costs. . . . I do not mean just your architecture and your tradition of letters, I mean the way the people live.'"[116] When fascism appears in *Black Lamb*, it represents not only a threat to the endurance of such cultural particularity; it represents habit stripped of virtue—a disregard for "the way the people live" in favor of empty routines and cognitive grooves forged through milieu control. West limns a different vision of politicized reflex in her depiction of Yugoslavia, one that depends upon an embodied tradition fashioned over centuries and millennia.

Perhaps the best way to understand the positive ideal of national reflex in *Black Lamb* is through the book's formal emphasis on the long historical processes of the nation. Virginia Woolf suggested in *Three Guineas* that new literary techniques would need to be devised to adequately address the variegated phenomena that is a national "atmosphere." "Atmosphere," she explained is a "very mighty power": "Atmosphere not only changes the sizes and shapes of things; it affects solid bodies, like salaries, which might have been though impervious to atmosphere. An epic poem might be written about atmosphere, or a novel in ten or fifteen volumes. But since this is only a letter, and you are pressed for time, let us confine ourselves to the plain statement that atmosphere is one of the most powerful, partly because it is one of the most impalpable, of the enemies with which the daughters of educated men have to fight."[117] Woolf understood the social environment of the nation as a force that daily worked to condition the reflexes of the populace such that society itself became "a gramophone whose needle has stuck" in grooves of thought (including the domestic "fascism" of patriarchy).[118] Though Bloomsbury was an explicit target of West's critique in *Black Lamb*, it is tempting to see Woolf's thoughts on "atmosphere" as an invitation to the kind of project West was then pursuing.[119] Woolf's assertion that it would take an epic of "ten or fifteen volumes" to adequately address the effects of atmosphere on "solid bodies" very neatly describes West's massive tome, which models in formal terms the work of history in creating a reflex community. Eschewing the economizing principle of propaganda, *Black Lamb* insists, instead, on long temporalities—both those of the national history and of the reading experience itself. The national habits that West so resolutely documents are, importantly, not the "tropisms" of regimentation, but practices with antecedents in a long, collective history. These cultural practices, like art itself, are both conditioned by the national history and primary modes of reproducing cultural particularity across time. Documenting the national milieu by attempting "to show the past side by side with the present it created," *Black Lamb* represents collective identity as the product of material conditioning, one that must be safeguarded at all costs.[120] It is in this sense that *Black Lamb* is a modernist epic. Rather than working to establish a new *narrative* of the nation as an imagined space, as recent critics have suggested, West undertook a project in which all questions of narrative and myth subserve the binding power of a physical environment to sustain the practices and values of a people.

What ultimately makes England and Yugoslavia the same kind of reflex community for West is that each is united by habits born of a long national history. In the epilogue to her travels, West argues that England coheres as a national community because it has, like Yugoslavia, retained its embodied traditions in the face of mass economic change. In West's idea of modern history, the English are habit-bound in a purposive way since their habits are the organic growth of contact with a long tradition that equips citizens with the capacity to think about and actively shape a complex world. The modernization of England did not result in fascism, she argues, because England is "controlled by a national tradition, which transcends the traditions of town and country, and by this was kept from the shame which comes of ignorance of good and evil."[121] This, then, is why Yugoslavia is so important to West; because it is a place that has not been completely undone by the shock of modernization, it retains the material and cognitive traditions necessary for moral agency. It instantiates not only a mode of life at odds with the currents of capitalist development, but one whose embodied traditions equip citizens with the spiritual capacities to confront fascism.

At times *Black Lamb* can seem like a naked effort to rally nationalist sentiment in the service of wartime anti-fascism. But to read West's book as mere agitprop is to miss the literary and philosophical complexity of a text that, after all, offers few ready-to-hand political messages. Even as *Black Lamb* casts fascism as a system built on empty tropisms, the text displays a remarkably canny sense of the ways in which political reflex could be made to respond to the crises of the twentieth century. Deploying the language of Pavlovian reflex in a strategic way, West suggests that habit can be either ballast amid the crises of modernity or the defining problem of modernity itself. In this sense, Rebecca West brings the competing valences of reflex into the heart of literary modernism, measuring both its limitations and its utility for a nation on the precipice of war.

Modernity's Metronome

By the time the Second World War began in 1939, the image of Pavlov's dog—the animal trained to respond, without thought or volition, to the most arbitrary of signals—had already become a useful figure for understanding the citizenry of repressive regimes. How else to account for the popularity of fascist governments if not as the application of new forms of ideological coercion? It is the dystopian literature of the period that no doubt made the connection between the Russian scientist and repressive governments most dramatically. If habit is the flywheel of society, as William James asserted, writers like Huxley and Orwell saw conditioned reflex as a way of making society into a perpetual motion machine, one free of the cognitive frictions we recognize as spontaneity, individuality, and agency. But the Pavlovian nightmare of *Brave New World* would soon come to be seen not just as the vision of the future but as diagnostic of the world being built by repressive regimes; with Cold War writers like Meerloo and Hunter, citizens of Nazi Germany and Soviet Russia came to represent an inversion of the Western democratic ideal. Appropriating the language of scientific experiment while stoking nascent anxieties about the scientist as social engineer, literary and non-literary writers cautioned against the dangers implicit in mass cultural conditioning. In so doing, they worked to enforce a sense of difference between national communities that could be leveraged in the field of public opinion, building support for anti-fascist and anti-communist political projects alike.[122] Yet, as we have seen, the association between Pavlovian reflex and repressive regimes was hardly limited to dystopian literature or the gutters of the political press. Even for a writer as positively disposed to Pavlov as Rebecca West, the effects of conditioned reflex were easily observed in the ordinary behaviors of Germans and their constitutive failures to navigate the demands of everyday life.

Much of the notoriety that came to attach itself to Pavlov rested on the fact that his work seemed to offer conclusive proof that there are real limits to that most Western of fetishes, individual agency. Rebecca West herself wrestled with this question. In her 1933 biography, *St. Augustine*, she writes, "If we examine ourselves carefully we cannot claim to have free will. We exercise what looks like a free faculty of choice, but the way we exercise that faculty depends on our innate qualities and our environment, and these always bind us in some way or another to the neuroses which compel us to choose death rather than life. We cannot break this compulsion by the independent efforts of our minds, for they cannot function effectively unless they learn to depend on tradition."[123] West was convinced of the truth of what materialists suggested about agency, but this doctrine served only to fuel a belief in the importance of human connection and tradition in the broadest sense. For others, however, Pavlov's work constituted something of an existential threat because it cast doubt about the origins of such seemingly essential aspects of individuality as political belief and even national identity. The fact that intellectuals and propagandists alike repeatedly drew on the language of conditioning in portrayals of fascism underscores the depths of Western apprehensions about the politics of reflex. It is worth noting that when Edward Hunter coined the term "brainwashing" in 1950, he was not doing so as a mere journalist, as he pretended. As an expert in propaganda who had worked during the Second World War for the Office of Strategic Services (the institutional predecessor to the CIA), he wrote with a clear political agenda. The specter of "brainwashing" was itself an effort to brainwash citizens. The purchase of "brainwashing" as a concept suggests that the Pavlovian citizen is not something that exists *out there* in Germany or Korea or Russia; instead, it reflects Western anxieties about its own growing dependence on political reflex.

Such anxieties are palpable in both the literary and non-literary discourses on totalitarianism, especially after the Second World War, when the depth of collaboration between Nazi officials and ordinary citizens became widely known. Prior to the war, as we have seen, the politics of conditioned reflex were still partially untainted by the associations they would later acquire. As this chapter has demonstrated, even as writers like Rebecca West utilized ideas of Pavlovian reflex in their critiques of repressive regimes, modernists were not able to regard the politics of reflex as an evil tout court. At the same time that they appropriated the language of conditioned reflex in order to understand fascist and totalitarian politics, modernists used these ideas in order to conceptualize a positive ideal of national cohesion, free of the racial and hereditary foundations central to fascism. In West and contemporaries like Eliot, the shared milieu of the national community represented a powerful force for ensuring the endurance of a moral and aesthetic tradition—those particularizing qualities threatened in equal measure by economic modernization and the ongoing political reorganization of Europe. For these modernists, literature was doubly important in this political project. As West argued in *The Strange Necessity*, literature was a unique vehicle for the synthesis of individual experience—a way of testing cultural values on the page as facts of physiology. But these modernists also understood literature as something capable of exerting real influence on the national milieu; emphasizing the embodied experience of readers over the hermeneutic practice of individual interpreters, they imagined a mode of literature capable of reproducing the binding values of the national community through reflex. In the work of West, we can witness an ongoing effort to use the literary tools of modernism to reimagine the nation as a reflex community grounded in this positive notion of Pavlovian science.

Recognizing the utility of conditioned reflex to these modernists is an instructive reminder of just how central such ideas became to Western political practice in the twentieth century. Pavlov's discoveries would survive the historical contexts of midcentury to become foundational to a number of political fields where the methodological injunctions of behavioral science took hold, including economics, psychology, public relations, education, and management. The effort to turn the study of behavior back toward observable fact and quantification marked an important effort to rein in psychoanalytic practice and the philosophical speculations of vitalism, of course, but it also proved central to fields that saw cognitive and embodied economies as the currency of mass life. As we will see in the afterword of this book, the paradigm established by Pavlov and put into practice by public relations experts survived the early twentieth century to become deeply entrenched in the political life of our own century.

One early twentieth-century field in which Pavlov's and Watson's ideas were to find utility was sociology. As Rebecca West was attempting to extract political lessons from *Conditioned Reflexes*, sociologists in France and Germany were inquiring into the place of automatic behaviors within modern social structures. By the late 1930s, the idea of "conditioning" central to Pavlov's work could be taken for granted by these thinkers; writing in 1939, the pioneering sociologist Norbert Elias could note, simply, that the term had already been "precisely defined" by Watson.[124] As we will see in the next chapter, the study of habit by sociologists paralleled modernists' own interest in and concern with the politics of reflex. Like their modernist contemporaries, these sociologists recognized the importance of embodied traditions and reflexes to the constitution of national communities. The "social units that we call nations," Elias argued in *The Civilizing Process* (1939), are centrally defined by their "institutionalized tradition[s]" and "the schemata by which the emotional life of the individual is molded."[125] As with West, Elias and his peers understood physiological categories of conditioned reflex and affective "molding" as foundational to the cohesion and endurance of national communities across centuries. Prioritizing automatic, embodied behaviors over national myths and shared stories, these sociologists adapted early twentieth-century theories of habit in ways that broadly mirror those of modernists. Yet, as we will see in the next chapter, the specter of affective molding also produced in Samuel Beckett a modernism in which habit and embodiment created some difficult political and aesthetic problems.

5 Higher Degrees of Automaticity
Habitus, Samuel Beckett, and Late Modernism

Pavlov's *Conditioned Reflexes* was greeted by early readers as auguring solutions to some of the most trenchant problems of the early twentieth century. But, as we have seen, almost as soon as writers were citing Pavlov as a source of political optimism, his name would become a byword for the degradations of mass life as a whole. Any application of his ideas threatened to undermine the values of a liberal political order, many argued, a sense that would become widespread from the 1930s onward. But for at least some of his initial readers, Pavlov's fame registered less as a danger to democracy than as a problem for literary culture. In 1929, when Samuel Beckett published an essay celebrating Joyce's *Work in Progress*, he invoked Pavlov and his literary champion, Rebecca West, as forces in the impoverishment of readers: "The form that is an arbitrary and independent phenomenon can fulfil no higher function than that of stimulus for tertiary or quartary conditioned reflex of dribbling comprehension. When Miss Rebecca West clears her decks for a sorrowful deprecation of the Narcisstic [sic] element in Mr. Joyce by the purchase of 3 hats, one feels that she might very well wear her bib at all her intellectual banquets, or alternatively, assert a more noteworthy control over her salivary glands than is possible for Monsieur Pavlov's unfortunate dog."[1] Writing nine years before the publication of his first novel, Beckett took issue with West's argument in *The Strange Necessity* that literature is a form of physiological stimuli. In West's vision of modernism, Beckett saw justification for those impoverished readers who preferred simple reflex ("dribbling comprehension") to the life of the mind. Literary form that is divorced from content, form that is "an arbitrary and independent phenomenon," can never mean more than the ringing of a bell. Such writing may provoke a response from readers, but in so doing it treats them as little more than "Pavlov's unfortunate dog."

Juxtaposing West's Pavlovian theory of literature with Joyce's formal agenda, Beckett's remarks suggest the virtues of the "higher function[s]" of the human organism over the automatic or reflexive. Written at the outset of a long and varied literary career, such comments might well be taken as auguring some of Beckett's most important aesthetic and philosophical attachments. Indeed, scholars have broadly seen the elevation of consciousness over the body as central to Beckett's literary project. In large part, this analysis can be attributed to the peculiar formal agenda of Beckett's work; excising plot, character, and setting to a radical degree, his work often seems to channel the reader's attention to a narrative or dramatic voice—a kind of literary consciousness that is anything but embodied. As Ulrika Maude has pointed out, scholarship since the 1950s has emphasized consciousness while marginalizing the body as an element inherently foreign to Beckett's work: "The prominence of the body and its decrepitude was accredited to the body's inherent otherness; what truly mattered in Beckett was the mind and its capacity to move beyond matter."[2] Yet, as even casual readers of Beckett know, his works are dominated by characters whose bodies announce themselves in unusually prominent ways; characters are plagued by bodies that hunger, ache, and misbehave, including bodies that twitch, tic, or jerk in ways that are often frustratingly opaque to readers. Such habits and reflexes occupy a central place in his thinking for the same reason as they did in other modernists—as a site of the political pressures constitutive of twentieth-century modernity. Yet even as his work reflected a perception that social life was increasingly dominated by automatic behaviors, it also grappled with a problem implicit within the studies of reflex. Bergson, for his part, noted that habit is that which we cannot represent to ourselves. "When we mechanically perform an habitual action," he writes, "unconsciousness may be absolute; but this is merely due to the fact that the representation of the act is held in check by the performance of the act itself, which resembles the idea so perfectly, and fits it so exactly, that consciousness is unable to find room between them."[3] For Beckett, the question of whether it was possible to bring back into consciousness those behaviors that, by nature, dwell below the threshold, would become a motivating concern throughout his oeuvre. In the years that followed his critical analysis of Rebecca West, Beckett would engage in his own extensive reading in reflex psychology, ultimately creating a series of literary experiments centered on the central but inenarrable role of automaticity in mass life.

In order to fully unpack the philosophical and historical dimensions of this problem in Beckett, this chapter focuses on a discipline that was directly shaped by the politics of reflex: sociology. Like modernism, sociology was from its origins concerned with automatic behaviors, including the use of behavioristic models for understanding social life. Though some notable sociologists at the turn of the century expressed unease about the discipline's proximity to behaviorism, by the late 1930s several sociologists were actively attempting to forge a framework for understanding the role of the body in establishing social values. Marcel Mauss and Norbert Elias, for example, independently revived earlier sociological interests in habit, offering theories of "habitus" that helped explain the role of automatic behaviors in endowing citizens with political dispositions. For these thinkers, everyday behaviors represented a system of training the body and thereby ensuring the acquisition and transmission of cultural dispositions; through automatic behaviors, they argued, citizens become entrenched in their political identities and come to embody the mores of their milieu.

These sociologists were motivated by the same thing that modernists like Beckett felt—that our environments condition us to behave in ways that are laden with political meaning even when our behaviors are not manifestly political in nature. Their studies engaged many of the questions that animated the politics of reflex as a whole—including issues of bodily susceptibility, individual autonomy, and agency—but their analyses of automatic behaviors reflect the rising intensity of such preoccupations within the historical moment of late modernism. Elias, for example, read the twentieth century as an era in which reflex played an unprecedented role, leading, as he explained in *The Civilizing Process*, to "a higher degree of automaticity" than any preceding era. Such a perspective is consonant with those of earlier writers, of course, but these sociological studies also suggested just how stealth these automatic behaviors are.[4] For Mauss and Elias, some of the most important mechanisms for creating political identities necessarily elude our conscious apprehension. Our automatic behaviors, they argued, are so intimate and so "natural" to us that we are often unaware of their importance and almost never capable of explaining the political dispositions they encode.

This chapter demonstrates a convergence between sociological studies of habitus and late modernism's preoccupation with automaticity. Like their contemporaries in sociology, late modernists discerned an intensification of reflex in the social realm even as citizens seemed to become less capable of distinguishing between automaticity and agency. Beckett's early work—

particularly his first novel, *Murphy*—draws much of its energy from the very theoretical problem outlined by Mauss and Elias, namely the tendency of habits to elude our conscious minds. In this respect, Beckett's novels intensify some of the dominant political and aesthetic concerns that we have seen in other modernists. But whereas earlier modernists like Lewis were animated by fear of hidden manipulators, Beckett's literary worlds diffuse reflex into far less centralized agencies. Rather than attempting to disclose the secret machinations of an invisible government, Beckett emphasizes the unknowable sources of such automatic behaviors; at the same time that characters are rigorously conditioned, they remain only vaguely aware of how environment affects them, their reflexes becoming nearly impossible to articulate or explain. In this sense, Beckett's work from the 1930s to the 1950s reflects an understanding of the "higher degree of automaticity" necessary to the twentieth century, concerns that broadly manifest in the work of other late modernist writers.

Yet, as this chapter will show, Beckett's later work also turned away from automaticity as a source of outright anxiety. His work at midcentury came to share with sociologists a sense that even the intensification of automaticity could also encode new forms of knowledge and power—indeed, that automaticity might help us survive the violence and upheaval of historical catastrophe. This movement in Beckett's later career, I show, reflects shifting cultural attitudes about automaticity. The latter half of the twentieth century witnessed disciplinary shifts for which automaticity—the central term of the behaviorist paradigm—ceased to maintain the political urgency that had animated the modernist moment. But if literary writers and cultural theorists charted a new intellectual course *away* from the body after midcentury, the same cannot be said of political theorists and tacticians, who remained committed to the science of behavior and its political promises.

From Habit to Habitus: The Sociology of Reflex

More than a century after sociology became a fully institutionalized discipline, it is easy to forget that its early days witnessed intense internal debate about its methods and objects of analysis. Sociology entered academia as an upstart, and early days saw key figures worrying over how to properly distinguish the field from rival disciplines, especially psychology. Issues of automaticity, habit, and reflex entered these debates as foundational figures like Émile Durkheim and Max Weber sought to establish institutional space for sociology and endow it with intellectual currency. Both thinkers were intrigued by nineteenth-century discourses of reflex and saw automaticity as crucial in establishing social meaning. In Weber's estimation, habits are endowed with "the dignity of oughtness"; by this he meant that habitual actions seem necessary and correct to their performers, even though they are almost always arbitrary and specific to a given society.[5] Some of the most significant aspects of social life are not those beliefs we consciously hold, he claimed, but rather those that are "ingrained by habituation" and are "often a matter of almost automatic reaction to habitual stimuli."[6] Early sociologists shared Weber's interest in automatic behaviors as one among many objects of inquiry, but the rising institutional clout of behaviorism in the early twentieth century discouraged many from fully embracing these categories. In Watson's work, the term "habit" deliberately elided physiological reflexes and cultural customs. He proposed to use the science of reflex to study patterns of behavior that sociologists themselves had identified as central to their new discipline. Watson's use of the term "habit" thus created problems for a field that was intent on establishing itself as autonomous from rival disciplines. Though automatic behaviors represented an important facet of social life, leading figures like Durkheim argued that sociologists ought to abandon the study of habit altogether. As Charles Camic explains, "The idea of habit remained, in Durkheim's mind, too closely associated with [reflex] psychology to merit inclusion in his sundry pronouncements about what the discipline of sociology ought to study; to make the concept part of sociology could only risk the whole cause by suggesting that the new field was not such an autonomous one after all."[7] As behaviorism solidified its position in America and abroad in the teens and 1920s, sociologists recoiled from its central terms, with the result that subsequent pillars of the field tended to stress volitional behaviors over automatic ones.

Though the first generation of sociologists ceded "habit" to behaviorism, Watson's emphasis on the susceptibility of the body proved to have enduring fascination to key figures in the history of sociology. Pavlov and Watson had individually asserted the importance of the body in mediating information, and they had implied that bodily susceptibility was key to establishing social values. But if sociologists were going to avoid the territory established by these thinkers, they would need a new term to describe the operation of habit in the social realm, a conceptual space that would be filled by "habitus." By scuttling the long familiar "habit," sociologists hoped to distance themselves from physiology and behaviorist psychology. As Nick Crossley explains, in the work of early twentieth-century sociologists, "habit belongs to the empirical domain and to a scientific conception of human beings," while " 'habitus' is used to capture the habitual basis of human perception, thought and motor activity in a discourse which explicitly disavows the empiricism and naturalism with which the concept of 'habit' is tinged."[8] "Habitus," in short, was an attempt to reopen the conceptual terrain that behaviorism had foreclosed in early sociology.

Sociological inquiry about "habitus" framed the physical body as a conduit between society and the enduring social values of subjects. As Pierre Bourdieu would later gloss the term, habitus "is that which one has acquired, but which has become durably incorporated in the body in the form of permanent dispositions."[9] This may sound rather similar to the project of behaviorism, which stressed the role of the physical body in establishing social attitudes. But sociologists were not interested, as Watson would become, in forging behaviors or in understanding dispositions that were temporary and specific to individuals. Instead, sociologists of habitus looked to the physical conditioning of bodies, particularly through ritualized and iterative actions, as the secret location of *collective* social values.[10] For European sociologists of the interwar period, it was possible to understand our conscious political beliefs as little more than the inward rationalization of what was already manifest in socially conditioned behaviors. They argued that by shaping outward habits (especially of children), communities enforce norms of behavior and entrench political attitudes without requiring the conscious participation of citizens. As Bourdieu would later explain, "the methodological manipulation of the body . . . is a way of obtaining from the body a form of consent that the mind could refuse."[11]

Drawing on classical ideas about how physical action inscribes durable dispositions—what Aristotle had called "hexis"—Norbert Elias and Marcel Mauss individually attempted to carve out new disciplinary space for the study of automatic behaviors. That Elias, a German, and Mauss, a Frenchman, returned to these questions simultaneously reflects the urgency around the study of reflex and the growing purchase of behaviorism in the period. For both thinkers, "habitus" was a valuable concept for understanding not just *how* people acquire their political dispositions, but the nature of twentieth-century modernity itself. Moreover, their theories were congruent with a growing sentiment in the period that modern collectives demanded ever more automatic behaviors from populations at the expense of individual autonomy. As we will see, Beckett's novel *Murphy* stands as a prime example of this characteristically late modernist relationship to habit. His early novels not only dramatize the political work of automatic behaviors, but they do so with a keen attention to the theoretical problems outlined by Mauss and Elias—the intimacy of habitus that renders deep-seated dispositions unnarratable.

In a 1935 essay entitled "Techniques of the Body," Mauss returned to earlier sociological concerns with habit in order to suggest that societies are constituted in part by bodily behaviors that are learned and collectively shared. Habits, he writes, "do not vary just with individuals and their imitations; they vary especially between societies, educations, proprieties and fashions, prestiges."[12] These collective habits include an extremely wide array of behaviors, from methods of marching and sitting, to ways of giving birth and having sex. But for Mauss the key insight about "body techniques" was not simply that communities are bound by the idiosyncratic ways of physically doing things, but that automatic behaviors are mechanisms for encoding social dispositions across time. Techniques of the body are, he writes, "training systems"; by repetitively doing certain kinds of actions, even unconsciously, we acquire values as embodied social knowledge, dispositions that entrench us in political communities.[13] While we may feel that such actions are *"of a mechanical, physical or physico-chemical order,"* even the unconscious operations of the body are in fact repositories of the values that distinguish cultures from one another. Thus, the fact that a "pious Muslim" individual "will go to any lengths to avoid using anything but his right hand" when eating is not simply a reflection of religious codes of purity and piety, but one of the many mechanisms by which collective values are learned and incorporated in the body.[14] Such body techniques are the product of overt education and policing, of course, but in Mauss's view they are substantially the product of our submersion in a physical environment. By merely inhabiting a culture, we are trained in the body techniques of our communities, and thus grow to do, feel, and think in regularized ways. Like behaviorists, who understood bodily susceptibility as the motive force of human action, Mauss suggests that the most important aspects of social identity are those that are automatic. "Everything in us all is under command," he writes.[15]

In and of itself, Mauss's treatment of habits as a collective phenomenon helped sociology regain the disciplinary ground that Weber and Durkheim had ceded to behaviorism. But Mauss's understanding of habitus remained fairly preliminary in his 1935 essay; he offers general observations and lists many of the kinds of activities that might encode political or social values, but he attempts little systematic analysis of how specific actions perpetuate specific values. Norbert Elias, in his 1939 book *The Civilizing Process*, offered a more robust account of the political meanings embodied in these habits, and outlined an extensive history of how they have been taught across the modern era. In two volumes stretching to about six hundred pages, *The Civilizing Process* looks at a large body of writing on etiquette and deportment from the late medieval period, through the European Renaissance, the Enlightenment, and the twentieth century. Reading this discourse with an eye toward the formation of nation-states, Elias elaborates a theory about the preeminent value of bodily conditioning and habit formation within political life.

Elias's and Mauss's interest in habitus cohered around a shared understanding of the role of the body in mediating political values and the importance of iterative behaviors as an engine of social reproduction. As Mauss implied, by training physical bodies to accord with collective practices, societies perpetuate social values and the "symbolic life of the mind."[16] Elias gave this suggestion greater specificity in *The Civilizing Process* by outlining how habitus evolved across the modern era. In early modern writing on etiquette he discovered that the policing of habits constituted a form of what he called "affective molding"—a way of conditioning specific kinds of political dispositions.[17] By disciplining mundane behaviors—from table manners and mores on spitting and defecating, to rules about sexuality and sleeping—political communities ensured the perpetuation of cultural values in an embodied form. Habits, Elias wrote, are "embodiments of a . . . mental and emotional structure."[18] Through "the totality of socially instilled forms of conduct," he argues, not only are social systems constituted, but with them entire architectures of the mind.[19] Such affective molding, Elias showed, constituted an enormous discourse in the early modern period, where it helped establish courtly society as a culturally distinct and superior class. But the rise of the bourgeoisie in the modern era saw the extension of affective molding to emerging national communities as well. In this modern context, the molding of affect did not require the strict policing that Renaissance writers like Erasmus had called for. Instead, habits are substantially learned through a social milieu—an environment that conditions the reflexes of its inhabitants. And this process of social habituation works because it creates in citizens what Elias called "an inner automatism":

To a large extent, however, the conduct and instinctual life of the child are forced even without words into the same mold and in the same direction by the fact that a particular use of knife and fork, for example, is completely established in the adult world—that is, by the example of environment. Since the pressure or coercion of individual adults is allied to the pressure and example of the whole surrounding world, most children, as they grow up, forget or repress relatively early the fact that their feelings of shame and embarrassment, of pleasure and displeasure, are molded into conformity with a certain standard by external pressure and compulsion. All this appears to them as highly personal, something "inward," implanted in them by nature.... Later it becomes more and more an inner automatism, the imprint of society on the inner self, the superego, that forbids that individual to eat in any other way than with a fork. The social standard to which the individual was first made to conform by external restraint is finally reproduced more or less smoothly within him, through a self-restraint which may operate *even against his conscious wishes.*[20]

For Elias, it is the ordinary behaviors of everyday life—those things that do not rise to the level of conscious effort—that safeguard collective dispositions. The use of a knife and fork, for example, is not manifestly political in any sense, but such habits encode values of cleanliness, proportion, order, class, and the like. And whereas courtly society overtly disciplined behaviors in order to maintain class distinctions, the modern era witnesses the dispersal of affect molding into every facet of life. In Elias's analysis, the modern period depends far less on disciplinary structures than on the example provided by a broadly shared milieu; it is "by the example of environment," not overt education, that subjects acquire the inward dispositions that knit them to a national community. Moreover, individuals subject to the example of environment do not experience their training as anything other than nature itself. What began in the early modern period as a carefully constructed effort to condition behaviors results in the "inner automatism" of modern subjects—an economy of affect that regulates so efficiently as to make cognitive reflexes seemingly invincible. In the twentieth century, the government of thought and action becomes so complete, Elias avers, that subjects may fail to overpower such habits *even by conscious effort.*

In Elias's analysis, we can see the close relationship between midcentury sociology and behaviorism. If thinkers like Durkheim had explicitly distanced themselves from "habit" as tainted by behaviorism, Elias's work reflects a less antagonistic relationship to reflex psychology. Indeed, when Elias writes about the "conditioning" of subjects, he notes that "American behaviorist literature," and Watson in particular, had usefully defined terms like "habit formation," and that such a vocabulary was "useful and even indispensable in investigating the past."[21] Though *The Civilizing Process* cites a large archive of writing about the molding of affect, like a variety of thinkers in the period Elias stresses just how important the relationship between bodies and physical environments is. Just as Mauss emphasized the role of physiology in the study of sociology, the body for Elias is "indissolubly linked to what we call the 'psyche.'"[22] In analyzing the body in this way, Elias and Mauss offered a robust sociological engagement with theories of reflex championed by behaviorists and argued for the increasingly important role that automatic behaviors play in national communities.

We have already seen a rough cognate of Elias's and Mauss's models of habitus in the political thinking of Rebecca West. While West was ignorant of modernist-era sociology, she intuitively understood the power of iterative behaviors in transmitting the kinds of cultural knowledge that T. S. Eliot associated with "tradition." But West also implied that social reproduction was waning across the West in the interwar period. This attitude set West at odds with a number of later modernists (including Beckett) as well as her sociological contemporaries. In Elias's sweeping account, it is in the twentieth century, not in courtly society, in which social reproduction reaches its most perfected state. The fact that the early modern society actively policed behaviors in order to mold affect suggests that such controls were necessary to perpetuate values. The innovation of the twentieth century, according to Elias, was the creation of forms of conditioning that make "socially desirable behavior," such as the desire for work, "automatic."[23] In the progressively differentiated world of mass society, he saw the creation of environments that were both more stealth and more totalizing than at any time in history, leading to a "higher degree of automaticity" among citizens.

It should be noted that in these early theories of habitus, automatic behaviors, even when ubiquitous, are rarely regarded as wholly pernicious. Modern forms of habituation are neither "better" nor "worse" than medieval affective structures for Elias since, in his opinion, modernity "goes hand in hand with liberations of the most diverse kinds."[24] This understanding is retained in much later commentary, which tends to stress that habitus is not a strict system of control but rather a kind of "know-how"—the embodied knowledge that aids in necessary cognitive and behavioral economies. In this respect, such definitions of habitus seem to share perspective with the pragmatist tradition, including John Dewey, who was interested in the positive as well as the negative entailments of habitual behaviors. But Elias also explains that the modern era produced citizens more automatic and "freer of spontaneous emotions" than their historical antecedents.[25] Indeed, the gloss "know-how" misses a key feature of "habitus," namely that subjects usually do *not* know the significance of the habits they share in common. This aspect of "habitus" shares more with an emerging midcentury brand of philosophy typical of the Frankfurt School than it does with the American pragmatist tradition. For example, Erich Fromm, who like Elias fled Germany in the early 1930s, wrote about the collapse of rationality in his 1941 book, *Escape from Freedom*. There he argued that the model citizen of mass society is not the rational individual, but the "the human automaton."[26] An "atmosphere of subtle suggestion" saturates "social life," he writes, leading to the "automatization of the individual in modern society."[27] We can recognize the congruence of Elias's ideas about the tightening of affect with other elements of the Frankfurt School, as well, including Adorno and Horkheimer's characterization of the "administered world" in *Dialectic of the Enlightenment* (1944), and Herbert Marcuse's attempts to diagnose the "pre-conditioning" of Western thought through public opinion and the mass media in *One-Dimensional Man* (1964). Collectively, these works inflect Elias's analysis of habitus, and speak to a widespread concern about the rising power of automaticity at midcentury and the contradictory nature of habitus. Read from this critical perspective, habitus is not "know-how" but rather something more like "unknow-how" since it short-circuits our ability to know explicitly or challenge the ways we have been conditioned to do and feel.

Late modernist figures were likely to agree with Elias's understanding of the twentieth century as an era that had witnessed what he called "the cultivation of new and stricter constraints" on behavior.[28] Wyndham Lewis's idea that the state itself leveraged bodily susceptibility in order to create social automata would become widespread during the late 1930s and endure long into the Cold War. Critics like Tyrus Miller, Jed Esty, Daniel Belgrad, and Michael Szalay have suggested the extent to which the formal and thematic concerns of late modernist writers were informed by the political intensifications of the interwar and postwar periods, including fascism and corporatism, most prominently. At the center of these diverse analyses is a shared agreement that late modernism is marked by a concern with individual autonomy amid the incursion of politics into everyday life. Miller, writing of the British context, has suggested that "the systematic and active organization of society by the state, a process greatly intensified by the need to mobilize human and material resources for the war and again by the economic crisis of 1929, was experienced by many artists as an encroachment on their authenticity and autonomy, a devaluation of their individual experience."[29] Whether states relied on the science of reflex as thoroughly as nascent fields like public relations is doubtful. But artists of the period certainly felt that the ability of individuals to break free of, or even identify, socially sanctioned habits was severely constrained. In the American context, for example, concerns about non-routinized behavior gave rise to a vibrant midcentury modernism that took up Lawrence's signature concern; as Belgrad explains, the American avant-garde of the midcentury was united by a shared belief "that cultural conditioning functioned ideologically by encouraging the atrophy of certain perceptions and the exaggeration of others," and that a culture of spontaneity was necessary to escape such conditioning.[30]

Among late modernist writers, it is perhaps Beckett more than any other who consistently signals a concern with autonomy and automaticity. While in his novels, the state and state-run institutions often appear as forces that condition behavior, the state typically does not occupy the central place that it did in the politics of modernists like Lawrence and Lewis. In Beckett's novels, the political milieu tends to recede from the foreground along with the collective values enforced through iterative behaviors. In this respect, the sociological analysis of the 1930s offers a useful way of understanding a theoretical problem explored by Beckett's work, namely the stealth nature of habitus. As Elias noted, the most important social and political values encoded by habitus lie beyond the "waking consciousness" of ordinary people—indeed, they may remain altogether invisible to our rational mind.[31] To study habitus, Elias explained in a later book, meant "bringing back into consciousness . . . things which have been forgotten" because they have been remembered only at the level of the body.[32] Habitus, by definition, is unsayable. As sociologist Paul Connerton explains, the performers of habitual actions are always "reminded of something with cognitive content," but content that cannot be explicitly put into words.[33] And it is precisely because habitus cannot be put into words that "the cognitive content of what the group remembers in common exercises such persuasive and persistent force."[34] For late modernism, this quality of automaticity raised a difficult aesthetic problem. How do you represent the increasingly reflexive nature of society if such reflexes are resistant to conscious analysis? How do you make manifest the production of dispositions that are stealth? In *Murphy*, Beckett would give the higher degrees of automaticity described by sociologists their most extensive treatment.

Murphy and the Whole Physical Fiasco

Preoccupied at every step with the relation between mind and body, Beckett's first novel, *Murphy*, is a quintessentially modernist novel of reflex. Set in mid-1930s London and centered on a character desperate to avoid the habits abundantly in evidence around him, *Murphy* tells the story of an Irish migrant as he attempts to first avoid work, and later find it, in an effort to save his girlfriend, Celia, from the degradation of prostitution. This narrative is symmetrically matched by the tale of a group of Murphy's Irish friends who travel to London to find the elusive hero, only to discover that he has been killed by an explosion at the sanatorium where he has taken work. In many ways a modernist picaresque, *Murphy* is a novel rife with the kinds of environmental determinisms we have seen in the work of earlier modernists. The eponymous Murphy is constantly aware of his status as a body, and much of the novel's plot concerns his attempts to access a genuine "consciousness" of pure interiority—a self uncorrupted by the body and its susceptibility. Beckett employs Cartesian philosophy and a host of more contemporary psychological models in the novel to trouble the firm distinction between body and mind, a distinction that Murphy himself seeks to uphold. In section six of the novel, the narrator offers an account of "Murphy's mind," not "as it really was" but "what it felt and pictured itself to be."[35] In his own mind, Murphy imagines himself "hermetically closed to the universe without," the "mental experience" and the "physical experience" being separate qualities entirely.[36] Throughout the novel Murphy endeavors to uphold this distinction so that he may maintain personal autonomy and avoid what he calls "the whole physical fiasco."[37]

While Murphy's mind "pictured itself to be" a space apart from the physical world, the novel itself consistently problematizes the firm distinction between body and mind. In writing the novel, Beckett drew on his own substantial knowledge about Pavlov, behaviorism, and related psychologies, studies he undertook shortly after decrying Rebecca West's admiration of Pavlov. In his "Philosophy Notebook" (now held at Trinity College Dublin), Beckett took note of the near-simultaneous discovery of conditioned reflex by Pavlov and his rival, Vladimir Bekhterev, as well as definitions and summaries of the work of behaviorists like Watson. These notes suggest an extensive study of trends in reflex psychology, including knowledge of Edward Thorndike's experiments on animal behavior and the studies of minor American behaviorists like Max Meyer, A. P. Weiss, and Walter S. Hunter, all of whom Beckett saw as part of a philosophical tradition reaching back to antiquity. In the notebook, Beckett differentiates between behaviorism and Pavlov's conditioned reflex, but he concludes that Watson merely "applies conditioned reflex concept to all human habit formation," including matters of emotion, thinking, and language.[38]

Beckett made use of these studies throughout *Murphy*, using images of automaticity and reflex to remind readers that neither Murphy nor his friends are free of conditioning from their environment. In some ways, the novel's attention to bodily susceptibility, including its overt references to reflex psychologists and scientists like Pavlov, suggests a strong indebtedness to behaviorism, even a possible retort to the concern with consciousness in Beckett's modernist predecessors. Joshua Gang has made this point, arguing that *Murphy* takes a behavioristic approach to character, replacing "the representation of covert mental states with the representation of overt behaviors and actions."[39] But the analysis of *Murphy* as a strictly behaviorist novel misses the social dimensions of Beckett's work—its interest in reflex as a vehicle of politics. As Beckett noted in his "Philosophy Notebook," behaviorism had a "biosocial" dimension since Watson claimed "that, given control of a healthy child's environment, he could turn him into anything he chose."[40] Indeed, in *Murphy* we can see this biosocial dimension at work in ways that directly mirror contemporaneous theorizations of habitus. Not only does *Murphy* employ a quasi-behavioristic approach to character, but it develops a sociological understanding of how environments instill habits that dwell below the threshold of conscious apprehension. In *Murphy*, we witness Beckett exploring the sociological meanings of habits even when characters like Murphy himself aren't aware of their conditioning or explicitly disavow it. Dramatizing the success of habit even against one's conscious wishes, *Murphy* underscores the higher degrees of automaticity that Elias described as a constitutive feature of twentieth-century life.

Throughout the novel, Beckett foregrounds the effect of an environment in establishing socially sanctified behaviors, particularly the habits of economically productive subjects. As the novel opens, the reader finds Murphy in his apartment, bound to a rocking chair and attempting to rock himself into a kind of trance state. As he slowly drifts into unconsciousness (or what he considers genuine "consciousness"), he hears a cuckoo clock, which, "having struck between twenty and thirty, became the echo of a street-cry, which now entering the mew gave *Quid pro quo! Quid pro quo!* directly."[41] The language of economic exchange that Murphy mistakenly attributes to the clock is a message that is coded in the noise of the street—it is the message that the everyday environment communicates. Subtly conditioning Beckett's characters to understand themselves primarily as financial actors, such forms of environmental stimuli conscript his characters into prescribed modes of thought and action that are socially productive and, like the clock itself, purely automatic. As a result of this environment, images of economic automatism saturate the novel from beginning to end, becoming the modus operandi of most of Beckett's characters. Mr. Kelly, Celia's infirm uncle, is a prime example. Upon learning of Celia's liaison with Murphy, Mr. Kelly asks, "Is he, has he, anything at all?"[42] Beckett links this economic reflex to the cuckoo clock, suggesting that Mr. Kelly's mind works, in this regard, like "clockwork."[43] In turning Celia's love for Murphy into an economic matter, Mr. Kelly exhibits a kind of reflex that dominates the novel. Like Murphy's Irish friends who would locate him in London for what they might extract from him, Mr. Kelly is a character who is capable of behaving only in the ways sanctioned by his environment. As Beckett's narrator will say, these characters are "puppets."[44]

Beckett's preoccupation with habituated behaviors is hardly unique in his wider body of work, but *Murphy* is unusual because it offers a pointed analysis of the sources and social utility of such reflexes. Throughout the novel Beckett stresses that the economic habits of his characters are not the product of an overt program of indoctrination but rather of contact with their social environment. As Murphy hears the *"quid pro quo"* of the cuckoo clock in the opening scene, the narrator comments that "these were sights and sounds that he [Murphy] did not like" because they "detained him in the world to which they belonged."[45] This world—what Beckett's narrator variously calls the "big world" and "outer reality"—is a realm of physicality, a world in which the most ordinary forms of social existence entail exposure to stimuli that conditions the mind in predetermined ways.[46] "Everywhere," Miss Counihan admits late in the novel, "I find . . . the mind at the cart-tail of the body, the body at the chariot-wheels of the mind."[47] While questions of embodiment are largely figured in philosophical terms, especially the Cartesian dualism with which Murphy understands his own phenomenal experience, Beckett also frames reflex in terms of an economic doctrine promulgated by the social milieu. If Beckett's characters are puppets, they are manipulated via a "psychosomatic fistula," an imaginary aperture that allows the environment to direct them toward economic productivity, even against their overt wishes.[48]

While bodily susceptibility is a primary concern of the novel, characters are rarely aware of the ways commonplace interactions with their environment condition them. Even the state—an ostensible force for overt discipline—impinges on characters' subjectivity in only the most minor of ways. One of the few representatives of the state in the novel is a civic guard at the Dublin General Post Office, whose momentary appearance goes a long way toward explaining the interface between the body and politics in Beckett's novel. Attempting to disperse a crowd that has gathered to watch what it thinks will be a confrontation, the civic guard commands the spectators to move along. The narrator reports, "The crowd obeyed, with the single diastole-systole which is all the law requires."[49] The crowd obeys the directive of the guard with an automatic reflex that mirrors corporeal processes that happen independent of cognition, namely respiration. The relationship between individuals and social collectives, Beckett suggests, is pulmonary in character; his characters internalize the protocols of their political environment through a process of habituation, of incorporation, that resembles the body's constant and automatic appropriation of the physical environment. Characters assimilate such influences unconsciously; they are no more aware of their political reflexes than they are of their own breathing.

The use of physiological language to describe a political relationship was not a matter of simple convenience for Beckett. Already in his short 1930 book, *Proust*, Beckett had closely aligned respiration and habituation. There he wrote, "The laws of memory are subject to the more general laws of habit. Habit is a compromise effected between the individual and his environment, or between the individual and his own organic eccentricities, the guarantee of a dull inviolability, the lightning-conductor of his existence. Habit is the ballast that chains the dog to his vomit. Breathing is habit. Life is habit."[50] Environment is the dog's vomit of *Murphy*—the stimuli to which Beckett's characters are blinded through habituation. Unable to consciously acknowledge the environment that conditions their thoughts and actions, they passively incorporate it into their routines and desires. Air, in fact, would become a recurrent metaphor for late modernist writers confronting the political intensities of the period. Orwell's 1939 novel, *Coming Up for Air*, imagines the "air" of the social environment as inescapable. Returning to a decidedly corporate London from a much-changed village of his youth,

Orwell's protagonist despairs of escaping the pervasive economic and political habits of industrialized England: "How can you, anyway? It's in the air you breathe."[51] In Beckett's own novels, "air" functions as a metaphor for the pervasive force of environments in general. The narrator of *The Unnamable* (1953), for example, repeatedly refers to the air as a force that engulfs his genuine individuality: "Air is to make you choke."[52] He goes so far as to wonder whether he is capable of speaking in a voice of his own, or simply reproduces what the environment gives him: "Perhaps it's not a voice at all, perhaps it's the air."[53]

In *Murphy*, air becomes a metaphor for the political environment that the protagonist would seek to escape. As the character Neary notes, the last time he saw Murphy, he was "saving up for a Drinker artificial respiration machine," or iron lung, "to get into when he was fed up breathing."[54] This wish reflects Murphy's desire to escape the "big world" and the effects of physical stimuli. Murphy aspires to be like Mr. Endon, a patient he later encounters at a sanatorium for the mentally ill, the Magdalen Mental Mercyseat. Murphy imagines that Endon has completely removed himself from the social realm and now experiences only pure interiority. Significantly, the staff at the asylum keep Endon under suicide watch for fear he may willfully cease to respire—by inducing "Apnœa."[55] To stop breathing is, Murphy imagines, to avoid the whole physical fiasco that encroaches upon his autonomy.

Critics have generally looked favorably on Murphy's efforts to escape this fiasco in his turn toward work at the Mercyseat. Richard Begam, for example, has argued that "reducing Murphy to a puppet is presumably something Beckett wants to avoid, and one way to read the novel is as an extended attempt on Beckett's part to preserve his hero from the mechanization that defines the other characters."[56] Beckett certainly invites such an interpretation in his consistent efforts to differentiate Murphy from the altogether worldly desires of his friends. As his narrator will say, "All the puppets in this book whinge sooner or later, except Murphy, who is not a puppet."[57] Critics have read Murphy's refusal to take on gainful employment as a revolt against capitalism's preference for wealth above all else. Lidan Lin, for example, has suggested that Murphy is nothing less than "a subversive idealist resolved to forswear the conventional Protestant ethic" whose calculated indolence makes him a "heroic defender of human dignity against a dehumanizing materialist culture."[58] However, such interpretations require a calculated disregard of Beckett's own efforts to undercut Murphy's self-image. After all, section six presents Murphy's mind *not* "as it really was" but *"what it felt and pictured itself to be.*"[59] In fact, Murphy is marked by what the narrator calls a "deplorable susceptibility."[60] This susceptibility to the physical world is signaled as early as the opening page of the novel, where Murphy is depicted sitting "naked in his rocking-chair of undressed teak."[61] The slippage between subjects and objects—here the naked body and the unvarnished furniture—suggests a more general susceptibility, one that belies Murphy's fantasy of personal autonomy. Just as Mr. Kelly is likened to the cuckoo clock, and by extension to the world of economic activity, so Murphy is affected by the physical world he inhabits, his physical desire for his girlfriend Celia serving as a primary motive of behavior throughout the novel.

Andrew Gaedtke has noted that Beckett drew on gestalt psychology, particularly the language of "figure" and "ground," to dramatize Murphy's inability to fully distinguish himself from his environment. The novel, he explains, "condenses a series of fundamental distinctions between self and world, mind and body, objects of desire and the absence of desire, and stages the consequences of their radical failure."[62] We can see notes of this influence in Beckett's nonfiction, as well, where he suggested that the slippage between subject and object was a new phenomenon, one particular to his epoch. In his 1934 essay, "Recent Irish Poetry," Beckett celebrates "the younger Irish poets" who "evince awareness of the new thing that has happened . . . namely the breakdown of the object."[63] "The thermolaters," he continues, "would no doubt like this amended to breakdown of the subject. It comes to the same thing—rupture of the lines of communication."[64] In part, we can understand Beckett's diagnosis of the "new thing that has happened" as part of a broader late modernist position vis-à-vis the representable world, which would manifest as a more radical foregrounding of the artistic medium than earlier artists had allowed.[65] But Beckett's insistence on the novelty of this "collapse" points in equal measure to the political realm of late modernism. As Tyrus Miller has noted, the political climate of late modernism overwhelmingly caused writers to accentuate "the fragility and permeability of the human body and its uneasy fit within spaces around it," resulting in a strong thematic emphasis on "corporeal automatism."[66] *Murphy*, with its overt coupling of corporeal susceptibility and ideological habits, calls attention to the "collapse" of subject and object. In his efforts to avoid the physical world, Murphy reflects an ascendant sense of automaticity, directly mirrored in the aesthetic priorities of late modernism—a world in which, as Elias suggested, the molding of affect had reached a new and more perfected efficiency.

Murphy repeatedly attempts to avoid the "physical fiasco" and the *quid pro quo* of his environment by constructing scenarios in which he can live "without initiative," thereby disavowing behaviors that might be the product of his conditioning. For example, early in the novel Murphy agrees to seek work only if Celia will supply him with a horoscope that might guide his way, "a corpus of incentives based on the only system outside of his own in which he felt the least confidence, that of the heavenly bodies."[67] This horoscope, based on the strict determinism of the solar system, conscripts Murphy to a set course of action, determining both when he can seek employment and what type of work he may accept.[68] The horoscope represents a positive idea of control; in contrast to the occult conditioning of the physical world, it serves as an arbitrary but perfectly knowable set of constraints. However, Beckett ironizes this "solution." The horoscope—itself a commercial product bought for sixpence in Berwick Market—is consistently aligned with social institutions of the state and the law.[69] Most importantly, Murphy does not simply consult his horoscope in order to divine what may come to pass or to inform him about the choices that lay before him; rather, he *obeys* the horoscope in absolute submission to its authority as if in submission to his social environment. In using the horoscope as an intermediary between himself and the physical world, Murphy is no different from his friends Neary and Miss Counihan, who use Pythagorean philosophy to determine their everyday actions. None of these characters are exempt from the economic habits promoted by their environment. The systems of thought to which they consciously subscribe displace questions of agency; the environment recedes from their conscious thoughts even as they remain susceptible to its influence.

This facet of Murphy's dilemma can be seen most directly in the institution of the asylum, the last stop in his efforts to avoid the physical fiasco. In the Mercyseat, Murphy hopes to practice "vicarious autology"—the study of self through the study of others.[70] The patients there appear uniquely free from the habits of society at large, in Murphy's estimation. By gaining proximity to them, he hopes to perfect his own techniques of introspection. However, to see the asylum as Murphy does—as a space apart from the political environment and material conditions of the "big world"—is to ignore the asylum's special role within the political currents of the period. Murphy's turn to the asylum is ironic for two reasons. First, mental asylums in England had, in the 1930s, become much more tightly entwined with the state. Legislative changes in the 1930s granted the state a far greater mandate than it ever had in matters of mental health, a fact that is foregrounded in Beckett's repeated efforts to situate the Mercyseat within institutions of legality, administration, jurisdiction, and certification.[71] Second, in seeking autonomy from bodily conditioning in the asylum, Murphy enters an institution explicitly geared toward molding affect through regimes of conditioning. In his studies of "total institutions" in the 1950s, Erving Goffman suggested that one of the signature attributes of the asylum is its capacity to breach the walls of personal autonomy. Outside the asylum, he writes, "the individual can hold objects of self-feeling—such as his body, his immediate actions, his thoughts, and some of his possessions—clear of contact with alien and contaminating things. But in total institutions these territories of the self are violated; the boundary that the individual places between his being and the environment is invaded and the embodiments of self profaned."[72] Asylums become in this context a symbol of political life in which the sovereignty of the individual body was increasingly felt to be violated.

In the work of Beckett's contemporaries, the asylum would come to symbolize the extremes of milieu control as a state enterprise. Just as the "air" of Beckett's novels implies an inescapable political climate that unconsciously conditions subjects, late modernist writers often drew on imagery of the asylum to metaphorize a loss of personal autonomy. In *Coming Up for Air*, Orwell's protagonist is disappointed to find that Binfield House, the ancestral "big house" near his childhood home, has been converted into a hospital of sorts: "Well—it's not what you'd call an ordinary hospital. More of a sanatorium. It's mental patients, reely. What they call a Mental Home."[73] Evelyn Waugh's *Brideshead Revisited* (1944) opens with a similar scene, his protagonist returning to the ancestral home of an old friend amid the carnage of the Second World War. Here the big house of British cultural legacy is superseded by "the municipal lunatic asylum," which houses "the undisputed heirs-at-law of a century of progress."[74] In both Waugh and Orwell, the ancestral house is juxtaposed with the mental asylum, the former denoting the space of individual autonomy and the latter its total collapse. As Andrew John Miller has argued, the big house signified for modernists "an autonomous space in which decisions can take shape . . . a sphere of sovereignty that provides a stay against the onslaughts of modernity."[75] By the period of late modernism, however, the big house was succeeded in the cultural imaginary by an institution for the management of mind—a symbol for the collapse of personal autonomy and the molding of affect through milieu control.

With the asylum, Beckett chose a setting dramatically ill suited to Murphy's efforts to avoid the reflexes engendered by the physical world. For all Murphy's attempts to avoid the *quid pro quo* of his social environment, the asylum is actually a space of rehabilitation, where patients' affects are molded for productive ends. The narrator notes that the Magdalen Mental Mercyseat is "a sanatorium, not a madhouse," meaning that it only admits those "whose prognoses were not hopeless."[76] The Mercyseat's aim is simple: to "translate the sufferer from his own pernicious little private dungheap to the glorious world of discrete particles"—the "outer reality" of capitalist productivity.[77] Yet Murphy imagines the asylum as a space of resistance in which patients enjoy contemplation of a self untainted by the physical world. The patients appear to Murphy "not as banished from a system of benefits but as escaped from a colossal fiasco."[78] This "fiasco" is the same "physical fiasco" that Murphy says he would like to escape.[79] Outside the asylum, he reflects, "one was prisoner of air"; in the asylum, however, he thinks he has found a "respirable vacuum."[80]

But Beckett goes out of his way to suggest just how untenable Murphy's position is. As he abets in the rehabilitation of patients toward the larger aims of society, Murphy is himself rehabilitated as an economic actor. This is evident not just in the fact that Murphy has a job and thus participates in the economy, but that his job requires submission to a routine of iterative procedures. While the patients receive specialized psychiatric interventions, Murphy's therapy consists simply of doing his job and living "without initiative."[81] His duties consist of mundane physical tasks: "He would be expected to make beds, carry trays, clean up regular messes, clean up casual messes, read thermometers, write charts, wash the bedridden, give medicine, hound down its effects, warm bedpans, cool fevers, boil gags, sterilize when in doubt, honour and obey the male sister, wait hand, foot and mouth on the doctor when he came, look pleasant."[82] These ordinary labors require Murphy's surrender to a physical regime of bodily habits, a regime that finds its fullest manifestation in the "rounds" that he does during his night shift. Like a clockwork figure, Murphy is required to visit each of the patients in turn during a sixty-minute interval. This inflexible system is the "higher law" of the Magdalen Mental Mercyseat.[83] Ostensibly, this system exists only to ensure that workers are complying with the rules of employment, but in Murphy's case such physical routines offer Beckett the opportunity to reflect on the inability of his protagonist to transcend the world of embodiment and the *quid pro quo* of his political context. It is not so much that such iterative behaviors establish a new habitus for Murphy, but that his failure to recognize his habits as a form of productive labor shows how profoundly he has already been conditioned by his milieu.

In *The Civilizing Process*, Elias had suggested that the asylum was one possible destination for those resistant to molding through social processes. Writing about the intensification of habitus in the twentieth century, he argues, "Today the circle of precepts and regulations is drawn so tightly about people, the censorship and pressure of social life forming their habits are so strong, that young people have only two alternatives: to submit to the pattern of behavior demanded by society, or to be excluded from life in 'decent society.' "[84] Impulses that do not correspond to socially sanctified affective structures, he writes, are generally deemed "pathological" or excised from "waking consciousness."[85] In *Murphy*, we see both of these outcomes. On the one hand, the behaviors that do not conform to the "outer reality" of capitalist productivity, particularly those of patients, are rehabilitated for productive economic ends. In the character of Murphy, on the other hand, we see the erasure of habitus from one's waking consciousness.[86] Murphy remains in every conceivable way a part of the physical and political universe he tries to escape, even though—and perhaps especially *because*—he does not recognize this to be the case.[87] He never thinks of his work at the Mercyseat as part of the physical fiasco, and this in itself is telling of the way in which habit functions within Beckett's novel. In this sense, *Murphy* is typical of late modernism's engagement with the politics of reflex. Here, just as theorists of habitus described, the environment has become so powerful and so deeply entrenched in political and social processes that attempts to overcome one's conditioning through conscious action is fated to fail. In this context, all behaviors are ultimately little more than the product of one's conditioning. For Beckett and his contemporaries, one could no more escape the higher degrees of automaticity than one could escape the air.

Beckett's Trilogy: From Politics to the Aesthetics of Reflex

When the idea of "human automatism" entered social theory in the early twentieth century, it was often tied to visions of a utopian future. Through a new, scientific approach to human behavior, social theorists envisioned the emergence of a society that would be more peaceful, more prosperous, and above all more efficient. But social programs grounded in the physical conditioning of bodies rarely delivered on these promises; instead of a brave new world, the early part of the century witnessed the molding of affect and the manufacture of consent that seemed only to exacerbate the problems endemic to mass society. It is no coincidence, then, that as modernism's own utopian aspirations began to wane after the 1930s, writers cathected their anxieties on the very same discourse that had promised so much. What began in the modernist era as an inquiry into the nature of the human body and its modes of economizing energy would become an anxiety about the metastatic creep of environment and the total degradation of individual autonomy. Beckett's first novel is quite different in this regard than the work of modernists like Lawrence, Lewis, or West; Murphy's desire to escape the political entailments of embodiment may reflect an anxiety that we see represented elsewhere in modernism, but it tells only the story of failure. The essential human condition of bodily susceptibility opens characters to corruption from a physical world they can never escape, a world that threatens to subvert their conscious desires, trespass upon their personal autonomy, and even invalidate a self distinct from the object world.

While concerns with reflex and embodiment remain throughout Beckett's oeuvre, around midcentury a fissure opened in his thinking. As we will see, the anxieties that animate *Murphy* shifted after the Second World War as Beckett moved away from fiction and toward drama. And yet the stress that he laid on automaticity in *Murphy* continued to dominate his novels; his trilogy *Molloy, Malone Dies*, and *The Unnamable* takes up *Murphy*'s interest in the entailments of human automatism, particularly how the unconscious and unspeakable nature of habitus might be registered formally. However, as these novels pushed the concerns of *Murphy* forward, they also threatened to obscure the *political* questions that had animated modernism's engagement with the science of reflex. When sociologists like Mauss and Elias elaborated their theories of habitus, the non-consciousness of automatic behaviors represented a kind of methodological problem since subjects cannot name or articulate the social meaning of iterative behaviors. As Bourdieu later explained, people are "subject to the censorship inherent in their habitus, a system of schemes of perception and thought which cannot give what it does give to be thought and perceived without *ipso facto* producing an unthinkable and an unnameable."[88] According to this understanding, the very familiarity and supposed naturalness of entrenched schemas of perception render us incapable of either recognizing our habits or of offering detached accounts of them. They are unnarratable.

Beckett dramatized this problem in the character of Murphy, but in his trilogy such concerns demanded a literary form in which the inenarrable might be registered. Characters in these three novels are often driven to the point of incapacitation by compulsions that manifest in empty automatisms. Their iterative behaviors—such as Molloy's endless quest to sort, organize, and suck stones—do not carry the political resonance of productive labor that we witness in *Murphy*. And yet each novel conspicuously emphasizes the bodily susceptibility of characters in relation to powerful institutions. Just as Murphy laments his "deplorable susceptibility," Molloy bemoans drowning "in the spray of phenomena."[89] "It is at the mercy of these sensations," he complains, "that I have to live and work."[90] In the almost entirely discursive world of *The Unnamable*, the narrator complains even more bitterly of his bodily susceptibility: "I'm tired of being matter, matter, pawed and pummeled endlessly in vain."[91] The physical bodies of characters are easily lost in the trilogy's formal experiments, including its progressive winnowing away of character, plot, and setting, but they are important to the overall agenda of the trilogy. Characters like Molloy, Malone, and the Unnamable are conscious of their bodies not just because they often fail, but because their bodies are conditioned by powerful forces. These forces, however, are by no means straightforwardly political since the characters themselves never succeed at fully understanding or narrating their relationships to these institutions. This dynamic is particularly pronounced in *The Unnamable*. There the eponymous narrator worries over the "delegates," whose "lectures" constitute the sum total of his understanding of himself and his world. Much of this novel concerns the Unnamable's sense that his speech and his very sense of self has been scripted by these shadowy delegates, including the primary delegate, "Mahood." Try as he may to explain his circumstances or his actions, the narrator cannot convince himself that his voice is genuinely his own. Mahood's voice, he says, "has often, always, mingled with mine, and sometimes drowned it completely . . . as though woven into mine, preventing me from saying who I was, what I was."[92] The eponymous narrator is "unnamable" precisely because he feels himself to be a product of conditioning, but he can neither fully articulate the nature of his conditioning nor perceive toward what ends it might be directed. In the other novels of the trilogy, characters report that powerful institutions control their habits, but more than this they cannot say. Molloy admits that his actions are the direct consequence of the "imperatives" of his "prompters," which produce his actions and retain their efficacy through "habit."[93] Moran's search for Molloy is likewise the product of mysterious forces, a synod called Obidil, whose directives Moran obeys "simply from force of habit."[94]

In each case, the political significance of these habits is occluded from the narrative even as the trilogy grapples with how to narrate the inenarrable. Already in *Molloy* the force of environment creates a narrative blockage that prevents characters from giving an account of themselves and the world that constitutes them. Moran is "plunged in it [the world] beyond recall," meaning that he can neither narrate the world nor tell his own story. Molloy notes that a "mist . . . rises in me every day and veils the world from me and veils me from myself."[95] As in *Malone Dies* and *The Unnamable*, the homology between environment and self creates a sense of subjective ineffability; by virtue of their inability to explain the environment they inhabit, both Molloy and Moran become incapable of accessing an individuality that is not conditioned by the physical world. As Molloy relates, "My sense of identity was wrapped in a namelessness often hard to penetrate."[96] This problem reaches its climax in *The Unnamable*, where Beckett's narrator laments that he can be certain of nothing about himself or his environment, and that even as he imagines himself a head enclosed in a jar, he cannot be certain that this is the case, or that Mahood didn't whisper "this suggestion in my ear, adding, I didn't say anything."[97] The Unnamable's situation is the most extreme of the entire trilogy, since he fears that every act, no matter how subversive in intent, may be nothing other than reflex demanded by his environment.

Given the central emphasis that the trilogy places on automaticity, it is tempting to see it as continuing the core project of *Murphy*. At the same time, however, the trilogy pursues issues of reflex in a way that undercuts the politics of Beckett's first novel; indeed, it is entirely possible that there is *no* political project at work in the trilogy at all. The characters of the trilogy may be automata, but their behaviors are often bafflingly opaque. What political or social function does Molloy's stone sucking serve? What is the political agenda of Molloy's "prompters" or of the Unnamable's "delegates"? Even as characters are seemingly dominated by their conditioning, readers are left in the dark about the political meanings of these narratives. In this respect, Beckett's trilogy stands at odds with the majority of modernism's engagement with the politics of reflex. We might even say that with the trilogy, reflex becomes part of an *aesthetic* agenda rather than a political one. In these novels, we see all the hallmarks of earlier modernisms, but the genuine political urgency that animated Wyndham Lewis, D. H. Lawrence, and others is absent. The far-reaching concern of earlier modernists with how the science of reflex was being integrated into modern political practice is here replaced by an almost academic interest in how bodily life impacts knowledge of ourselves and our world. In this regard, Beckett's novels might mark a deflation of modernism's utopian aspirations. In *A Singular Modernity*, Fredric Jameson has argued that modernism is characterized by "an apocalyptic dissatisfaction with subjectivity itself and the older forms of the self."[98] We have seen this feature of modernism abundantly already, where literary form seeks to create new kinds of readers, disposed to better forms of agency, individuality, or collectivity. However, with Beckett, the self appears as hopelessly tied to the physical world that conditions it. Rather than attempt to produce new readers better able to confront the unnamable conscription of thought and action, Beckett offers a literature of "pure interrogation."[99] This is a literature that takes the habitual body as its primary term but offers nothing like a political agenda. In this sense, the trilogy brings the concerns of literary modernism—concerns with agency, habit, individuality, rationality, and embodiment—to full fruition. But in so doing the trilogy also marks a dead end in modernism's attempts to offer an affirmative response to the politics of reflex.

What Remains?

Beckett never lost his interest in bodies, reflex, and power, concerns that often endow his work with more than a hint of pessimism. But he also never fully abandoned hope in the cause of human liberation. Even as his work registered the higher degrees of automaticity native to the twentieth century, it expressed an enduring faith that some part of the self always exists uncorrupted by the physical and political world, a subjective remainder that exceeds the onslaughts of one's conditioning. Traditionally read as an existentialist emphasis on "being," this remainder is the reservoir of human intransigence that animates Beckett's novels—a site of hope at the heart of his diverse literary project. But, with the promise of a self that exceeds the physical, Beckett is also brought to something of an impasse. Beckett's novels disclose how the act of perception works—how we know (or more often *don't* know) the systems in which we are enmeshed. In so doing, they invite us to reckon with the power of habit within our everyday experience but without promising any release from it. In the dramatic works he produced starting in the 1950s, however, Beckett presents a different understanding of habit. As Elias knew, the most important values of a culture are entrusted to bodily habits. In the embodied record, cultures can endure even as institutions fail. In Beckett's dramas, regularized and automatic behaviors—not our ability to overcome them—offer characters the ability to survive in the face of an indifferent cosmos.

This attitude can probably best be seen in the first dramatic work to follow his decades of novel writing, *Waiting for Godot* (1953). Set like the novels in a decontextualized space, *Godot* prioritizes the physical bodies of characters (now physically present on the stage) and the routines and habits to which they are subject. However, unlike his novels, Beckett's play takes a far more evenhanded approach to automaticity by suggesting that although habit is akin to death, it is also utterly necessary to human survival. In the closing scene of the play, Beckett registered this tension. As Estragon sleeps, Vladimir offers one of his longest monologues of the play:

> Was I sleeping, while the others suffered? Am I sleeping now? Tomorrow, when I wake, or think I do, what shall I say of today? That with Estragon my friend, at this place, until the fall of night, I waited for Godot? That Pozzo passed, with his carrier, and that he spoke to us? Probably. But in all that what truth will there be?
>
> (*Estragon, having struggled with his boots in vain, is dozing off again. Vladimir looks at him.*)
>
> He'll know nothing. He'll tell me about the blows he received and I'll give him a carrot. (*Pause.*) Astride of a grave and a difficult birth. Down in the hole, lingeringly, the grave digger puts on the forceps. We have time to grow old. The air is full of our cries.
>
> (*He listens.*)
>
> But habit is a great deadener.
>
> (*He looks again at Estragon.*)
>
> At me too someone is looking, of me too someone is saying, He is sleeping, he knows nothing, let him sleep on. (*Pause.*) I can't go on! (*Pause.*) What have I said?[100]

This scene occurs at the end of the play, just before the boy appears to tell them that Godot won't be coming today. Here Beckett revisits a key aspect of his discussion of habit in *Proust*. In his 1930 book, habit appears as a force that "paralyses our attention" and constitutes the very "suffering of being."[101] But, as in his later dramatic works, habit does retain some utility; while it is "a minister of dullness," it also acts as "an agent of security" since it allows us to synthesize sense data that would otherwise overwhelm the sensorium.[102] Such "security" may well be acquired at a high price in Beckett's novels since it entails a politics that obscures what Beckett called our "first nature."[103] We get more than a glimpse of this degradation in *Godot*. The two-act structure, for example, suggests the endless repetition of days, each populated by the ever-unchanging routines of the protagonists—Estragon's nightly beatings and dreams, Vladimir's difficult urination, the visitation of Lucky and Pozzo, and so forth. These repetitions have a tragic aspect, suggesting the hopelessness and brutality of Estragon's and Vladimir's existence. Their habits paralyze their attention and are the very substance of their suffering. In this sense, one can see the iterative aspects of *Godot* along the same lines as the trilogy's emphasis on physical tics and routines, such as Molloy's stone sucking. These automatic behaviors are bodily manifestations of a universe that lacks intrinsic meaning. Just as Molloy will go on, unsuccessfully seeking sustenance from his stones, Vladimir and Estragon will never succeed in meeting Godot or even in understanding what they might gain by so doing. Habit is the ballast that chains them to their execrable existence.

But here, as often in Beckett's dramatic works, habit has a purpose that is absent from his novels. For all the insistence that habit is a kind of sleep or even a death-in-life, in *Godot* it is Vladimir's and Estragon's routines and habits that are essential to their survival. This is true in a practical sense; the pair's inability to break the routine of their lives forces them to stay together and prevents them from killing themselves. But even more importantly, through their habits the pair is able to create meaning, however fleeting, in their otherwise meaningless struggles. The universe of *Godot* is famously replete with contingency; Estragon, Lucky, and the boy's brother are all beaten, as Lucky's monologue has it, "for reasons unknown."[104] Time does not pass according to any knowable order, and despite their best efforts to understand their world logically, Vladimir and Estragon are simply at the mercy of an unpredictable and indifferent cosmos. And yet, they attempt, time after time, to make sense of their situation. When Estragon inquires what they have asked of Godot, for example, he and Vladimir engage in one of their many attempts to construct a framework of understanding. They posit that they have asked Godot for a "kind of prayer" or a "vague supplication," and that Godot would need to consult his friends, family, agents, correspondents, books, and/or bank account, as is only natural.[105] These comedic actions constitute one of the many habitual behaviors that the characters employ in their attempts to create meaning in a universe that is intrinsically devoid of it. These routines also allow the characters to establish interpersonal roles that help them endure amid temporal contingency. Vladimir will always remain the dominant intellect who struggles with his boots, while Estragon will remain the dim-witted interlocutor who has no one to tell about his dreams. These roles are not just comedic fodder. Unlike in *The Childermass*, where Wyndham Lewis cast the social roles of Satters and Pullman as clichés demanded by their ideological environment, in *Godot*, interpersonal habits ground characters across time. Such roles may not satisfactorily replace their desire to locate an *intrinsic* meaning in their circumstances, but they do allow characters to establish meaning on an ad hoc basis. It may be the case that habit is "a great deadener," as Vladimir says, but for all the traumas that they endure, waiting day after day, physically susceptible to the beatings and starvation visited upon their bodies, Didi's and Gogo's habits are their salvation—indeed their only hope. For better or worse, it is what allows them to go somehow on.

This turn in Beckett's thinking was not unique to *Godot*. Critics have rightly noted that Beckett's dramatic works stress habitual behaviors in overwhelmingly positive terms. Ulrika Maude, for example, links Beckett's work to the nineteenth-century French philosopher Félix Ravaisson, whose *Of Habit* (1838) was influential on Bergson and anticipated later pragmatist efforts to understand the necessity of cognitive and behavioral economies. In Beckett's stage work, it is the positive economy of physical grace that Maude sees as predominating. She writes, the laws of habit that he articulated in *Proust* "only grow stronger in Beckett's late work."[106] In plays like *Come and Go* (1966), *but the clouds* (1977), *Quad* (1981), and *What Where* (1983), linguistic and behavioral repetitions are the foundation of character and the substance of dramatic action (such as it is). In these plays, Maude writes, "any sense of self resides precisely in and emerges out of these mechanical, near-automated actions."[107] In *Godot* we can see the first instance of what Maude has described. Vladimir's and Estragon's habits structure their relationship, endow their lives with the possibility of meaning, and allow them to define their beings, even if only temporarily. The automatisms of Beckett's novels are, in other words, recast as facts that must be embraced (or at the very least negotiated) rather than overcome. One can see here a through line from Rebecca West, in whose depiction of Yugoslavia habits carry embodied knowledge that allows cultures to endure through the upheavals and violence of mass modernity. Beckett's drama, born in no small part from the violence and contingency of the Second World War, similarly locates in habit the capacity to survive. Habitus may entail a condition of unknowing, but as Elias and Mauss both understood, it is also a kind of noncognitive knowledge—a mechanism that permits values and meaning to endure across the upheaval of peoples, clans, or nations.

This element of Beckett's drama offers a fascinating counterpoint to his novelistic work, both because it marks a divergence in his thinking about automaticity and because it tracks a larger intellectual and cultural shift. While at midcentury the body still performed a crucial function in the political sphere, its prominence in social theory was somewhat on the wane. To be sure, bodily susceptibility did retain currency in some intellectual corners, particularly existentialism and phenomenology, but it held a comparably minor place in social theory after midcentury. When the body mattered at all, it increasingly entailed a positive notion of economy akin to that promoted by pragmatist philosophers. In key intellectual movements of the second half of the century, we can glimpse this new intellectual terrain; in continental philosophy and cybernetics, thinkers established the preeminence of categories like "discourse" and "information" over concern with their mediation through physical bodies. Even Marshall McLuhan's pioneering studies of "media ecology," directly inspired by Wyndham Lewis, shifted away from the physiological models of behavior favored by early twentieth-century thinkers to see media as something experienced by minds.[108] Though the body never entirely dropped out of any of these fields, it occupied a far different status in the intellectual landscape than it had during the early years of the century. The fact that these fields turned away from the body might lead us to conclude that materialist theories of human automatism were ultimately disproven, and that modernist concerns with reflex were therefore somehow misplaced.

Yet to dismiss modernist concerns with the higher degrees of automaticity in this way would be to misunderstand just how important reflex has been to political life since the modernist era. Even if concern with automaticity in social theory diminished after midcentury, the study of behavior never left political or commercial practice. As we will see, our own era has birthed techniques and technologies that have dramatically enhanced the ability of powerful interests to lay prescribed tracks of thought and action. Today we find ourselves largely without a grammar for describing and confronting systems that would seek to "nudge" us toward predictable and profitable outcomes. The critical vocabulary of reflex invented by modernists is perhaps their most important legacy to contemporary readers; their efforts to assess and confront the politics of reflex offer us intellectual and artistic resources that are now urgently needed if we are to bring back into consciousness those things that have been made unnamable.

Afterword

Choice Architects, Where Is Your Vortex?

The Politics of Reflex in the Twenty-First Century

When we look at the political history of the early twentieth century, it is hard to write off the new freedoms afforded by mass modernity. The legal rights of enfranchisement, the weakening of class and familiar structures, and the novel possibilities for the expression of sexuality are all fundamental features of a historical period uniquely concerned with the individual and its liberation. But the modernist period was also subtended by a pervasive sense that these freedoms were either beset by countervailing forces or the mirage of a more primary kind of control. As we have seen throughout this book, modernist writers and their contemporaries regarded the twentieth century in these contradictory terms: at once a moment of radical newness in art and culture, and an era dominated by robots, hollow men, and automata incapable of escaping the grooves of thought and action patterned by society. Though it would be possible to discount these concerns as the anxious by-products of mass social upheaval, I have argued in this book that they arose from a genuine sensitivity to shifts in the political and scientific landscape. Employing understandings of reflex and bodily susceptibility central to nineteenth-century sciences, social theorists of the twentieth century understood politics not as a way of gaining affirmative assent, but rather a contest for the capacity to influence, herd, and condition the behavior of citizens. In 1899 Bernard Bosanquet argued that social life in the new century would be "increasingly constituted by adjustments which have become automatic," and that the state itself should be in the business of christening those reflex behaviors it deemed most conducive to "orderly action" and "co-operative existence."[1] By the early decades of the twentieth century, political and social theorists turned toward materialist science, recasting agency and autonomy as constructs of little value to the new era, ideas that challenged modernists to rethink the role of embodiment in public life, the virtues of individuality and collectivity, and the political agenda of their own work.

As I have shown throughout this book, discourses of automaticity saturated the political and social thinking of a host of intellectual and artistic fields of the early twentieth century. But what is perhaps surprising about this history is not the successes of reflex as a political idea but rather the relatively diminished role it has played since. The body may have lost much of the critical purchase it once had in intellectual fields that animate literary studies and critical theory, but automaticity remained crucial to fields intent on channeling the behavior of citizens in the commercial and political realm.

Today we are in a historical moment that sees political behaviors in terms remarkably similar to those of the modernist era. Just as modernists attempted to grapple with the political implications of reflex, governments and industry in the twenty-first century increasingly see behavioral modification as a more efficacious and profitable way of orchestrating social order than the laborious and unruly task of winning affirmative consent. Autonomy, agency, and the rationality of citizens—the primary terms at issue in the politics of reflex—have all once again come under the duress of social and political institutions that regard these values as stumbling blocks to greater efficiency. This is so much the case that we often fail to appreciate the role that automaticity plays in public life today. What in an earlier moment might have seemed like a conspiracy of mass manipulation is today openly discussed by political and commercial interests, who have employed the science of behavior to covertly shape our actions as consumers and citizens. Indeed, the politics of reflex may only be reaching its maturity now, in an era of networked information that allows more sophisticated and targeted ways of conditioning reflexes than were possible even a generation ago. In this context, modernism is arguably more important than ever before since it developed an artistic and intellectual vocabulary for understanding the perils and virtues of a world in which our reflexes are becoming the object of ever more intense competition. If we are to adequately confront the politics of reflex as they come to dominate our century, we will need to understand its genesis and the responses it has engendered.

Here I want to focus attention on a 2008 best-selling book entitled *Nudge: Improving Decisions about Health, Wealth, and Happiness*, written by behavioral economist Richard Thaler and legal scholar Cass Sunstein. Though this book has made a direct and palpable contribution to a contemporary politics of reflex, I propose here to think of *Nudge* and the strategies it elaborates as a popular distillation of what can be seen in a variety of contemporary disciplines. *Nudge* sharply articulates a political logic endemic to the twenty-first century, one that can be traced through major institutions of the neoliberal order, including statecraft, technology, advertising, and propaganda. These institutions are all inheritors of the techniques first imagined in the early twentieth century, but now undertaken at scales and at speeds that behaviorists, public relations experts, and propagandists could not have imagined. As we shall see, the political logic of Thaler and Sunstein's work demonstrates just how important the politics of reflex remain today and suggests the urgency with which its imperatives are pursued by governments, political campaigns, corporations, and the titans of Silicon Valley.

The premise of Thaler and Sunstein's book is simple and compelling; the authors argue that through the "emerging science of choice," policy makers have the opportunity to shape the conditions under which citizens make choices, and may thus "nudge" us to behave in specific ways.[2] Synthesizing decades of research on reflex and the science of decision making, they argue that policy makers should capitalize on the predictably irrational patterns of human behavior in order to orchestrate specific social outcomes. They call this practice the architecture of choice. "A choice architect," they explain, "has the responsibility for organizing the context in which people make decisions."[3] They give the example of someone who designs ballots in an election, noting that "there is no such thing as a 'neutral' design."[4] Placing candidates in any order at all will have a predictable effect on how people vote. These issues of design lurk everywhere—in bureaucracies, infrastructures, markets, and so forth. The layout of physical details and information can prove decisive in "nudging" people to make the decisions desired by the designers themselves. "Small and apparently insignificant details can have major impacts on people's behavior," they write. "'Everything matters.'"[5]

In making this argument, Thaler and Sunstein were distilling and applying the findings of decades of research in psychology, particularly those of the Israeli researchers Daniel Kahneman and Amos Tversky. Kahneman and Tversky's work demonstrated that, regardless of background or education, people tend to rely on biases, prejudices, and shortcuts (what they term "heuristics") in making judgments. This facet of human behavior arises out of a need to economize our attention and energy, as William James knew at the end of the nineteenth century. But Kahneman and Tversky demonstrated that these irrational judgments are regular and systematic—and that they suffuse our daily lives. We tend to be what Kahneman calls "fast thinkers," meaning that when we make decisions we mostly depend on "the entirely automatic mental activities of perception and memory," rather than the "slow thinking" of rationality.[6] For Thaler and Sunstein, this predictable irrationality is precisely why choice architecture works. While we like to imagine ourselves as guided by rationality, some of the most important elements of social life depend on this "Automatic System," which "does not involve what we usually associate with the word *thinking*."[7] Whereas we tend to see overt cognitive effort as the wellspring of our behaviors, for Thaler and Sunstein our reflexes play a far more significant role than we usually admit. "People tend to be somewhat mindless, passive decision makers," they write.[8] And this is the case even in arenas where reflex would seem inadequate, such as elections, where voters "rely primarily on their Automatic System."[9] Though this model of decision making undercuts certain fundamental ideas about agency and autonomy, it also offers an opportunity to choice architects, they explain. By exploiting the "automatic system," policy makers of all sorts have the opportunity to produce what, in another context, we would all "rationally" desire, but which our usual cognitive economies inhibit. We can be *nudged* into performing what the choice architect considers the objectively "rational" action.

It bears noting here that this model of decision making has become exceptionally influential in recent years. Kahneman and Tversky's work led to a paradigm shift in economics, including the development of behavioral economics, which has challenged the rational action theory that underwrote much of twentieth-century economics. And Thaler and Sunstein's work has spurred innovation by governments hoping to capitalize on the predictably irrational behavior of citizens. In May of 2008, one of David Cameron's advisors distributed copies of *Nudge* to high-ranking government officials in the United Kingdom. Only a few weeks after becoming prime minister in 2010, Cameron would commission the Behavioral Insights Team—more commonly known as the "Nudge Unit"—to use the behavioral sciences to create policies and procedures that account for (and take advantage of) inherent human reflexes. According to Tamsin Rutter of the *Guardian*, this approach to human behavior now "permeates almost every area of government" in England, making its services in high demand at the United Nations, the World Bank, and among the world's governments. "Nudge teams" have since been established in Australia, Singapore, Germany, and elsewhere. And in the United States, the book won Cass Sunstein a position in the Obama White House as Administrator of Information and Regulatory Affairs.[10]

These governmental efforts to put the lessons of the behavioral sciences into practice on their own citizens have, to some extent, been limited to the work of policy matters—public sanitation, pensions, smoking cessation, taxes, charitable giving, and so forth.[11] In one sense, then, we can laud nudging as a practical way of approaching political life; nudging proceeds from the recognition that automatic behaviors are inherent to human nature, and that our social and political systems must account for them. As Sunstein and Thaler note, people are susceptible to influence; there is "no way of avoiding nudging in some direction."[12] In this sense, nudging shares fundamental features with modernist-era thinking about automaticity. Just as Pavlov and Watson showed the power of environmental cues to conscript behavior, choice architects take as a given our lack of autonomy as subjects. In this respect, nudging is a direct descendant of the philosophical pragmatism of James and Dewey, which treated automatic behaviors as inevitable and necessary to social life. We depend, James wrote, on "the effortless custody of automatism" in order to successfully inhabit the world.[13] The goal, pragmatists argued, is not to eliminate our reflexes, which would be impossible, but to cultivate those that are most useful to us. Who could possibly argue that nudges that make us healthier, or more prosperous, or that help us conserve the planet, are nefarious? Shouldn't all our systems help us make the most "rational" choices? Shouldn't we embrace systems that nudge us to behave for the social good?[14]

Compelling as this account is, nudging raises a number of ethical problems when we consider the significance of choice architecture as a political project. Thaler and Sunstein cast their work as libertarian, meaning that it only *encourages* specific choices. The very term "nudge" suggests something subtle—a push or a prod, but not a shove. "Nudges are not mandates," they write.[15] And yet it is hard to imagine how an individual could choose to reject a nudge since the most effective nudges are invariably those that are not explicitly marked as such. In fact, it is probable that people respond best when they are not even conscious of being nudged at all.[16] Though Thaler and Sunstein are careful to assert the democratic virtues of such a technique, nudging treats citizens as the unwitting subjects of manipulation. As Mark White explains in *The Manipulation of Choice* (2013), nudging "is very much coercive, and in some ways more insidious than 'old school' paternalistic policies. . . . Rather than telling people what to do or not to do, or influencing them explicitly," nudges "have an intrinsically covert nature, designed as they are to piggyback on people's cognitive biases and dysfunctions to 'guide' them into the 'right' choices."[17] In this sense, choice architects are more akin to Bernays's "invisible government" than Thaler and Sunstein might imagine. Like the PR expert, the choice architect endeavors to manipulate the habits of the populace from behind a veil, all the while costuming itself in the rhetoric of democracy.

This characterization of choice architecture would surely strike Thaler and Sunstein as a contentious misreading. Choice architects work to guide behavior in ways that serve the social good; they aren't an elite class of puppet masters. However, their definition of "choice" suggests something else about the appeal of their model of human behavior. Often for Thaler and Sunstein, choice is a singular action; it occurs in discrete moments. For example, they discuss highways designed to nudge drivers in ways that lead to fewer accidents, delivering stimuli to drivers at just the right moment to change dangerous behaviors. Such nudges are limited in time and space. But what about other choices, the ones that we make over time and in consultation with a much wider array of input, such as our choice of candidate, affiliation with a particular party, or even our brand loyalties? As Kahneman and Tversky knew, these kinds of choices are shaped by the social environments we inhabit and the ways we are conditioned to associate ideas, not by the specific context in which our decisions are formally recorded. And, in fact, this is where Thaler and Sunstein's term gains its most significant political purchase. Choice architecture recognizes the importance of these larger contexts as the premier space of political activity, codifying a political logic of the twenty-first century that can be found in a wide variety of enterprises that seek to conscript the "automatic system" and nudge us to behave in specific ways.

Digital technologies increasingly provide political tacticians new ways of understanding the reflex behaviors of citizens and the kinds of stimuli likely to influence their behaviors. Though most people today have a rudimentary idea of how their engagement with platforms like Google and Facebook entails the production of personalized, proprietary data for private firms, rarely do we appreciate just how vast such stores of data are and their use in shaping our behaviors, attitudes, or personalities. Data, it must be noted, is not limited to the information we voluntarily supply to platforms, such as information on purchasing habits or our professional and personal networks. Data is an expansive term, incorporating what can be scraped and intuited from all manner of collateral actions we take online. In her analysis of these technologies, Shoshana Zuboff calls this data "behavioral surplus," and suggests that such data is actively collected in an effort to anticipate and proactively shape the behavior of users. She explains that through our engagement with a growing array of digital technologies—including smart homes, wearable devices, mobile phones, payment terminals, and the internet itself—we produce information that is "fed into advanced manufacturing processes known as 'machine intelligence,' and fabricated into *prediction products* that anticipate what you will do now, soon, and later."[18] Companies like Google can thus "infer and deduce the thoughts, feelings, intentions, and interests of individuals and groups with an automated architecture that operates as a one-way mirror irrespective of a person's awareness, knowledge, and consent, thus enabling privileged secret access to behavioral data."[19] Most of these processes occur well out of view of the public, meaning that we are rarely aware of how our "choices" are being nudged. This information is easily purchased from data brokers, and social media in particular has made its use a shockingly easy procedure, allowing political campaigns and advertisers to reach and monitor populations precisely suited to their aims.

Perhaps the most widely discussed form that this use of information has taken in recent years is "microtargeting," a method for creating content that is personalized to individuals based on known patterns of behavior. Microtargeting is a relatively new term, but it grows out of a long-standing effort in public relations to "segment" the population into groups that are susceptible to different kinds of stimuli. The idea was pioneered in the 1930s by Paul Cherington, director of research at the J. Walter Thompson agency, where John B. Watson himself had been a vice president. Today, researchers have developed empirical methods that allow a far greater degree of accuracy about how to segment populations, sorting us into microgroups whose responses to stimuli can be predictably mapped and analyzed using sophisticated computation models of human behavior. The interface of computation and psychology is a booming area of commercial and academic inquiry. At the University of Cambridge's Psychometrics Center, for example, researcher Michal Kosinski was able to create a model in 2012 that could accurately predict human behavior based on a relatively small number of Facebook "likes."[20] According to *Das Magazine*, "with a mere ten 'likes' as input his model could appraise a person's character better than an average coworker. With seventy, it could 'know' a subject better than a friend; with 150 likes, better than their parents. With 300 likes, Kosinski's machine could predict a subject's behavior better than their partner. With even more likes it could exceed what a person thinks they know about themselves."[21]

Though by no means the only domain of such techniques, elections represent the clearest site of this logic in the contemporary world. By aggregating tens of thousands of data points about what you watch or purchase online, the causes to which you donate, your religious affiliation, your geography, your sexual orientation, your voting record, your daily rhythms, and so on, what emerges is a profile that moves well beyond old-fashioned demography. Political campaigns are today able to automate the creation of individualized profiles that predict our behaviors with startling accuracy. Moreover, data of this sort allows campaigns to test political messages on specific populations, receive prompt feedback on their efficacy, and instantaneously refine those messages that prove effective. In so doing, they are often able to predict with a high degree of precision whether a given person is likely to donate to a campaign, attend a rally, and vote for a given candidate—or what might discourage someone from voting at all.

The Obama presidential campaign of 2012 did not invent these techniques, but it successfully deployed them in ways that were groundbreaking at the time. With its much-touted use of data, the campaign endeavored to predict the behavior of specific individuals within the electorate and to subtly shape those behaviors. Through an unprecedentedly experimental agenda, the campaign was able not only to identify citizens by name, but to assess exactly how to motivate them. As Sasha Issenberg wrote in the *MIT Technology Review*, the 2012 presidential cycle saw the empirical approach to electoral behavior reach maturity, delivering "an almost perfect cycle of microtargeting models."[22] These models allowed the campaign to reach out to voters knowing precisely how likely they were to vote for the Democratic ticket, and what kind of messaging would galvanize less-motivated voters. For example, mailers would be specifically targeted to their recipients, using language and imagery most likely to appeal to biases and known dispositions, on a topic known to be a sensitive part of their political makeup. Door-to-door volunteers were sent to the homes of citizens most susceptible to the campaign's platform, armed with scripts targeted to that voter's own predispositions. The campaign aggressively worked to test these messages, but also to make well-informed hypotheses about how a given topic in the mass media was likely to sway the electorate. This behavioral approach constituted a kind of sea change in the landscape of campaigning; whereas previous campaigns relied on small samples of the electorate to devise their messaging strategies, the Obama campaign created the first "narrowcast" campaign, targeting individuals and empirically assessing the susceptibility of voters to rhetoric, imagery, style, and the like. And just as Thaler and Sunstein asserted that "everything matters" in the architecture of choice, Obama data experts were able to show the predictable and often strange ways that voters react to even non-political information. For example, no matter what state a voter hailed from, they were much more likely to support Obama if they were contacted by a volunteer claiming to be in California. What emerged from these efforts was an understanding of the extent to which voters were capable of being nudged to support a particular candidate. Issenberg explains, "The campaign didn't just know who you were; it knew exactly how it could turn you into the type of person it wanted you to be."[23]

The presidential campaign of Donald Trump in 2016 learned these same lessons, though in a slightly different media context. His campaign assembled a database of 220 million American citizens, with between four thousand and five thousand data points about each one. This data ultimately dictated every aspect of the campaign—"travel, fundraising, advertising, rally locations—even the topics of speeches," according to Steven Bertoni.[24] Employing computational models of human behavior developed by researchers at the University of Cambridge (and made famous by Cambridge Analytica), the Trump campaign focused intensively on monitoring engagement of both supporters and detractors. At the height of the campaign, the Trump camp was deploying more than one hundred thousand unique digital advertisements to targeted voters *every single day*; those that proved to have the most enthusiastic engagement were then scaled up and deployed to more users. And just as the Obama campaign adopted the perspective that "everything matters," Trump's data specialists saw that very minor changes to his website—including wording, imagery, and even the color of the "donate" button—could yield more engagement and larger donations.[25] But perhaps most strikingly of all, microtargeting allowed experts to strategically map which portions of the electorate were most easily discouraged from voting— what a senior campaign official described as a voter suppression operation.[26] By accurately mapping those portions of the electorate that were most dissuadable, and then strategically targeting them with content proven to be effective, the Trump campaign was able to lower turnout among groups at the center of Hillary Clinton's coalition, including idealistic white liberals, young women, and African Americans.

From one perspective, the use of data by political campaigns is really nothing more than a highly efficient way of delivering information. In some respects, this is what we should all want—targeted information to tell us how candidates or campaigns are catering to our individual interests. However, this assessment misunderstands the way we respond to information specifically targeted to our cognitive biases. Already by the 1920s, critics were well aware that stereotypes have the capacity to override our rational agency. In *Public Opinion* (1922) Walter Lippmann explained, "The subtlest and most pervasive of all influences are those which create and maintain the repertory of stereotypes. We are told about the world before we see it. We imagine most things before we experience them. And those preconceptions, unless education has made us acutely aware, govern deeply the whole process of perception."[27] As Lippmann understood, our need for economical forms of perception, like stereotypes, is extremely powerful, and makes us susceptible to influences that gratify our biases. This is what makes new forms of electoral data so powerful; because they map and exploit our preconceptions about the world, we are often incapable of responding except in the ways desired by choice architects. Our understanding of political candidates and complex issues will be channeled into grooves of perception, and information that challenges our cognitive economies will be discarded. This makes us uniquely sensitive to manipulation. As a recent academic study on microtargeting explained, immersion in the informational milieu of social media means that an "audience can be coached and influenced into choices that can be in contradiction to their actual beliefs."[28] These techniques not only cater to us; they prime us to respond to the world automatically and to obey choice architects we have never seen and whose desires may run contrary to our own.

    The technological revolution in this area has been swift, and it will likely constitute a major challenge to our conceptions of human autonomy, choice, and democracy in the near future. In her book *The Age of Surveillance Capitalism* (2019), Shoshana Zuboff examines this technological revolution in detail, arguing that it successfully marries a neoliberal economic ideology to the experimental agenda of behaviorism—"the prediction and control of behavior" that Watson imagined in 1913. For Zuboff, these technologies represent a new stage of economic history that she calls "surveillance capitalism," in which our behaviors are encoded as data and used to actively intervene across a wide range of social domains. Google is a good example. In its earliest days, the company sought to understand user behaviors to predict how they would use the platform, and thus improve the user experience. Eventually, however, the company discovered that their "predictions" could be even more robust if they actively intervened in user behaviors. Zuboff writes: "Eventually, surveillance capitalists discovered that the most-predictive behavioral data come from intervening in the state of play in order to nudge, coax, tune, and herd behavior toward profitable outcomes. Competitive pressures produced this shift, in which automated machine processes not only *know* our behavior but also *shape* our behavior at scale. With this reorientation from knowledge to power, it is no longer enough to automate information flows *about us*; the goal now is to *automate us*."[29] This stage of capitalism represents a challenge to fundamental conceptions of autonomy and choice that define our sense of being human. Whereas industrial capitalism threatened the natural world, this new capitalist paradigm threatens to corrupt human nature, specifically what Zuboff calls "the right to the future tense." She explains that in this economic era, "the mental agency and self-possession of the right to the future tense are gradually submerged beneath a new kind of automaticity: a lived experience of stimulus-response-reinforcement aggregated as the comings and goings of mere organisms."[30] This is nothing less than a realization of the behaviorist social agenda, but it is quite a different animal than totalitarianism, in her view, since it does not prioritize group conformity, but rather celebrates differences of all kinds as long as they can be encoded as behavioral data. We need not be the conformist automata of mass society or the Pavlovian dogs of totalitarian regimes. "All of that is superseded," she writes, "by a digital order that thrives within things and bodies, transforming volition into reinforcement and action into conditioned response."[31]

Consider, for example, the problem of social networks, an industry whose business model is built almost entirely on the collection and sale of data about its billions of global users. Trafficking in data has become a lucrative business for governments and the private sector alike, with highly targeted information about "individual attributes, activities, and preferences" leading to new kinds of "behavioral advertising," as legal scholar Julie E. Cohen writes. Such data can go hand in glove with old fashioned regimes of control, including real-time surveillance or the censoring of news.[32] But more frequently, it leads to an experience of information that is so highly targeted that we can no longer effectively maintain anything like autonomy before it. Such targeting impinges upon our liberty, but in a way that is different than liberal theory typically allows. Cohen explains, "The prevailing conception of liberty as the absence of constraint is not particularly useful for describing the ways in which different digital architectures affect the experiences

Choice Architects, Where Is Your Vortex?

of network users."[33] She notes that "regulation by code is different and more troubling than regulation by physical architecture because of the immediate and fine-grained control that code permits."[34] Data about users of social media—which includes most readers of this book—has become a valuable commodity not just because it gives politicians and advertisers a window into *how* a population thinks. Data provides access to constructing *what* a population thinks. This reality seems to have reached an inflection point only recently, with a number of former social media experts publicly sounding the alarm. Tristan Harris, a former design ethicist at Google, recently explained this phenomenon in a TED Talk entitled "How a Handful of Tech Companies Control Billions of Minds Every Day."[35] Harris explains that the sheer ubiquity of smartphones means that our choices as consumers and citizens are more and more dependent on only a handful of people who have the power to say, "That group over there, I want to schedule these thoughts into their minds."[36] Those with the most money can "target a lie directly to the people who are most susceptible. And because this is profitable [for social media companies], it's only going to get worse."[37] Chamath Palihapitiya, a former vice president of user growth at Facebook, was even more blunt in remarks at Stanford, where he deployed the language of brainwashing: we are being "programmed" by social media without realizing it.[38]

If this sounds like a paranoid analysis of digital media, it bears repeating that this industry works in concert with some of the most sophisticated science of human behavior. The Persuasive Technology Lab at Stanford, for example, pairs behavioral psychology with technology, specifically asking how technology can be used to alter what we think and what we do. This kind of research has led designers to develop techniques for increasing our engagement with online platforms. By using the schedules of reinforcement pioneered by B. F. Skinner (and perfected by casinos), social media companies attempt to maximize the time we spend on their sites, making us more valuable to advertisers. Richard Freed explains, "Users never know when they will get the next 'like' or game reward, and it's delivered at the perfect time to foster maximal stimulation and keep them on the site. Banks of computers employ AI to 'learn' which of a countless number of persuasive design elements will keep users hooked. A persuasion profile of a particular user's unique vulnerabilities is developed in real time and exploited to keep users on the site and make them return again and again for longer periods of time."[39] This all creates a kind of feedback loop: the more time we spend using networked media, the better companies are able to engage us, and the more susceptible we are to being "nudged." And as computer technology improves, these companies will only get better at predicting and channeling our behaviors to fit the desires of their clients. Already in 2006, B. J. Fogg, a behavioral psychologist who founded the Persuasive Technology Lab, explained before the Federal Trade Commission, "We can now create machines that can change what people think and what people do and the machines can do that autonomously."[40] More recently, Facebook has begun offering advertisers something even more tantalizing; as a confidential presentation by the company explained, their AI can "predict future behavior," allowing clients the ability to target people according to decisions they have yet to make.[41] And though the company has downplayed its ability to influence elections, Facebook has in the past touted its success in doing just that.[42]

One of the challenges to placing this recent history in conversation with the politics of reflex of the modernist era is that we tend to think of information as something that interacts with the circuitry of minds rather than involving the entire sensorium of the body. As we have seen, modernists and their intellectual contemporaries did not make this distinction. In Watson's work, for example, language is always treated as a kind of physical stimulus; no matter whether it is heard or read, language is registered by the body before ever involving cognitive processes. It was only later, with midcentury cybernetics, that information was reduced to mathematical data and dematerialized, as Katherine Hayles noted in *How We Became Posthuman* (1999). Returning to a modernist emphasis on material embodiment has offered some recent critics purchase on the political consequences of networked life. In *Configuring the Networked Self* (2012), Cohen argues that reckoning with the role of embodiment in information networks powerfully challenges the "first-order commitments" of liberal political theory—commitments "to individual autonomy, to an abstract and disembodied vision of the self, and to the possibility of rational value-neutrality."[43] Modernists understood that the role of material stimuli in producing automatic behaviors challenged the traditional emphasis laid upon rationality, autonomy, and agency within democracies. As we have seen throughout this book, modernists responded to these issues in a variety of ways, but always with a sense that mass modernity presented a new problem in its tendency to demand ever more automatic forms of behavior. And the problems that modernists first encountered over a hundred years ago have only grown more acute. The media we daily imbibe in the twenty-first century has a deep and measurable effect on what we consciously and unconsciously believe, and on the choices we make—or rather on the "choices" we are nudged into making.

There is some argument to be made that choice architecture of this sort is not nearly as powerful as critics fear. After all, digital media companies and data scientists both have a product to sell, meaning that we should not mistake their rhetoric for what they are actually capable of achieving. Furthermore, the tools used by advertisers and political campaigns are, in some cases, available to all of us. Anyone can use them to promote any agenda or to sell a product—this book, for example. In this sense, the contemporary informational milieu can seem somewhat more democratic than the centralized mass media of a hundred years ago. But this perspective misses both the fact that these recent technologies require a degree of knowledge and sophistication not typically available to ordinary citizens and the fact that the open and anonymous nature of these platforms poses serious challenges to democratic politics.[44]

The recent history of Russian intervention into foreign elections presents a striking instance of this challenge, one that nicely encapsulates the enduring value of reflex within contemporary political life. In many respects, Russian efforts to nudge voters in the British Brexit campaign and the American presidential election of 2016 resemble quite closely what the Obama campaign pioneered in 2012. As Clint Watts and Andrew Weisburd write in *Politico*, Russian operatives merely "borrowed from this playbook and targeted audiences vulnerable to their influence across the West."[45] This activity has taken many forms, but in most cases it has entailed a surgical effort to sway voters by targeting regions and contests in which a small swing can produce consequential outcomes. In both the United States and Britain, "it took a nudge of just a few percentage points in each case to achieve victory."[46] And as in recent US presidential elections, choice architects have taken advantage of the rapid scalability of digital media. By trying out an array of messages, imagery, and themes through automated bots, and doubling down on those that gain traction online, these influence campaigns have strategically identified biases most likely to nudge the electorate. In this sense, these campaigns attempt to undermine the agency of citizens, pitting their "automatic systems" against their capacity for rational action. As Molly McKew explains, part of the agenda of these campaigns is not just to elect candidates that will work on behalf of Russian interests; they are intended to erode faith in democratic institutions and "convince [citizens] to make decisions against [their] own best interests."[47] She notes that these influence campaigns—which involve the industrial production of fake news, hacking, and saturating social media to ensure that specific kinds of information trend—are not propaganda in the traditional sense, since they do not work to convince citizens of an "alternative truth" but instead erode "our basic ability to distinguish truth at all."[48] In a truth-free world, what alternative do citizens have but to rely on their cognitive biases and reflexes?

The road from conditioned reflex to Twitter bots, AI, and "fake news" may seem like a long one. But Russia's recent efforts to nudge Western electorates fall squarely within the tradition established in the early twentieth century. Though information warfare is classed under various terms of art in Russian statecraft, one term specifically pegs such efforts to the longer history of automaticity: "reflexive control." Timothy Thomas, writing in the *Journal of Slavic Military Studies*, defines the term as "a means of conveying to a partner or an opponent specially prepared information to incline him to voluntarily make the predetermined decision desired by the initiator of the action."[49] Here, as so often within the politics of reflex, "decision" really must be understood to mean something that is not agential—a choice that is not chosen but rather "predetermined." Reflexive control is an object of considerable study in Russia, one that emerged in the 1960s but built on early twentieth-century military tactics.[50] It brings together scientists and national security experts under the auspices of the government and academic institutions; an academic journal called *Reflexive Processes and Control* was founded in 2001, and the Russian Academy of Science's Institute of Psychology runs a laboratory "that studies elements and applications of the reflex in considerable detail."[51] By understanding the reflexes of an adversary population, political planners can anticipate and thus exploit the automaticity of citizens and military officials, provoking behaviors from adversaries that go against their own best interests. But if Russia's application of these ideas represents a prominent manifestation of the politics of reflex, I do not want to suggest that its efforts in this arena are in any way unique. For one, it is probable that geopolitical forces besides Russia have used similar techniques under the same behavioral paradigm. But even more importantly, Russia's influence campaign is cognate with what already happens in sophisticated corporate or public relations campaigns. According to Philip N. Howard of Oxford's Computational Propaganda Project, Russia's uses of digital media in recent years depends on "regular ad technology that regular advertisers use."[52] Brad Parscale, the head of Trump's 2016 digital efforts (and campaign manager in his 2020 reelection bid), made the same point, explaining that there is nothing wholly novel in such techniques: "I always wonder why people in politics act like this stuff is so mystical. It's the same shit we use in commercial, just has fancier names."[53] The scale and stakes of these political campaigns may differ from what we usually associate with PR, but the underlying techniques are no different. Both proceed from an understanding that choice is a ghostly thing; even when we seem to be making rational decisions, we are often in thrall to our automatic systems and the stealth stimuli of everyday life.

In considering these recent political techniques—whether they be in domestic politics, ordinary corporate campaigns, or geopolitics—perhaps the most surprising thing is not just how pervasive the logic of nudging has become; it is the seeming poverty of our critical vocabulary for naming and addressing it. We hear so much about attempts by bad geopolitical actors to "hack" elections, or the use of "data" by political campaigns. But we almost never hear anything about why these techniques are so effective. Hobbled by a cybernetic notion of information, we talk little about the ability of political actors to map our reflexes, subvert our rational agency, and channel our behaviors toward ends that may go against our own best interests. And if we do talk about these things at all, it is with no small degree of resignation before the immense digital architectures and the corporate powers behind them. Such an economic and political order makes us not just automata, but, as Zuboff writes, "exiles from our own behavior," and "shorn of meaningful alternatives for withdrawal, resistance, or protection."[54] What good does encrypting your data really do when the entire information economy depends on harvesting behavioral surplus? What solace is there in individually logging off when elections and political dispositions are increasingly shaped by the choice architecture or our collective digital life?

The literary and intellectual history of the twentieth century may not offer solutions for reforming or escaping the choice architecture of our own historical moment, but it should at least offer us a starting point for building a critical vocabulary for it. In 1919, just after Wyndham Lewis returned from the front, he published what would be the last document of the abortive Vorticist movement—a manifesto on design entitled *The Caliph's Design: Architects, Where Is Your Vortex?* In the urban landscape, Lewis detected a lack of conscious design, one that made citizens susceptible to the worst and more puerile elements of modernity. Looking at the modern cityscape, he asks, "Exactly what set of circumstances, what lassitude or energy of mind working through millions of channels and multitudes of people, make

... every stitch and scrap of art-work that indefatigably spreads its blight all over a modern city, invading every nook, befouling the loveliest necks, waists, ears, and bosoms; defiling even the doormat . . . ?"[55] Since the common man, susceptible to this environment, "in a sense, *is* the houses, the railings, the bunting or absence of bunting," the result can only be boredom, commercialism, and a society desiccated of all vitality.[56] A modernist or Vorticist architecture, on the other hand, would account for bodily susceptibility but without strictly determining the thoughts and actions of city dwellers. He entreats architects, "It is life at which you must aim. Life, full life, is lived through the fancy, the senses, consciousness. These things must be stimulated and not depressed."[57] His exhortation stands as a reminder of the power that today's choice architects wield. As Lewis and his modernist contemporaries knew, human automaticity is a fundamental feature of political life, one that modern science made accessible for the first time. If we want to make the politics of reflex legible, and if we want to build political strategies or intellectual tools that restore our access to the future tense, we would do well to study the varied ways in which the early twentieth century met and failed to meet the challenges that the politics of reflex entailed.

In philosophical vitalism, for example, we encounter one of the earliest and most searching critiques of materialist science and the political world it enabled. The work of modernists like Lawrence and Hulme testifies to the cultural need for such a critique and the literary forms it might take. Like Bergson, both writers understood dogmatic ways of thinking as endemic to mass modernity, and both worked to imagine literary modes that might help revitalize the body politic through appeals to spontaneity, affect, and the unpremeditated. As we have seen, however, vitalism's rejoinder to the politics of reflex was not a wholly successful project; the opposition between thought and spontaneity stressed by writers like Lawrence endured beyond the 1920s to become central to certain iterations of fascism. Nevertheless, the effort to catalyze agency in readers without appealing to cognitive clichés represents a fully realized, modernist attempt to confront the problems of an increasingly automatic society, one that may appeal to contemporary readers. In our era, in which our thought processes have become objects of urgent competition, we might view the vitalist perspective as one among many possible ways of challenging systems that reduce citizens to little more than algorithmically regular machines—indeed, a reminder of the power of political movements that answer the predictive logic of choice architecture with the language of spontaneity.

In public relations, we encountered perhaps the clearest through line from the early twentieth-century politics of reflex to our own. If Edward Bernays and his early colleagues were never anything close to constituting a true "invisible government," his vision of an automatic society is, arguably, more than ever at hand. Today, the sprawling industries of advertising, consulting, and PR are very much what Bernays imagined, equipped with a set of techniques for assessing the habits and opinions of the masses and orchestrating them for paying clients. Understanding the global history of PR and the assumptions about human behavior that underwrote it is essential to any critical assessment of twenty-first century life. But just as important is understanding how to respond to the considerable power wielded over bodies by choice architects. Lewis's analysis of secret manipulators stands as a searching and rigorous attempt to find a politics adequate to a world in which we are ruled by "invisible" governors. In his fiction and nonfiction, we see an attempt to create literary forms that mirror a society structured to turn citizens into the passive, reflexive receptacles of rulers' desires. If his tendency to see a secret agency in any zeitgeist led Lewis to a self-defeating fanaticism, it nevertheless represents a prescient understanding of how new industries would attempt to nudge political behaviors. His work of the 1920s and early 1930s constitutes one of the most serious and prolonged attempts to stake conceptual and aesthetic ground in which agency and individuality might stand a chance against the new, organized efforts to condition the reflexes of citizens.

Though behaviorism's innovations came to occupy a more central place in the contemporary politics of reflex than Pavlov's, conditioned reflex remains important to political practice as well as a powerful source of anxiety. As we have seen, Pavlov became a staple of thinking about agency and totalitarianism, particularly after the Second World War, when "brainwashing" and "Pavlovian" entered the political lexicon to denote the erasure of independent rationality, typically through state-sponsored means. Returning to the legacy of conditioned reflex now helpfully defamiliarizes a rhetoric that remains common to our contemporary moment. Who has not thought of those with whom they disagree as sheep devoid of will, bots mindlessly reiterating the party line, or puppets brainwashed by propaganda? This rhetoric powerfully plays upon enduring anxieties about autonomy, agency, and individuality even as it honors their centrality to the modern sense of self. At the same time, in the work of a modernist writer like Rebecca West, we can see how our lack of autonomy might take on positive political values. West understood that while human automaticity might feature prominently in authoritarian regimes, it could also act as a bulwark against the centrifugal forces of modernity, entrenching citizens in common ways of doing and thinking that bind them to a time and place. In her writing, the nation works best when it organically conditions citizens, creating reflex communities in which values are shared, and in which we are made resilient against the forces of modernity. Her engagement with the politics of reflex represents a more pliable one than we saw in writers like Lewis and Lawrence since it recuperates some automatic behaviors for productive ends. While her affirmation of the nation as a privileged space may appear suspect amid the new nationalist movements of recent years, her literary politics suggest that our susceptibility to material stimuli might help us work collectively even if doing so challenges the privileged place we tend to allot to personal agency.

In West's vision of reflex communities, we can see a more evenhanded approach to automaticity than is apparent in the work of earlier modernists. In this sense, her political project shares much with philosophical pragmatism. But pragmatism, as we have seen, elided the relationship between automaticity and social structures and tended to see habits and reflexes as transhistorical phenomena. It would fall to sociologists of habitus like Norbert Elias and Marcel Mauss to uncover the history of reflex in modern social structures. These sociologists saw the twentieth century as a moment unique in its tendency to promote automatic behaviors, yet they shared with pragmatists a sense that reflex could promote liberty just as easily as it could promote control. In the work of Beckett, we encountered a cognate approach to automaticity. Informed by reflex psychology, Beckett's first novel, *Murphy*, treats automatic behaviors with disdain; here, characters are anxious to avoid the behaviors promoted by their environments but prove incapable of distinguishing reflex behaviors from volitional ones. In his later work, however, Beckett modulated toward seeing habit with the same ambivalence as sociologists; in plays like *Waiting for Godot*, habit is a political problem, but it also is the ground for shared understanding and stability in an existential void. From both sociologists and Beckett emerges a sense that some of the most consequential elements of social life are also those that are hardest to consciously apprehend, and yet neither treats them with the outright anxiety of writers like Lawrence and Lewis. If Beckett was wary of the higher degrees of automaticity that Elias described, he nevertheless saw that collective habits have their virtues—that, indeed, they might just be the physiological bedrock that allows us to survive and even flourish.

Differences between the era of the wireless and the world of digital networks are significant; our world allows for the covert orchestration of behaviors to an extent that modernists could not have imagined. Modernist literature and early twentieth-century discourses of automaticity may not offer complete "solutions" to the politics of reflex, then, but they do offer a roadmap to some of the critical orientations and ideological pitfalls that the politics of reflex have generated. I think of this as something like an anatomy of the various ways in which critics and artists have attempted to turn the facts of human physiology to their own benefit. Across the distance between then and now, modernists communicate a powerful set of strategies for understanding, managing, and taking control of the political and social world we call "modernity." Our ability to do and think in concert with and beyond collectives, particularly international collectives, may, after all, be the difference between a planetary future in which our modernity is fully realized or one in which it is prematurely short-circuited. If these early twentieth-century interventions into the politics of reflex do not offer us anything like the "vortex" that Lewis exhorted architects to create, they nevertheless compel us to identify the role of reflex in the choice architecture of our century. If nothing else, this history will help us to understand the continuities and discontinuities between then and now, and it will empower us to build systems in which access to our behaviors is not a commodity to be bought and sold. Moreover, they may help us build the foundations for a new politics in which reflex becomes a source of vitality rather than part of an ever-tightening gyre of control, nudging us always to submit.

Notes

Introduction. Prescribed Tracks

1. Lewis, *Blasting and Bombardiering*, 207.
2. Lewis, *Time and Western Man*, xi.
3. Bosanquet, "Social Automatism," 167.
4. Lewis, *The Art of Being Ruled*, 45.
5. Shklovsky, "Art as Technique," 721.
6. Schoenbach, *Pragmatic Modernism*, 19.
7. Woolf, "On Being Ill," 101.
8. Woolf, "Modern Fiction," 213.
9. In *Mrs. Dalloway*, for example, Woolf casts physical habits as constitutive of selves. Peter Walsh ruminates, "Rigid, the skeleton of habit alone upholds the human frame" (48). In her later work, such as *Three Guineas* (1939), consciousness stands not as an autonomous object requiring new literary modes but something entangled in the materiality of the body. Woolf feared that without a literature capable of diagnosing the effects of environmental conditioning, the world would become dominated by cognitive clichés, behavioral formulas, and political forms like fascism.
10. In *Modernism, Technology, and the Body*, Tim Armstrong argued that by the late nineteenth century, the body had come to be regarded as deficient for the conditions of modernity, leading to a host of new, compensatory technologies (including prostheses, hormone therapies, electricity, etc.). "Modernity," he argues, "brings both a fragmentation and augmentation of the body in relation to technology; it offers the body as lack, at the same time as it offers technological compensation" (3). The cultural history of these technologies provides the context for Armstrong's analysis of modernist literature, which he understands as exhibiting a desire to render the body "part of modernity by techniques which may be biological, mechanical, or behavioural" (6). Armstrong's study laid the groundwork for some later scholars who emphasized the interface between bodies and technology,

including Danius, who stresses technologies like photography, the cinema, and the wireless in the emergence of modernist aesthetics. A more extreme analysis of the body has emerged in some recent criticism, where the body becomes not the secondary term in a dualist framework but the only term. In *Cold Modernism: Literature, Fashion, Art*, Jessica Burstein offers an account of a "cold" modernism in which "the mind plays no role; or, in a slightly less extreme form, in which the mind is so physicalized as to have no more or less purchase than pure anatomy" (13). In her analysis, the self—long understood as the ultimate fetish of the most varied modes of modernist literature—is supplanted by a body that is so wholly a *thing* as to preclude selfhood. Joshua Gang has made a similar argument in relation to Samuel Beckett, arguing that his first novel, *Murphy*, "replaces the representation of covert mental states with the representation of overt behaviors and actions" ("Mindless Modernism," 120). As Gang sees it, this mode of modernism emphasizes the knowable behaviors of the body over a much vaunted (but unobservable) consciousness.

11. Mao, *Fateful Beauty*, 35.

12. Coole and Frost, "Introducing the New Materialisms," 7.

13. Althusser's essay, "Ideology and Ideological State Apparatus (Notes towards an Investigation)," delineates a theory of political behavior in which the material conditioning of bodies plays a key role. According to Diana Coole and Samantha Frost, this theory stresses the material basis of political identity and the value of embodied, habitual practice within the acquisition of ideology. Althusser, they explain,

> draws attention to the way 'ideas' are inscribed in actions whose repetitive, ritualized performances are borne by concrete individuals who are thereby practically constituted as compliant or agentic subjects. While such performances are institutionalized in rituals and ceremonies, they also become sedimented at a corporeal level, where they are repeated as habits or taken for granted know-how. . . . It is indeed this nonreflexive habituality and the way it imbues objects with familiarity that makes artifacts, commodities, and practices seem so natural that they are not questioned. It is in this sense that ideology or power operate most effectively when embedded in the material practical horizons and institutions of everyday life (34).

14. The work of a writer like Stein often emphasizes the physical and mental repetitions of daily life, including textual habits, but invites readers to recognize the aesthetic pleasures that such habits entail. While this aesthetic approach to habit does carry a politics, such concerns tend to be of a secondary concern. This was part of the reason that Wyndham Lewis treated Stein with such disdain. In *The Childermass* (1928), he mocked her syntactic repetition by having his characters "stein" (50), and in *Time and Western Man* he diagnosed her style as reflecting the

"mental habits" of "mass-democracy" (60). The conjunction between modernism and pragmatism has already been well documented by scholars. In *Pragmatic Modernism*, Schoenbach notes that Stein, James, and Proust all had direct biographical connection to William James and his philosophy of habit. For a treatment of Stein, cf. Will, *Gertrude Stein*; Wald, *Constituting Americans*; and Olson, *Modernism and the Ordinary*. On Henry James, see Phipps, *Henry James*. On Proust, see Sachs, *Marcel Proust*.

15. Lawrence, *Kangaroo*, 294.
16. Lewis, *Time and Western Man*, xi.
17. Woolf, *Three Guineas*.
18. Elias, *The Civilizing Process*, 447.
19. In *Human Programming*, Scott Selisker examines the circulation of the human automaton figure within the American twentieth century. He makes a strong case for the role of Watson and Pavlov in establishing tropes of "non-American" behaviors in the postwar period. Among other things, he shows just how pervasive the language of conditioning has become in attempts to understand behaviors that do not square with putatively American ideals of agency and autonomy, including the behaviors of cult members and terrorists.

Chapter 1. Automatic Man

1. Rebecca West declared America "a Robot civilisation" upon visiting New York for the first time in November of 1923 (*Selected Letters*, 64). Wyndham Lewis used the word "robot" throughout the 1920s. In *The Art of Being Ruled*, he argued that democratic man is a "Robot" "manipulated by the press" (106). In the preface to *Time and Western Man*, he stated his desire to create a class of readers that would be "a new race of philosophers, *instead* of 'hurried men,' speed-cranks, simpletons, or robots" (xvi). For more on Čapek's contribution to modernism's imagination of automata, see Segel, *Pinocchio's Progeny*.
2. Descartes, *Discourse*, 31.
3. Descartes, *Discourse*, 72.
4. The history of the word "automaton" is quite telling of the fate of the concept in the long history of modernity. Originally meaning "a being or thing having the power of spontaneous motion or self-movement" ("automaton," definition 2, *Oxford English Dictionary*), "automaton" derives from *autos*, meaning "self," and *matos* meaning "thinking, animated." However, already by the late eighteenth century, "automaton" took on the definition we know it by today: "a person who acts, or appears to act, in an inhuman, mechanical, or unemotional way" ("automaton," definition 3c, *Oxford English Dictionary*). This change in definition reflects a shift in ideas of agency itself. In the introduction to his 1879 book, *A Textbook of Physiology* (1879), Michael Foster explained, "Automatic . . . has recently acquired a meaning

almost exactly opposite to that which it originally bore, and an automatic action is now by many understood to mean nothing more than an action produced by some machinery or other. In this work I use it in the older sense, as denoting an action of a body, the causes of which appear to lie in the body itself." These changes in the meaning of "automatic" and "automaton" reflect shifting notions about the locus of agency. What begins with Descartes as a "self-acting" phenomenon, in which the body and brain work in a single unified way to produce an effect, becomes by the nineteenth century a matter of bodies behaving independent of the mind.

5. Boakes, *From Darwin to Behaviourism*, 87.

6. Offray de la Mettrie was specifically impressed by the automata designed by Jacques de Vaucanson. Vaucanson's most famous android was *The Digesting Duck* (1739), an automaton that, when fed a grain of rice, would void seemingly genuine excrement. Equally famous were the "Jaquet-Droz automata" (ca. 1770), which, among other things, could write Descartes's phrase "Cogito ergo sum." For more on Vaucanson's duck, see Cottom, *Cannibals and Philosophers*. For a cultural history of the android and its influence on later industrialists and roboticists, see Wood, *Edison's Eve*.

7. Leys, *From Sympathy to Reflex*, 2.

8. Boakes, *From Darwin to Behaviourism*, 109.

9. The contrast between speculative and experimental methods is probably most clearly seen in German physiology, which in the early nineteenth century was profoundly indebted to idealism. This "romantic physiology" constituted something of an interlude between periods of intense experimental inquiry about reflex, with the work of Müller, Ludwig, du Bois-Reymond, and Helmholtz (the so-called Berlin School of physiology) constituting some of the most important experimental work on reflex in the mid-nineteenth century. See chapters five and six of Rothschuh's *History of Physiology*.

10. *The American Journal of Psychology*, 71.

11. Canguilhem, "The Living and Its Milieu," 11.

12. Zola, *Thérèse Raquin*, 4.

13. Zola, *Thérèse Raquin*, 54.

14. American naturalists were less interested in categories of heredity and environment than French naturalists, but the scientific question of determinism played a central role in their fiction. In line with thinkers like John Stuart Mill and T. H. Huxley, American naturalists did not foreclose the possibility that humans were both determined by circumstance and endowed with free will. For an analysis of the influence of this "compatibilist" perspective on American naturalism, see Roberts, "Determinism." For an analysis of naturalism's limited appeal to British writers of the same period, see Joyce, *Modernism and Naturalism*.

15. Eliot, *Middlemarch*, 117. Numerous critics have called attention to Eliot's

emphasis on the body, including Marc Redfield, Sally Shuttleworth, and Douglas Mao. John R. Reed offers a contrasting analysis in *Victorian Will*. In Reed's estimation, Victorian concerns with agency cohere not around scientific challenges to liberal models of the self but religious ones. He writes, "The most characteristic attitude toward will during Victorian years was supernatural, that is, human will was seen primarily in relation not merely to the necessary choices of daily life but to the great design of providence" (11). In Eliot's novel, he sees "a Godwinian world where free will was a useful but illusory notion" (309).

16. Prince, *The Nature of Mind*, 105.
17. Brain, "The Pulse of Modernism," 402.
18. Brain, "The Pulse of Modernism," 402.
19. Pavlov, *Lectures on Conditioned Reflexes*, 41.
20. Pavlov, *Lectures on Conditioned Reflexes*, 41, 95.
21. Watson, *Behaviorism*, 16.
22. R. M. Yerkes quoted in Gaedtke, *Modernism and the Machinery of Madness*, 52.
23. Watson, "Psychology as the Behaviorist Views It," 158.
24. Schmitt, *The Crisis of Parliamentary Democracy*, 29.
25. Lewis, *Time and Western Man*, 155.
26. Gramsci, *Selections from the Prison Notebooks*, 242.
27. Gramsci, *Selections from the Prison Notebooks*, 265.
28. Gramsci, *Selections from the Prison Notebooks*, 242.
29. Gramsci, *Selections from the Prison Notebooks*, 301.
30. Gramsci, *Selections from the Prison Notebooks*, 302.
31. Kang, *Sublime Dreams of Living Machines*, 232.
32. Taylor, *Principles of Scientific Management*, 125.
33. In *Labor and Monopoly Capital* Harry Braverman outlines the history of scientific management, noting that at its heart Taylorism sought to manage workers' conscious and unconscious reactions to new labor relations themselves. Braverman writes that management's role in production "was to render conscious and systematic, the formerly unconscious tendency of capitalist production. It was to ensure that as craft declined, the worker would sink to the level of general and undifferentiated labor power, adaptable to a large range of simple tasks, while as science grew, it would be concentrated in the hands of management" (120–121).
34. Gramsci, *Selections from the Prison Notebooks*, 303.
35. Gramsci, *Selections from the Prison Notebooks*, 244.
36. Bernays, *Propaganda*, 37.
37. Bernays, *Propaganda*, 55.
38. In order to manufacture public support for the overthrow of the Arbenz government, Bernays played on American prejudices, successfully planting a variety of news stories that fabricated ties between the Guatemalan government and com-

munism at large. For more on Bernays's influence in twentieth-century mass culture, including his famous "Torches of Freedom" campaign for Lucky Strikes, see Ewen, *Captains of Consciousness*, and Curtis, *The Century of the Self*.

39. Nineteenth-century British physiologists like Thomas Laycock and William Carpenter defined human cognition in terms of bodily reflexes that operate without the need for our conscious mind. For Laycock, a physiologist at the University of Edinburgh, the materialist paradigm of psychology suggested that ideation and volition were in large part informed by a process of mental incorporation that did not require the conscious participation of the individual subject. As Adam Crabtree summarizes, for Laycock, "a person's brain could convert stimuli from outside or inside into meaningful actions without the person being aware of what was occurring" (Crabtree, "'Automatism,'" 52). According to this view, ideation and volition were almost entirely understandable in terms of a physiological unconscious, grounded in the automatism of the body and mind. Several decades later, Carpenter would formalize this theory, arguing that our behaviors are influenced by the bodily registration of stimuli that we do not readily apprehend, a process he dubbed "unconscious cerebration." For more on the intellectual history of the unconscious, see Whyte, *The Unconscious before Freud*, which documents its role in Enlightenment and Romantic-era thought, as well as nineteenth-century philosophy and science.

40. Mao, *Fateful Beauty*, 46.
41. Simmel, "Metropolis and Mental Life," 325.
42. Beckett, *Proust*, 516.
43. Beckett, *Proust*, 515.
44. Beckett, *Proust*, 516.
45. Schoenbach, *Pragmatic Modernism*, 19.
46. In some contexts, habit was taken as a near synonym to those ostensibly anti-modern terms "tradition" and "custom." One of the origins of such ideas lies not in the context of mass society, but rather in Victorian attitudes toward aesthetics. In the conclusion to *The Renaissance*, Walter Pater wrote, "To burn always with this hard, gemlike flame, to maintain this ecstasy, is success in life" (189). This gemlike flame of being is explicitly linked for Pater to habit: "In a sense it might even be said that our failure is to form habits: for, after all, habit is relative to a stereotyped world, and meantime it is only the roughness of the eye that makes any two persons, things, situations, seem alike" (189). Though Pater's analysis of habit lacks the vitriol of Beckett's, it captures an attitude that critics would later take to be representative of modernism's orientation toward habit.

47. Shklovsky, "Art as Technique," 721.
48. Spencer, "Philosophy of Style," 508.
49. Spencer, "Philosophy of Style," 508.
50. Shklovsky, "Art as Technique," 725.

51. Unlike the New Critics, Russian Formalists eschewed extraneous discourses in their efforts to create a methodology particular to literary criticism. However, this did not prevent them from drawing on Spencer explicitly in "Art as Technique" and the *Opojaz* manifesto. In fact, Formalism broadly arrogated to itself the language of the sciences. As Victor Erlich pointed out in his landmark study, *Russian Formalism*, the defining feature of Formalism was its effort to make literary experience itself the predominant critical concept. This ambition constituted a form of literary critical empiricism—what Formalist Boris Eikhenbaum called "the scientific study of fact" (quoted in Erlich, *Russian Formalism*, 72). Indeed, contemporary writers criticized Formalism for thinking of aesthetic perception in terms of "psychophysiological conditions" (quoted in Erlich, *Russian Formalism*, 178).

52. Erlich notes that while the terms of Russian Formalism were coded as "apolitical," the movement itself was highly political (79). This fact comes through in the concept of "defamiliarization" itself, which, as Fredric Jameson notes in *The Prison-House of Language*, is political by nature. Defamiliarization, he writes, is a way of "restoring conscious experience, of breaking through deadening and mechanical habits of conduct . . . and allowing us to be reborn to the world in its existential freshness and horror" (Jameson, 51). The Formalists' *Ostranenie* was to find a near analogue in Bertolt Brecht's *Verfremdungseffekt*, or estrangement-effect, which likewise employs Formalist idiom of habit but restored the politics that Formalists deliberately subtracted. Jameson writes, "The effect of habituation is to make us believe in the eternity of the present, to strengthen us in the feeling that the things and events among which we live are somehow 'nature,' which is to say permanent. The purpose of the Brechtian estrangement-effect is . . . to make you aware that the objects and institutions you thought to be natural were really only historical" (Jameson, 58).

53. Leavis and Thompson, *Culture and Environment*, 102.

54. Leavis, "Mass Civilisation and Minority Culture," 21.

55. Fromm, *Escape from Freedom*, 166.

56. Elias, *The Civilizing Process*, 447.

57. Leavis and Thompson, *Culture and Environment*, 32.

58. Gang, "Behaviorism and the Beginnings," 3.

59. Richards, *Practical Criticism*, 314. In *Science and Poetry*, Richards was slightly more circumspect about the role of environments in conditioning behaviors, though here the political urgency remains paramount. He notes that the behavior of citizens in general has multiple sources, including heredity, and that environment in particular "may be given too much importance, *though not in politics*" (35, emphasis added).

60. Richards, *Practical Criticism*, 339-340.

61. Richards, *Practical Criticism*, 254.

62. Leavis's work is marked by some ambivalence about reflex and habit. On

one hand, he worried about the economies of perception inculcated by mass society and regarded behaviorism as its gospel. Watson's work appears throughout his writings as the foundation of the "increasingly scientific direction" of advertising, one that led to the standardization of taste and values (Leavis, "Mass Civilisation and Minority Culture," 23). On the other hand, his anxiety about automatic behaviors was undercut by a faith in an organic, national community rooted in shared habits. In "Mass Civilisation and Minority Culture" he writes of tradition in much the same terms that T. S. Eliot employed in "Tradition and the Individual Talent"—as the "inherited codes of habit and valuation" of a community (17). In this sense, the politics of reflex proved quite alluring to Leavis; while he railed against behaviorism, he also identified it as a "scheme for using a civilised technique on behalf of a civilising education" (40), one that reflects the traits of those "highly intelligent and disinterested persons of scientific training who devote themselves to the future of humanity" (41).

63. Schoenbach, "'Peaceful and Exciting,'" 241.
64. James, *The Principles of Psychology*, 122.
65. James, *The Principles of Psychology*, 125.
66. Schoenbach, *Pragmatic Modernism*, 32.
67. Stein consistently employed habit as a formal device in her writing. Like many of her modernist peers, Stein was directly engaged with the science of reflex. As a student in Hugo Münsterberg's laboratory at Harvard in the 1890s, she wrote two research papers on "motor automatism" and was influenced by James's own work. But rather than foreground the political perils of automatism, Stein transmuted it into an object of aesthetic enjoyment in her literary work. Liesl Olson has made this point in *Modernism and the Ordinary*. She explains that Stein's iterative language often indexes not the mindless automatisms associated with mass society, but a kind of familiarity that endows value. She writes, "For Stein, repetition is the source of daily pleasure, not a staging of past trauma and certainly not a mark of failure" (97). In this sense, Stein reversed the Formalist distrust of the automatisms of perception in order to elaborate what Schoenbach calls a "pragmatic modernism."

Chapter 2. Vibrant Bodies, Automatic Minds

1. Münsterberg, *The Eternal Life*, 5-6.
2. Schwartz, "Bergson and the Politics," 278.
3. I know of only two critics who specifically read Lawrence's work in the tradition of philosophical vitalism. Richard Lehan has argued that modernism is inseparable from the discourse of Bergsonian vitalism and that Lawrence's work bears the direct traces of Bergson's influence. Sociologist Sean Watson has also cogently linked *The Rainbow* to a Bergsonian notion of affect, arguing that the "real

plot" of the novel "does not trace life in the domain of language, but in the domain of pure sensation" (Watson, "Bodily Entanglement," 27).

4. T. S. Eliot quoted in Levenson, *A Genealogy of Modernism*, 38; Lewis, *Blasting and Bombardiering*, 107; Bergson, *Introduction to Metaphysics*; Sorel, *Reflections on Violence*.

5. Bergson, *Creative Evolution*, 39.

6. Bergson, *Laughter*, 89.

7. Bergson, *Creative Evolution*, 27.

8. In *Laughter*, Bergson gives a shorthand definition of "life": "A continual change of aspect, the irreversibility of the order of phenomena, the perfect individuality of a perfectly self-contained series: such, then, are the outward characteristics—whether real or apparent is of little moment—which distinguish the living from the merely mechanical" (89). This definition stresses life as a temporal process. From any given moment in an organism's development (frozen, as if in space), we can neither deduce origins nor predict outcomes. The order of phenomena are "irreversible," meaning that organic life necessarily leads to outcomes that cannot be foreseen. It is the spatializing intellect of the sciences which would turn a process into "the merely mechanical" (89).

9. Bergson, *Creative Evolution*, 27-28.

10. Bergson, *Creative Evolution*, 31.

11. Gillies, *Henri Bergson and British Modernism*, 10.

12. Bergson, *Creative Evolution*, 30; Bergson quoted in Burwick and Douglass, *The Crisis in Modernism*, 3.

13. Bergson, *Laughter*, 32.

14. Hulme, "Notes on Bergson," 141.

15. Hulme, "Notes on Bergson," 142.

16. Bergson, *Laughter*, 18.

17. T. S. Eliot quoted in Burwick and Douglass, *The Crisis in Modernism*, 3.

18. Moses, *Out of Character*, 19.

19. In "Bergson, Vitalism, and Modernist Literature," Paul Douglass names the "inner circle of Bergson's primary influence," including Jacques Maritain, Nikos Kazantzakis, T. E. Hulme, John Middleton Murry, Julien Benda, Wyndham Lewis, and T. S. Eliot, even though some of these (Lewis, Eliot, and Hulme) later disavowed vitalism (112). Even granted these disavowals, Bergson's influence remained; a writer like Eliot, for example, "emulated Bergsonian principles and influenced many other writers" even after jettisoning vitalism (114). In the further reaches of Bergson influence, Douglass places Faulkner, Wallace Stevens, Henry Miller, Pound, Willa Cather, Frost, Stein, Woolf, and Nabokov, noting that all of them "probably read philosophical works by Bergson" and that "all certainly read works *inflected* by the philosopher's ideas" (114). Douglass also includes Picasso, Brancusi, and Matisse among his list of artists influenced by Bergson. For an

in-depth analysis of vitalism's role in twentieth-century painting, see Antliff, *Inventing Bergson*.

20. Douglass links Bergson's ideas to modernist concerns with "memory, flux, the *élan vital*, real duration, the parastic self, and the trope of metalepsis" ("Bergson, Vitalism, and Modernist Literature," 114). See also Gillies, *Henri Bergson and British Modernism*, which offers an analysis of Bergson's appeal to specific writers, including Eliot, Woolf, Joyce, Richardson, and Conrad.

21. Bergson, *Time and Free Will*, 237.

22. Bergson, *Time and Free Will*, 237.

23. Douglass, "Bergson, Vitalism, and Modernist Literature," 109.

24. Schwartz, "Bergson and the Politics," 288-289.

25. Bergson, *Introduction to Metaphysics*, 69.

26. Bergson, *Introduction to Metaphysics*, 17.

27. Bergson, *Creative Evolution*, 127.

28. Hulme's fascination with vitalism lasted only until 1913, particularly as he came to share Pierre Lasserre's critique of Bergson as an essentially Romantic thinker. But Hulme's "classicist" orientation was itself short lived. See the introduction to chapter three. As I note in that chapter, he staked out a new, anti-humanist position in a series of short essays published in 1915 and 1916. These essays cast vitalism as a ridiculous effort to replace religion with biology. Levenson's *A Genealogy of Modernism* offers a robust timeline of Hulme's philosophical turn away from Bergson and toward the political values of abstraction.

29. Looking back at this moment from the vantage of 1915, F. S. Flint declared Hulme, not Pound, the founder of Imagism. For a brief history of the Poets' Club and its role in Hulme's intellectual biography, see McGuinness, "Introduction."

30. Hulme, "Bergson's Theory of Art," 192.

31. McGuinness, "Introduction," xxxi.

32. Jesse Matz has noted that for Hulme, emphasis often falls on the artist, rather than the art, as the source of defamiliarizing. In *Time and Free Will* Bergson posited that artists are inherently better suited than the masses to break through habits of perception because they are in closer touch with a "deep" self. As Matz explains, Bergson held that "the authentic human mind exists beneath the surface of conventional thought and perception," positing two selves. "Facing practical existence, the mind increases its chances of real survival by developing an orientation toward action in space. In doing so, it develops a 'second self' that 'obscures the first,' causing 'our living and concrete self' to become 'covered over by an outer crust of clear-cut psychic states'" (Matz, "T. E. Hulme," 341). For Hulme, the artist is the type of the first self—one unencumbered by fixed habits: "He or she perpetually creates new language to convey immediate experience" (Matz, "T. E. Hulme," 345).

33. Hulme, "Bergson's Theory of Art," 199-200.

34. Hulme, "A Lecture on Modern Poetry," 55. In "Notes on Language and Style"

Hulme is especially insistent on the problems of prose as opposed to poetry. The central conceit of these notes is that most language, particularly in prose, is like a "counter." In algebra, "real things are replaced by symbols," like "counters" on a chessboard. In algebra, we know these symbols are just symbols, but in language we almost always mistake the representation for the thing itself: "We replace meaning (i.e. *vision*) by words. These words fall into well-known patterns, i.e. into certain well-known phrases which we accept without thinking of their meaning" ("Notes on Language and Style," 24). In poetry, on the other hand, the "cheapness" of prose is dispensed with through analogy (25). It must confront "the extraordinary difficulty of the living material" (26) and approach the "flux and real basic condition of life" (27). Some of Hulme's antipathy for prose may have come from Bergson himself. In *Introduction to Metaphysics*, one of his first examples of intelligence comes from a consideration of how characters are presented in novels (Hulme, *Introduction to Metaphysics*, 3). Novels thus appear in Bergson as a literary form well suited to conceptual language and spatialization.

35. Lawrence, *Letters*, vol. 1, 544.
36. Wallace, *D. H. Lawrence, Science, and the Posthuman*, 18.
37. Lawrence, *Fantasia of the Unconscious*, 54.
38. Lawrence, *The Rainbow*, 370.
39. Lawrence, *The Rainbow*, 372.
40. Lawrence, *Women in Love*, 198. It is a curious irony that Rupert Birkin, often taken to be Lawrence's mouthpiece in *Women in Love*, works as an inspector of schools. Such a social role squares well with his own social posturing early in the novel; as the narrator describes him, "he affected to be quite ordinary . . . taking the tone of his surroundings" (16). Birkin, in other words, affects to perfectly mirror the environment that conditions him even as he desires to give vent to a corporeal vitality unbounded by this environment.
41. Lawrence, *The Rainbow* 422, 426.
42. Lawrence, *Kangaroo*, 294.
43. Lawrence, *Letters*, vol. 2, 183.
44. "Allotropic," *Oxford English Dictionary*.
45. Lawrence, *Letters*, vol. 2, 182-183.
46. Though Lawrence could have read translations of *Interpretation of Dreams* (1899) and *The Psychopathology of Everyday Life* (1901), as Spitzer argues, there is "no evidence" that he engaged any of Freud's work or his English-language commentators (Spitzer, "On Not Reading Freud," 91). She notes that Lawrence grew particularly hostile toward psychoanalysis "after psychoanalytic theory chose *Sons and Lovers* as its case study *par excellence*," a novel which seemed to offer a clear manifestation of the Oedipal complex (93). See "On Not Reading Freud."
47. Lawrence, *Fantasia*, 93.
48. Lawrence, *Psychoanalysis and the Unconscious*, 6.

49. Lawrence, *Fantasia*, 106.

50. Lawrence, "Democracy," 79. Lawrence's fiction and nonfiction are replete with attention to the intellect and "idealism" as a form of automaticity. He variously defines "idealism" as "the fall into automatism, mechanism, and nullity" (*Fantasia*, 162) and "the little, fixed machine-principle which works the human psyche automatically" (*Psychoanalysis and the Unconscious*, 12).

51. Lawrence, *Kangaroo*, 295.

52. Lawrence, *Kangaroo*, 295.

53. Lawrence, *Psychoanalysis and the Unconscious*, 9.

54. Lawrence, "Education of the People," 129.

55. Lawrence, *Psychoanalysis and the Unconscious*, 47.

56. Lawrence, *Fantasia*, 162.

57. Lawrence, *Studies in Classic American Literature*, 26.

58. Lawrence's insistence on an "IT" that authors our deeds strongly resembles Freud's notion of "das Es," a concept controversially translated by James Strachey as "the id." Superficially similar to the id, Lawrence's "IT" disaggregates the unconscious and the pleasure principle that form the basis of Freud's concept.

59. Bergson himself was cognizant of the fact that his theory of embodied, intuitive action threatened to foreclose the philosophical possibility of agency. In *Creative Evolution* he suggests that the entirety of his thought was intended "to prove that the vital is in the direction of the voluntary" (224). But to be "in the direction of" the voluntary is not the same thing as voluntarism itself. In fact, even as Bergson's thought attempts to clear conceptual ground for human agency by problematizing "radical mechanism" and other positivist modes of inquiry, he is unable to demonstrate that the inherent creativity of life endows humans with agency. "The physical order is 'automatic'; the vital order is, I will not say voluntary," he writes, "but analogous to the order 'willed'" (231). This tension within vitalism rankled one of Lawrence's most vituperative critics, Wyndham Lewis, as we will see in chapter three.

60. Lawrence, *Sons and Lovers*, 11.

61. Lawrence, *Sons and Lovers*, 449.

62. The sexual encounter is only one of many forms of experience that Lawrence singles out for its consciousness-extinguishing quality. The non-sexual physical encounter of bodies, such as the fight between Baxter and Paul in *Sons and Lovers*, or the wrestling match between Birkin and Gerald in the "Gladiatorial" chapter of *Women in Love*, presents another aspect of the vital body. But Lawrence also spoke of the production of art in these same terms. Paul Morel's paintings, for example, are "produced unconsciously" (*Sons and Lovers*, 249), and Lawrence claimed of his own writing that "the novels and poems come unwatched out of one's pen" (*Fantasia*, 57).

63. Shklar, "Bergson and the Politics of Intuition," 635.

64. This is the conclusion reached by Anne Fernihough in *D. H. Lawrence*. She writes, "Lawrence's stance is, in the final analysis, apolitical, if by politics we implicate large, controlling organizations" (187).

65. Lawrence, *Sons and Lovers*, 567. A prominent example in the Anglophone context is Arthur Lovejoy, whose article "The Practical Tendencies of Bergsonism" appeared in the *International Journal of Ethics* in 1913. He reads Bergson along the lines of those who discerned an apolitical or perhaps asocial quality in vitalism. He concludes that if we follow Bergson's thought as a political philosophy, "we must, finally, turn away from the social life" because it requires discarding the intellect and language, without which society cannot exist (Lovejoy, "The Practical Tendencies of Bergsonism. I," 266). Lovejoy would be forced to reconsider this conclusion when exploring Sorel's politics in a subsequent article.

66. See Schwartz, "Bergson and the Politics," which documents not only Bergson's appeal on the religious right in France, but also his effect on leftists like Georg Simmel and Sorel. Interestingly, Schwartz notes that Walter Lippmann, the American journalist and critic of public relations, was influenced by Bergson (298). See chapter three for a discussion of Lippmann.

67. Nickels, *Poetry of the Possible*, 2.

68. Cf. Luxemburg's theory of revolutionary spontaneism in *The Mass Strike*; chapter two of Lenin's *What Is to Be Done?*, entitled "The Spontaneity of the Masses and the Consciousness of the Social-Democrats"; chapter two of Fanon's *Wretched of the Earth*, entitled "Spontaneity: Its Strength and Weaknesses"; and Gramsci's writing on Sorel in *The Prison Notebooks*. Ernesto Laclau and Chantal Mouffe provide a useful overview of some of these spontaneist philosophies, including Sorel's, in the first chapter of *Hegemony and Socialist Strategy*. See also Nickels, *Poetry of the Possible*, which demonstrates the appeal of these and other theories of political spontaneity to modernists like William Carlos Williams, Wyndham Lewis, Laura Riding, and Wallace Stevens.

69. Lawrence, "Democracy," 66.

70. Leavis, *D. H. Lawrence, Novelist*, 71, 73.

71. Leavis, *D. H. Lawrence, Novelist*, 21, 71. In *F. R. Leavis*, Richard Storer notes that Leavis was uncomfortable with works that were laden with "abstract sermonizing about spontaneity, impulse, primitive consciousness and so on" (63). For Leavis, the use of fiction as a means of disseminating ideas—any ideas—constituted a dangerous departure from the art's real calling, and it is on these occasions, such as in his dismissal of *The Plumed Serpent*, that Leavis finds in Lawrence the very elements of twentieth-century modernity Lawrence sought to repudiate.

72. For these critics, the novel serves as a prominent instance of Lawrence's racially essentialist tendencies, or they read the novel's depiction of indigeneity as a relatively benign figure for larger social problems. For criticism that emphasizes Lawrence's primitivism, see Terry Eagleton's chapter on Lawrence in *The English*

Novel, which sees a proto-fascism inherent in works like *The Plumed Serpent*. Many critics have mistakenly asserted that Lawrence fetishizes indigeneity by treating it as a solution to the problems of automatism. For these critics, Lawrence attributes to the indigenous population a degree of spontaneity elsewhere foreclosed, and it is for this reason that he is often accused of engaging in a nefarious form of primitivism. Brett Neilson, for example, has argued that *The Plumed Serpent* demonstrates that Lawrence "believes in the possibility of a complete restitution of precolonial modes of social and cultural organization in Mexico" (Neilson, "'Dark Page,'" 315). By insisting on the Mexican context of the novel as Lawrence's ultimate political objective, these critics fail to understand the way in which the novel works to imagine a mode of politics beyond "Mexican nationalism" and "Precolumbian modes of religious, cultural, and social life" (321). See also Mariana Torgovnick's discussion of Lawrence's primitivism in *Gone Primitive*.

73. Lawrence, *Letters*, vol. 4, 455.
74. Lawrence, *Letters*, vol. 5, 260.
75. Lawrence, *Letters*, vol. 5, 27.
76. Lawrence, *Letters*, vol. 4, 457.
77. Lawrence, *The Plumed Serpent*, 28.
78. Lawrence, *The Plumed Serpent*, 93.
79. Lawrence, *The Plumed Serpent*, 204-205.
80. Lawrence, *The Plumed Serpent*, 44, 77.
81. Lawrence, *The Plumed Serpent*, 112.
82. Lawrence, *The Plumed Serpent*, 52.
83. Lawrence, *The Plumed Serpent*, 106.
84. Lawrence, *The Plumed Serpent*, 105.
85. Sorel, *Reflections on Violence*, 238.
86. Sorel, "Letter to Daniel Halévy," 20.
87. Sorel, "Letter to Daniel Halévy," 115.
88. Unsurprisingly, Sorel's idea of myth coheres around a vitalist definition of agency. Because myth transcends the doctrinal character of political ideology, it understands political actors as driven by the same forms of agency that cannot easily be called "willed." As Judith Shklar has pointed out, for Sorel political freedom is a kind of creativity, "characterized by the absence of premeditation," and action "must emerge from some blind, nonrational inner impulse" (Shklar, "Bergson and the Politics of Intuition," 647).
89. In *"Ulysses*, Order, and Myth" Eliot calls the mythic method "a way of controlling, of ordering, of giving a shape and a significance to the immense panorama of futility and anarchy which is contemporary history" (177). Eliot's later lectures, *After Strange Gods*, likewise affirm the importance of collective habit as a virtue of national identity. See chapter 4 for a discussion of habit in Eliot's lectures.
90. Lawrence, *The Plumed Serpent*, 203.

91. Lawrence, *Apocalypse*, 91.

92. Lawrence, *Apocalypse*, 91.

93. Lawrence, *The Plumed Serpent*, 62.

94. Lawrence's essays do not always evince a blanket preference for the image. In "Art and Morality" he worries about the tendency of idealism to make us visualize ourselves as static subject: "We have learned to see, and each of us has a complete Kodak-idea of himself. . . . This is the habit we have formed: of visualizing *everything*. Each man to himself is a picture. The identifying of ourselves with the visual image of ourselves has become an instinct; the habit is already old. The picture of me, the me that is *seen*, is me" (164-165). This idea of the photographic image stands, then, in contrast with the vitalistic image, which inhibits stasis and promotes the passage through allotropic states.

95. Fernihough, *D. H. Lawrence*, 73.

96. Lawrence, *The Rainbow*, 192-193.

97. Judith Shklar has argued that Bergson's "entire philosophy is an effort to provide an aesthetic substitute" for something lost in twentieth century life, namely the substitution of positivism for religion, and that his writing thus reflects an effort to engage readers an intuitive rather than rational level (Shklar, "Bergson and the Politics of Intuition," 636).

98. Sorel, *Reflections on Violence*, 113.

99. Sorel, *Reflections on Violence*, 136.

100. Lawrence, "Morality and the Novel," 175.

101. Lawrence, "Why the Novel Matters," 195.

102. Lawrence, "Why the Novel Matters," 195.

103. Burwick and Douglass, "Introduction," 6.

104. The appeal of vitalism to fascist ideology is well documented. Mark Antliff has argued for the centrality of Sorel to fascism and fascist modes of modern art in *Avant-Garde Fascism*. Antliff's overall goal in this book is to counter the notion that modernism and fascism are diametrically opposed "by revealing the centrality of theories of art and of creativity to the fascist project initiated by Sorel's followers in France" (15). See also Sand, "Legend, Myth, and Fascism," which assesses the complicated legacy of Sorel's work in the context of fascist political philosophy. Patrick McGuinness offers a different perspective, arguing not that vitalism informed fascist doctrine but rather that fascism is a response to vitalism. He writes, "Bergson's is one of the most convincing arguments for the boundedness and limitation of the subjective, the individual, and it is but a small step from Bergson's ideas about flux, lack of unity, intuitive as opposed to intellectual apprehension . . . to the desire to respect or impose laws to live by in spite of them. Indeed, it is likely that Bergsonism gave a new urgency to political authoritarianism *for these very reasons*: not because one denied his findings but because one found them too convincingly dangerous to live by" (McGuinness, "Introduction," xxxv).

105. Eric Brandom's "Violence in Translation" offers a comprehensive discussion of Sorel's appeal across the political spectrum of the twentieth century, including the consolidation of Sorel as "a useful shorthand for radicalism gone wrong" in European and American contexts (734).

106. Pritchett, *The Living Novel*, 132.

107. Russell, *Portraits from Memory*, 114.

108. It should be clear that even in his most extreme visions of a vitalist revolution, Lawrence never embraces ethnonationalism. Lawrence spent several years in Italy during the 1920s, time that did little to convince him of the virtues of fascism. "Fascism, whatever else it does, spreads the grand blight of boredom," he wrote to Mabel Dodge Luhan in October of 1926 (*Letters*, vol. 5, 550). Boredom, of course, is a keyword for automaticity throughout Lawrence's novels.

109. Lawrence, *Kangaroo*, 107.

110. Lawrence, *Letters*, vol. 6, 321.

111. Levenson, *A Genealogy of Modernism*, 100.

112. Leavis, *For Continuity*, 143.

Chapter 3. Public Reflex

1. Hulme, "A Notebook," 426. Hulme's turn against vitalism seemed to be a logical outgrowth of a genuine philosophical maturation. Yet Jesse Matz has also suggested that Hulme's rejection of vitalism may have been a result of Bergson's ballooning popularity, particularly his appeal among women. See Matz, "T. E. Hulme."

2. Kenner, *Wyndham Lewis*, 113.

3. Lewis, *Time and Western Man*, xi.

4. Lewis is known to have attended lectures by Bergson at the Collège de France before he returned to England in 1908. These lectures were foundational for Lewis's antipathy toward vitalism, which has been well documented by critics. Bergson's influence on Lewis's early painting has been examined by Paul Edwards in *Wyndham Lewis: Painter and Writer*, and numerous critics—including Vincent Sherry ("Anatomy of Folly") and Michael North (*Machine-Age Comedy*)—have elucidated the relationship between Bergson's and Lewis's theories of laughter. Even as Lewis rejected vitalism as an anti-individualist and anti-intellectual philosophy, he remained committed to the vitalist agenda in many ways.

5. Lewis, *The Art of Being Ruled*, 119, 334.

6. Lewis, *Time and Western Man*, 92.

7. Lewis, *Paleface*, 176.

8. Lewis, *Paleface*, 196.

9. Lewis, *The Art of Being Ruled*, 196.

10. Watson, *Behaviorism*, 42.

11. Lewis, *Time and Western Man*, xi; Bernays, *Propaganda*, 37.
12. Nordau, *Degeneration*, 39.
13. Collier, *Modernism on Fleet Street*, 13.
14. Tarde, "Opinion and Conversation," 304.
15. The term "mass media" is itself a product of the interwar period. The first citation given by the *OED* is 1923, after which point "the media" itself may be taken to refer to the ever-expanding range of communications technologies increasingly at the center of political life.
16. Lasswell, *Propaganda Technique*, 34.
17. Miller and Dinan, *A Century of Spin*, 40.
18. Higham, *Looking Forward*, 116.
19. Higham, *Looking Forward*, 117.
20. Higham, *Looking Forward*, 125.
21. Grant, *Propaganda*, 5.
22. Lambert, *Propaganda*, 145.
23. Wald, *Constituting Americans*, 109.
24. North, *Reading 1922*, 68.
25. Mao, *Fateful Beauty*, 47.
26. In 1913, Walter Lippmann hailed Freud's work as "the greatest advance ever made towards the understanding and control of human character" (*Preface to Politics*, 85). However, by the 1920s, he came to see the limits of the psychoanalytic model for theorizing political thought, arguing in *Public Opinion* that "The psychoanalyst . . . almost always assumes that the environment is knowable . . . This assumption of his is the problem of public opinion. Instead of taking for granted an environment that is readily known, the social analyst is most concerned in studying how the larger political environment is conceived, and how it can be conceived more successfully" (17). The Freudian idea that humans are "governed by irrational unconscious impulses stemming from infantile fantasies" (Wald, *Constituting Americans*, 111) was not a central element of interwar public relations efforts. It would not be until midcentury that Freud's ideas gained wide acceptance among advertising and public relations experts, galvanizing several critical studies of such industries, including, most famously, Vance Packard's *The Hidden Persuaders*.
27. Watson, *Behavior*, 21.
28. Bernays, *Crystallizing Public Opinion*, 163
29. Bernays, *Crystallizing Public Opinion*, 113.
30. Lippmann, *The Phantom Public*, 20.
31. Lippmann, *The Phantom Public*, 20.
32. L'Etang, *Public Relations in Britain*, 28.
33. Lippmann, *Public Opinion*, 59.
34. Lippmann, *Public Opinion*, 10. The idea that citizens are capable only of perceiving what they have been prepared to perceive was already explicit in

William James's writings. In *Principles of Psychology*, he puts the matter succinctly: "*The only things which we commonly see are those which we preperceive*" (444). Preperception is a matter of habituation for James, or what later writers, following Pavlov, called conditioning. Unmediated perception of the real or the actual environment remained for Lippmann a physiological problem as much as a political one.

35. Angell, *The Press*, 16.
36. Lippmann, *Public Opinion*, 11.
37. Lippmann, *Public Opinion*, 131–132.
38. North, *Reading 1922*, 79. North notes that there was a close biographical connection between early PR experts and important institutions of literary modernism. Bernays's *Crystallizing Public Opinion* was originally published by Boni and Liveright, a firm that had distinguished itself by publishing *The Waste Land*, as well as work by Hemingway, Faulkner, Toomer, Cummings, Pound, and Barnes (North, *Reading 1922*, 77). According to North, Lippmann was also "a sometime fellow traveler of the avant-garde who frequented Mabel Dodge's salon before the war" (71). It is important to remember, too, that public relations worked in the field of culture, meaning that cultural artifacts like film could themselves be marshaled for political ends—a realization that would prove attractive to the students of Lippmann in England's Documentary Film Movement.
39. Wollaeger, *Modernism, Media, and Propaganda*, 13.
40. Lewis, *Time and Western Man*, 5, 354.
41. This project was initially conceived of as a single work entitled *The Man of the World*. Abandoned as impractical, the disaggregated project included what became the nonfiction works *The Art of Being Ruled*, *The Lion and the Fox*, *Time and Western Man*, and *Paleface*, his essay "Creatures of Habit, Creatures of Change," as well as the novels *The Childermass* and *The Apes of God*, among others. For more background, consult Edwards, *Wyndham Lewis*.
42. Lewis, *Paleface*, 161.
43. Lewis, *The Art of Being Ruled*, 17.
44. Lewis, *The Art of Being Ruled*, 44.
45. Lewis, *The Art of Being Ruled*, 45.
46. Lewis, *The Art of Being Ruled*, 105.
47. Lewis, *The Art of Being Ruled*, 94.
48. The question of "education" and the mass media was an important one in the foundation of New Criticism. In the introduction to *The Meaning of Meaning*, Ogden and Richards explain,

> None but those who shut their eyes to the hasty re-adaptation to totally new circumstances which the human race has during the last century been blindly endeavouring to achieve, can pretend that there is no need to examine critically the most important of all the instruments of civilization. New millions of par-

ticipants in the control of general affairs must now attempt to form personal opinions upon matters which were once left to a few. At the same time the complexity of these matters has immensely increased. The old view that the only access to a subject is through prolonged study of it, has, if it be true, consequences for the immediate future which have not yet been faced. The alternative is to raise the level of communication through a direct study of its conditions, its dangers and its difficulties. The practical side of this undertaking is, if communication be taken in its widest sense, Education (x).

What constituted such an education in this new media context was a matter of great debate, particularly as "education" was collapsed into categories like persuasion and propaganda. For Ogden and Richards, the growth of the mass media required a philosophical project that would allow differentiation between "the symbolic and the emotive" in a language system, thus restoring the conditions "under which a general revival of poetry would be possible" (viii). *The Meaning of Meaning* takes square aim at behaviorism's analysis of language, but it rarely uses the language of automatism to describe the effect of media on citizens. In his later works of the 1920s, however, Richards uses this very language, arguing that the media "threatens us by stereotyping and standardising both our utterances and our interpretations" (Richards, *Practical Criticism*, 339-340)—in short, turning citizens into mere repeating machines.

49. Lewis, *The Art of Being Ruled*, 106.
50. Lewis, *Time and Western Man*, xi.
51. In *Paranoid Modernism*, Trotter suggests that Lewis's nonfiction writing is a "mildly psychotic" (289) reaction to the class antagonisms of the period, and that this paranoia helped move him closer toward the fascist politics he embraced in the early 1930s. In *Modernism and the Machinery of Madness*, Andrew Gaedtke reads Lewis's work "within a broad discursive range of technological paranoia" (33), one that saw in the wireless the ability to hypnotize citizens.
52. In the early 1920s, Grierson did research at the University of Chicago on a Rockefeller Research Fellowship. During his time in the United States, he not only read Lippmann's *Public Opinion* but also traveled to New York to interview him.
53. Grierson, *Grierson on Documentary*, 207.
54. Grierson, *Grierson on Documentary*, 207.
55. Grierson, *Grierson on Documentary*, 165-166.
56. See Stephen Tallents's 1933 essay, "The Projection of England," which lays out the rationale of the EMB and the desire for "the projection of national personality" (208).
57. Grierson, *Grierson on Documentary*, 246.
58. Grierson, *Grierson on Documentary*, 191.
59. Quoted in L'Etang, *Public Relations in Britain*, 34.

60. In this respect, the example of radio is quite different than that of film. Unlike many countries, such as Russia, England did not benefit from the extensive investment of the state in the film industry. However, recognizing the power of film to engender foreign values, parliament passed the 1927 Cinematograph Films Act, which ensured a minimum production of British cinema. In so doing, it attempted to confront "the indirect propaganda carried" in Hollywood films and "the submergence of national habits and culture beneath those of another country" (Swann, *British Documentary Film Movement*, 10-11).

61. Cohen, "Annexing the Oracular Voice," 147.
62. Quoted in Cohen, "Annexing the Oracular Voice," 146.
63. Reith, *Broadcast over Britain*, 219.
64. Cohen, "Annexing the Oracular Voice," 144.
65. Cohen, "Annexing the Oracular Voice," 145.
66. Lewis, *The Art of Being Ruled*, 148.
67. Lewis, *The Art of Being Ruled*, 50.
68. Lewis, *Time and Western Man*, xix.
69. Lewis, *Time and Western Man*, xi.
70. Lewis, *Paleface*, 182.
71. Lewis, *Time and Western Man*, 212.
72. Bernays, *Propaganda*, 37.
73. Bernays, *Propaganda*, 37.
74. Bernays, *Propaganda*, 48.
75. Lippmann, *Public Opinion*, 158.
76. Lippmann, *Public Opinion*, 196.
77. North, *Reading 1922*, 69-70.
78. North, *Reading 1922*, 70.
79. Lippmann, *Public Opinion*, 158, emphasis added.
80. Lippmann's criticism of democratic practice should not be confused with a hatred of democracy itself. Unlike Bernays, who regarded occult conditioning as a necessary check on democracy, Lippmann saw such forces as a fundamental assault on the nature of participatory politics. As Richard Steel has noted, Lippmann was a lifelong writer for the popular press, a fact that underscores his enduring commitment to democracy. Nevertheless, his critique of democracy might easily be mistaken as mirroring the anti-democratic sentiments coalescing in Italy, Germany, and Spain in the interwar period. Indeed, in his next book, *The Phantom Public*, Lippmann went so far as to suggest that the uninformed public might be relieved of the responsibility of making public decisions altogether—a position closely mirrored by Lewis's *The Art of Being Ruled*.
81. Lewis, *The Art of Being Ruled*, 73. In *Modernism on Fleet Street*, Patrick Collier notes that the phrase "What the Public Wants" was "a catch-phrase of the 1920s and 1930s routinely invoked in commentaries on the press" (8). According to

Collier, the use of scare quotes around the phrase testifies "to that clause's ubiquity in the anxious commentaries of a culture in which the understood nature of 'the public' was in disorienting flux" (18).

82. Lewis, *The Art of Being Ruled*, 73-74.
83. Lewis, *The Art of Being Ruled*, 85.
84. Lewis, *The Art of Being Ruled*, 106.
85. Lewis, *The Art of Being Ruled*, 106.
86. Lippmann, *Public Opinion*, 158.
87. Bernays, *Propaganda*, 61.
88. Bernays, *Propaganda*, 78.
89. Bernays's sense that ideas should come to consumers and citizens *as if* they were their own had been anticipated earlier in the century in the writing of the American psychologist, Walter Dill Scott. In his 1908 book, *The Psychology of Advertising*, he suggested the preeminent role of "suggesting" in configuring consumer behaviors, explaining that "we reason rarely, but act under suggestion constantly" (215). Scott foresaw that a science of advertising would need to contend with the fact that most behaviors are the product of what has been suggested to us without our knowledge. Furthermore, the most effective advertisements were precisely those that allowed the consumer to act *as though* their choices were deliberate and rational: "An advertisement has not accomplished its mission till it has instructed the possible customer concerning the goods and then has caused him to forget where he received his instruction" (216).
90. Lewis, *The Art of Being Ruled*, 363.
91. Lewis, *The Art of Being Ruled*, 26.
92. Lewis, *Time and Western Man*, 12.
93. John Watson quoted in Hulbert, *Raising America*, 127.
94. Arvidson, "Personality," 799.
95. Lewis, *The Art of Being Ruled*, 148.
96. Lewis's analytic method has caused some amount of confusion for commentators, who have seen his work, and *Time and Western Man* in particular, as evidence of a theory of cultural logic avant la lettre. Reed Way Dasenbrock argues that, in an "essentially proto-structuralist" manner, *The Art of Being Ruled* rests on the notion that cultural and political phenomena are shaped by a "collective mentality" (Dasenbrock, "Afterword," 440) controlled by no one in particular. However, as Lewis himself explained it, what seems like a "popular movement of thought" (*The Art of Being Ruled*, 134) only appears as such to an observer unacquainted with the real forces creating such fashions.
97. Lewis, *Time and Western Man*, 136.
98. Lewis, *Time and Western Man*, 136.
99. Lewis, *Paleface*, 109-110.
100. Lewis, *The Art of Being Ruled*, 65.

101. Lewis, *The Childermass*, 322.

102. Wollaeger, *Modernism, Media, and Propaganda*, 26.

103. Lewis, *Time and Western Man*, 357.

104. Kenner, *Wyndham Lewis*, 97.

105. Lewis, *The Childermass*, 3.

106. Watson, *Behavior*, 20. Lewis repeatedly returned to this idea in his nonfiction. In *Time and Western Man*, he satirically suggested that "many animals, indeed most, are more dignified, much freer, and more reasonable than men, in the conduct of their lives: and the 'language habit,' as the behaviourist calls it, is a servitude for those who are unable to use it, but have to be content to be used by it" (303). In his 1934 book *Men without Art*, he concluded that man is "an animal in every respect upon the same footing as a rat or an elephant . . . except for what the behaviourist terms his word-habit" (231). From this Lewis concluded that "*the word . . . is the thing most proper and peculiar to him [mankind]*" (231), which means that art can help us to "recognize our animal limitations—our enormous physical and intellectual handicaps" (232).

107. Lewis, *The Childermass*, 72.

108. Lewis, *The Childermass*, 6.

109. Lewis, *The Childermass*, 24, 27, 27–28, 39, 40, 42, 56, 75, 77, 92, 80, 92, 110.

110. Lewis, *The Childermass*, 76, 92.

111. Lewis, *The Childermass*, 109, 158, 182.

112. Lewis, *The Childermass*, 133.

113. Jameson, *Fables of Aggression*, 160.

114. Lewis, *The Childermass*, 73.

115. Lewis, *The Childermass*, 223.

116. Lewis, *The Childermass*, 222.

117. Michael North makes this point eloquently. Lewis's fiction, he explains, "reverses the time-honored practice of realist fiction, which tends to work by revealing progressively deeper and more complex layers of human behavior. Lewis progressively narrows the choices available to his characters, slowly trapping them in the toils of their own small-minded habits, turning them inside out, as it were, to show that the deepest interior is really only the shabby backside of a cheap and worn-out surface" (North, *Machine-Age Comedy*, 125).

118. Lewis, *The Childermass*, 287. Lewis's overt efforts to throw the Bailiff's status into question surely challenge Kenner's claim that the Bailiff "is the menacing *will* behind the time-doctrines anatomized in *Time and Western Man*" (Kenner, *Wyndham Lewis*, 98). Whether he wills at all seems, instead, to be the question of the text.

119. Ayers, *Wyndham Lewis and Western Man*, 107.

120. See in particular *Men without Art*, which concentrates especially on the surface aesthetics of satire.

121. Lewis, *The Art of Being Ruled*, 231.
122. Gaedtke, *Modernism and the Machinery of Madness*, 10.
123. Lukács, "Realism in the Balance," 33.
124. Lukács, "Realism in the Balance," 33.
125. While, unlike Lukács, Lewis was an ardent proponent of formal experimentation, his critique of literary modernism shared much with Lukács's. Both insisted on the essentially de-agentializing and fatalistic ideology at work within modern culture, literary and otherwise; both saw modernists like Joyce as naively reproducing the ideological values at odds with individual agency; and both emphasized the necessity of a literature capable of making manifest the operations of ideology. Indeed, Lukács and Lewis might be modernism's most ardent critics—even as the latter was, in some sense, one of its most vocal proponents.
126. Jameson, *Fables of Aggression*, 73.
127. Jameson, *Fables of Aggression*, 73.
128. Edwards, *Wyndham Lewis*, 325.
129. Jameson, *Fables of Aggression*, 113.
130. Richards, "The Niceties of Salvation," 60.
131. Trotter, *Paranoid Modernism*, 290.
132. Bernays, "The Engineering of Consent," 115.
133. Bernays, *Propaganda*, 37-38.
134. Ewen, "Introduction," 25.
135. In this sense, Bernays's *Propaganda* can be read as a supremely self-conscious effort to orient the thoughts of its audience to the beneficial nature of social conditioning; it is a piece of propaganda *for* public relations itself, as Mark Crispin Miller notes. See his introduction to *Propaganda*.
136. Lewis, *Hitler*, 84.
137. Ayers reads *The Childermass* as a novel "dominated by a nihilism and antihumanism probably unrivalled in Modernist literature" (*Wyndham Lewis and Western Man*, 102). Such a reading only makes sense if we believe that Lewis came to accept the behaviorist position. Hugh Kenner has made this argument: "*Time and Western Man* had argued that the behaviorist, in reducing the person to a set of predictable gestures, was insulting the human race. In the same year Lewis was producing a body of fiction on the premise that people were nothing else" (*Wyndham Lewis*, 107). While Lewis's unrelenting criticisms of his peers often make such conclusions plausible, such analyses misrepresent his enduring desire to find literary and critical modes that would allow readers and artists to rupture the clichés and automatisms propounded by institutions like public relations. As Gaedtke has argued, Lewis's fiction and nonfiction constitute a "satirical campaign *against* what he perceived to be anti- or posthumanist cultural development" (*Modernism and the Machinery of Madness*, 36).
138. Lewis, "Plastic Art in Our Time," 26.

139. Lewis, *Men without Art*, 232.
140. Lewis, *Men without Art*, 232.
141. Lewis, *The Childermass*, 398.
142. Lewis, *Paleface*, 97–98.

Chapter 4. Pavlovian Nationalism

1. Packard, *The Hidden Persuaders*, 31.
2. Packard, *The Hidden Persuaders*, 31.
3. This figure comes from *The Holmes Report*, a publication dedicated to the global PR industry. See https://www.holmesreport.com/long-reads/article/global-pr-industry-now-worth-$15bn-as-growth-rebounds-to-7-in-2016.
4. Robert Boakes notes that Watson's popular press articles in the early 1920s "were of considerable help in making subscribers to the 'Behavior Research Fund' or trustees of the Rockefeller Memorial sympathetic towards arguments that investment in behavioural science would produce a technology to solve social problems" (*From Darwin to Behaviourism*, 240). The Behavior Research Fund was founded in 1925 without the participation of Watson, but the vast majority of the books and articles it helped produce were guided by Watson's thinking. The BRF was initially affiliated with the University of Chicago, where it made significant contributions to the study of juvenile delinquency.
5. It is worth noting just how closely aligned with business interests Watson's academic pursuits were. According to Stuart Ewen, Watson came to advocate for "transferring psychological development away from the traditional arenas of socialization (e.g., the family) and for making the realities of commercial life the guiding principles of child-rearing" (*Captains of Consciousness*, 82). These ideas would be directly pilloried by Huxley in *Brave New World*.
6. Richards, "*Behaviorism*," 374–375.
7. One of the major differences between the two is that Watson's research was centered on human subjects, whereas Pavlov was always limited to animals. The equivalent to Pavlov's dog was the "Little Albert" experiment, in which Watson attempted to change the unconditioned responses of an infant through the strict application of Pavlovian techniques. In this experiment, a child's innate desire to touch soft things (such as a rat, a rabbit, a dog, etc.) was conditioned away and replaced by a phobia of soft things. These simple experiments were intended to help unlock a much wider vista of conditioning in which fundamental characteristics of test subjects could be made or unmade at will. In *Behaviorism*, Watson wrote, "Give me a dozen healthy infants, well-formed, and my own specified world to bring them up in and I'll guarantee to take any one at random and train him to become any type of specialist I might select—doctor, lawyer, artist, merchant-chief and, yes, even beggar-man and thief, regardless of his talents, penchants, tenden-

cies, abilities, vocations, and race of his ancestors" (82). Scott Selisker has noted that "Orwell borrows his central torture scene [in *1984*], in which Winston is brought face-to-face with rats" from the "Little Albert" experiment, and that Orwell's treatment of language throughout the book was inspired by Watson's theory of language habits (*Human Programming*, 44).

8. "Books: Circles of Perdition," 116.

9. Despite West's large and variegated output, critics have tended to overwhelmingly stress her contribution to women's suffrage and women's writing. Victoria Glendinning begins her 1987 biography of West as follows: "The story of Rebecca West, who lived from 1892 to 1983, is the story of twentieth-century women" (*Rebecca West*, xv). Literary critics such as Jane Marcus, Phyllis Lassner, Debra Rae Cohen, and Bernard Schweizer have offered accounts of West's contribution to England's feminist movement, and West's work appears in numerous anthologies specifically concerned with gender, including Bonnie Kime Scott's anthology *Gender in Modernism* as well as Gilbert and Gubar's *The Norton Anthology of Literature by Women*.

10. Boakes, *From Darwin to Behaviourism*, 119.

11. Pavlov, *Conditioned Reflexes*, 26.

12. Pavlov, *Conditioned Reflexes*, 32.

13. Pavlov, *Lectures on Conditioned Reflexes*, 60.

14. Pavlov, *Conditioned Reflexes*, 7-8.

15. Boakes, *From Darwin to Behaviourism*, 120.

16. Anrep, "Ivan Petrovich Pavlov," 16-17.

17. Pavlov, *Lectures on Conditioned Reflexes*, 95.

18. Pavlov, *Lectures on Conditioned Reflexes*, 95.

19. Pavlov, *Lectures on Conditioned Reflexes*, 41.

20. Huxley, *Brave New World*, 258.

21. Huxley, *Brave New World*, 48. For more of Huxley's comments on Pavlov, see Huxley's 1932 radio broadcast, "Science and Civilization," as well as his 1958 essay, *Brave New World Revisited*. In the latter essay, Huxley explains that the communist police "draw their inspiration, not from the Inquisitor or the SS man, but from the physiologist and his methodically conditioned laboratory animals. For the dictator and his policemen, Pavlov's findings have important practical implications" (72). This essay reflects a postwar understanding of brainwashing as a singular event, rather than an ongoing process of social conditioning that *Brave New World* dramatizes. Under the laboratory-like conditions of the torture chamber, people become "more than normally suggestible," such that "practically everybody can be converted to practically anything" (75).

22. Boakes, *From Darwin to Behaviourism*, 130.

23. Huxley, *Brave New World Revisited*, 78.

24. Hunter, *Brainwashing*, 24.

25. Historian Claudia Koonz has suggested that the official Nazi policy of ideological coercion, *Gleichschaltung*, depended on an idea of human automatism. While "'Nazification,' 'coordination,' 'integration,' and 'bringing into line' all come close" to the meaning of the term, "none carries the mechanical overtones of *Gleichschaltung*" (*The Nazi Conscience*, 72). As she explains, "*Gleich* means both 'equal' and 'the same.' *Schalten* means 'to shift.' The conversion of A/C to D/C electrical currents is a *Gleichshaltung*. The removal of anyone who 'stained' or 'soiled' the nation was 'switching them off'—an *Ausshaltung*" (72). The specific forms that *Gleichschaltung* took included everything from semantic gestures of everyday speech and German public culture, to Hitler's image as an icon and symbol of the *Volk*. The mobilization of everyday stimuli to enforce ideological positions was seen by observers in the 1950s as the direct application of Pavlov's research.

26. Meerloo, *The Rape of the Mind*, 52.

27. Meerloo, *The Rape of the Mind*, 52.

28. Taylor, *Brainwashing*, 6.

29. Selisker, *Human Programming*, 66.

30. Arendt, *The Origins of Totalitarianism*, 587.

31. Arendt, *The Origins of Totalitarianism*, 588.

32. Lifton, *Thought Reform*, 420.

33. Because Pavlov's research demanded surgically transplanting salivary ducts, the extraction of digestive glands, and work with fistulas, many cast him as emblematic of a scientific disregard for animal suffering. Writers like Shaw thus naturally classed Pavlov as only the latest in a long line of vivisectionists. A review of West's *The Strange Necessity* in the *Sunday Express* (August 12, 1928) entitled "The Vengeance of Fido" reflected this opinion of Pavlov, writing that "art is, indeed, a strange necessity if it leads to Pavlovolatry and the condonation of ingenious cruelty in order to construct an aesthetic hypothesis." Pavlov himself appears as a "myop" in Shaw's short story, "The Black Girl in Search of God" (1932).

34. Wells, "Mr. Wells Appraises Mr. Shaw," SM1-2.

35. For more on utopian readings of Pavlov, see Baars, "I. P. Pavlov and the Freedom Reflex."

36. Mao, *Fateful Beauty*, 179.

37. West, *The Strange Necessity*, 73. West had a long-standing hatred for casinos. In her 1935 novel *The Thinking Reed*, she represents gambling as the stalest of determinisms for those who cannot synthesize the stimuli of their environment: "These master intelligences had banished beauty from the Casino because the lust of the eye may lead either to love or to thought, to coherent processes, ultimately to civilization, to the preservation of life. Within these walls those who hated life should be able to take refuge from it in number, pure number, its intricate and insignificant whims" (*The Thinking Reed*, 285).

38. West, *The Strange Necessity*, 61.
39. West, *The Strange Necessity*, 74.
40. West, *The Strange Necessity*, 59.
41. West, *The Strange Necessity*, 59.
42. West, *The Strange Necessity*, 99.
43. West, *The Strange Necessity*, 98.
44. West, *The Strange Necessity*, 195.
45. West, *The Strange Necessity*, 99.
46. West, *The Strange Necessity*, 99-100.
47. West, *The Strange Necessity*, 102-103.
48. West, *The Strange Necessity*, 143.
49. West, *The Strange Necessity*, 159.
50. West, *The Strange Necessity*, 160.
51. West, "Necessity and Grandeur," 47.
52. West, "Necessity and Grandeur," 42.
53. The nationalist implications of conditioned reflex are especially pronounced in West's postwar analyses of treason. In a manuscript essay housed in Yale's Beinecke Library entitled "Post-Mortem on Radio Propaganda," West pities radio traitors like William Joyce for trusting the stimuli of the airwaves over the bodily experience of a national environment: "They are the most piteous victims of the modern faith in internationalism: of our refusal to admit that a man understand the things which he can see and hear and touch and smell and taste better than those things which are beyond the experience of his senses" (8).
54. West, "Environment Matters Most," 10.
55. Connerton, *How Societies Remember*, 4.
56. Braddock, "Tradition and Archive," 100.
57. Eliot, *After Strange Gods*, 18.
58. Though anti-Semitism is by no means the major note of *After Strange Gods*, it is an explicit one. In outlining his theory of tradition, Eliot notes the importance of racial homogeneity within a national community. "Where two or more cultures exist in the same place," he writes, "they are likely either to be fiercely self-conscious or both to become adulterate. What is still more important is unity of religious background; and reasons of race and religion combine to make any large number of free-thinking Jews undesirable" (19-20).
59. It is telling that Eliot omits the second half of Leopold Bloom's definition of the nation: "A nation is the same people living in the same place. . . . Or also living in different places" (*Ulysses* 272). Unlike those living in a shared milieu, those living in different places would be dependent on the *imaginary* community that discourse make possible. Unlike Leopold Bloom, then, Eliot and West both considered the national a real, physical fact.
60. Eliot, *After Strange Gods*, 29

61. Eliot, *After Strange Gods*, 18, 29.
62. Eliot, *After Strange Gods*, 18.
63. Esty, *A Shrinking Island*, 39.
64. Esty, *A Shrinking Island*, 40.
65. As a counterpoint, it is worth noting that Pound shared this emphasis on embodied traditions but also yoked them to fascistic tropes of heredity and biological purity. Pound adapted the term "paideuma" from German ethnologist Leo Frobenius to signify "the mental formation, the inherited habits of thought, the conditionings, aptitudes of a given race or time" (Pound, "The Jefferson-Adams Letters," 148).
66. West's most overt invocation of Pavlov after *The Strange Necessity* is her 1931 essay "Woman as Artist and Thinker," which details the impediments to female artists, framing them as matters of conditioning.
67. Hitchens, "Introduction," xiii.
68. West, *Black Lamb and Grey Falcon*, v.
69. West, *Black Lamb and Grey Falcon*, 21.
70. MacKay, *Modernism and World War II*, 44-45.
71. West, *Black Lamb and Grey Falcon*, 1101.
72. West, *Black Lamb and Grey Falcon*, 1114.
73. *Black Lamb* enjoyed a resurgence in readership during the 1990s, when, in an effort to understand war-torn Yugoslavia and the roots of Slobodan Milošević's Serbian nationalism, readers turned to West's book. According to Brian Hall, West's prejudice in the book for Serbs had an indirect but conspicuous impact on American foreign policy. See Hall's essay in *The New Yorker*, "Rebecca West's War." For an alternate analysis of the effect of West's romanticization of Yugoslavs on foreign policy, see also Hansen, *Security as Practice*.
74. Schweizer, *Rebecca West*, 87, 88.
75. MacKay, *Modernism and World War II*, 45.
76. MacKay, *Modernism and World War II*, 64.
77. MacKay, *Modernism and World War II*, 64.
78. West, *Black Lamb and Grey Falcon*, 8.
79. West, *Black Lamb and Grey Falcon*, 9.
80. West, *Black Lamb and Grey Falcon*, 34.
81. West, *Black Lamb and Grey Falcon*, 32-33.
82. West, *Black Lamb and Grey Falcon*, 28.
83. West, *Black Lamb and Grey Falcon*, 35.
84. West, *Black Lamb and Grey Falcon*, 37.
85. James, *The Principles of Psychology*, 112.
86. James, *The Principles of Psychology*, 891.
87. Bergson, who strongly challenged materialist psychologies, repeatedly uses

the language of grooves in *Laughter*, writing about "the mind crystallising in certain grooves" (58) as one source of the comic.

88. Watson, *Behaviorism*, 166.
89. Chu, *Race*, 109.
90. West, *Black Lamb and Grey Falcon*, 37.
91. West, *Black Lamb and Grey Falcon*, 612.
92. West, *Black Lamb and Grey Falcon*, 1104.
93. West, *Black Lamb and Grey Falcon*, 1104-1105.
94. West, *Black Lamb and Grey Falcon*, 481.
95. West's idea that fascist propaganda was an ersatz replacement for the loss of tradition found some support within studies of propaganda in the 1930s. In his 1938 study, *Propaganda*, Richard Lambert made much the same point, arguing that most people "do not order their lives according to reason, but according to habit," and that "they found most of their opinions upon tradition—upon what is handed down to them by their family, their class, their government." In the absence of these traditions, they "do not revert to a process of pure rationality; they fall victims to another non-rational process of reaching decisions, *i.e.* propaganda." Propaganda becomes, in effect, "a kind of *substitute* for tradition" (157).
96. Woolf, *Three Guineas*, 169.
97. Orwell, *Coming Up for Air*, 25.
98. Orwell, *Coming Up for Air*, 205.
99. Orwell, *Coming Up for Air*, 171.
100. Lippmann, *Public Opinion*, 33.
101. Orwell, *Coming Up for Air*, 229.
102. West, *Black Lamb and Grey Falcon*, 302.
103. Much of the Cold War discourse on fascism and totalitarianism draws explicitly on the physiological model of the gramophone. In his seminal book, *Brainwashing*, Hunter presents the case of a "brainwashed" man named Malcom Bersohn, whose affect he considers typical of the brainwashed:

> His speech seemed impressed on a disc that had to be played from start to finish, without modification or halt. He appeared to be under a weird, unnatural compulsion to go on with a whole train of thought, from beginning to end, even when it had been rendered silly. . . . Bersohn appeared no longer capable of using free will or adapting himself to a situation for which he had been uninstructed; he had to go on as if manipulated by instincts alone. This was Party discipline extended to the mind; a trance element was in it. It gave me a creepy feeling (13).

Similar descriptions of the repetition compulsion and gramophonic quality of fascism are widely in evidence in the writing of the postwar period. The best examples outside of popular culture and Cold War propaganda are Hannah Arendt's depiction of fascism in *Eichmann in Jerusalem* and studies of the "authoritarian personality" by Theodor Adorno, Else Frenkel-Brunswik, Daniel Levinson, and Nevitt Sanford after the Second World War. In both studies, fascist or authoritarian behavior is characterized by rote adherence to routines of thought acquired through conditioning, what Adorno and his colleagues termed "stereotypy" (Adorno, et al., *The Authoritarian Personality,* 1950).

104. Mao, *Fateful Beauty,* 208.
105. Mao, *Fateful Beauty,* 208.
106. Eliot, *After Strange Gods,* 29.
107. West, *Black Lamb and Grey Falcon,* 43.
108. Hall, "Rebecca West's War," 78.
109. Hansen, *Security as Practice,* 160.
110. West, *Black Lamb and Grey Falcon,* 400.
111. West, *Black Lamb and Grey Falcon,* 638.
112. West, *Black Lamb and Grey Falcon,* 638–639.
113. West, *Black Lamb and Grey Falcon,* 639.
114. West, *Black Lamb and Grey Falcon,* 228.
115. West, *Black Lamb and Grey Falcon,* 10.
116. West, *Black Lamb and Grey Falcon,* 228.
117. Woolf, *Three Guineas,* 64.
118. Woolf, *Three Guineas,* 125.
119. There are many telling points of contact between *Black Lamb* and *Three Guineas* that suggest a less antagonistic relationship between Woolf and West than might be supposed. Chief among these is the use of images in both books. While recent editions of *Black Lamb* omit West's images, these images form an integral part of the text in much the way that Woolf's do. While Woolf's images demonstrate the operation of "atmosphere" in the spectacles of masculine pageantry, West's images of Yugoslav aesthetic and cultural practices establish a sense of the physical milieu and traditions that constitute the long history of the nation. These images militate in favor of forms of conditioning that were established over generations rather than those forged through the milieu of control and spectacle of fascism.

120. West, *Black Lamb and Grey Falcon,* 1089.
121. West, *Black Lamb and Grey Falcon,* 1129.
122. In some cases, especially after the war, writers used the notion of mass cultural conditioning not to substantiate national differences but to understand (and even sympathize with) the seemingly irrational behavior of traitors and Nazis. These analyses suggest that the citizens of repressive regimes were the passive victims of governmental malevolence; their lack of agency (if such it was) could be understood as the product of ubiquitous social forces beyond the control of

individual actors, and, in some cases, even sympathized with. One place in which we can see a grain of such sympathy is Rebecca West's own postwar analysis of sedition, *The Meaning of Treason*. In this text, West continued to insist that nations are bound by more than just territory or law because they are shot through with embodied traditions. To feel treason toward one's nation, West reasoned, is to rebel against the conditions of one's own making, and thus against one's own nature. This makes the traitor a neurotic in much the way Pavlov defined the term at the conclusion of *Conditioned Reflexes*—an animal conditioned to salivate when it gets shocked. West nevertheless sympathized with the traitor William Joyce, arguing that "there was certainly much to be loved in William Joyce" because behind his "political folly was a grain of wisdom, a degree of preference for the things that must be preferred if humanity is to survive" (*The Meaning of Treason*, 65). In Joyce, West recognized a hierarchy of values she so prized in the embodied traditions of Yugoslavia and England, even as his rebellion against his own reflex community made him a tragic and contemptible figure.

123. West, *St. Augustine*, 120.
124. Elias, *The Civilizing Process*, 246.
125. Elias, *The Civilizing Process*, 27.

Chapter 5. Higher Degrees of Automaticity

1. Beckett, "Dante . . . Bruno. Vico . . Joyce," 503.
2. Maude, *Beckett, Technology, and the Body*, 1. This view, founded in midcentury analyses of Beckett's existentialism, has found fortification in much recent scholarship, which has overwhelmingly sought to draft Beckett into the ranks of post-structural philosophers. Read in the light of thinkers such as Levinas, Deleuze, and Badiou, Beckett's work has been understood not only as an inducement to the ambitions of post-structuralism, but also as an instantiation of the philosophy itself. While critical conversations about the complex relationship between Beckett and post-structuralism have expanded exegetical and theoretical horizons, this "Blanchoting of Beckett" (Eagleton, "Introduction," 3), as Terry Eagleton terms it, has had the effect of muting the presence of the body within Beckett's work and consigning historical questions to positions of inferiority, if not irrelevance. For prominent examples, see Uhlmann, *Beckett and Post-Structuralism* and Gibson, *Beckett and Badiou*.
3. Bergson, *Creative Evolution*, 144.
4. Elias, *The Civilizing Process*, 447.
5. Weber, *Economy and Society*, 326.
6. Weber, *Economy and Society*, 25.
7. Camic, "The Matter of Habit," 1056.
8. Crossley, "Habit and Habitus," 145.

9. Bourdieu, *Sociology in Question*, 86.

10. In his article on the history of "habit" and "habitus," Nick Crossley argues that one of the reasons that "habit" lost intellectual currency within sociology is that it was "identified with mechanical behavioural responses of individual organisms, qua individual" ("Habit and Habitus," 143). If this is the case, it implies a misunderstanding within twentieth-century sociology, since the major pronouncements of both Pavlov and Watson suggested the larger political value to understanding and shaping collective reflexes as well.

11. Bourdieu quoted in Sterne, "Bourdieu, Technique and Technology," 381.

12. Mauss, "Techniques of the Body," 101.

13. Mauss, "Techniques of the Body," 108, 104.

14. Mauss, "Techniques of the Body," 108.

15. Mauss, "Techniques of the Body," 105.

16. Mauss, "Techniques of the Body," 105.

17. Elias, *The Civilizing Process*, 45.

18. Elias, *The Civilizing Process*, 45.

19. Elias, *The Civilizing Process*, 54.

20. Elias, *The Civilizing Process*, 105, emphasis added.

21. Elias, *The Civilizing Process*, 246n40.

22. Elias, *The Civilizing Process*, 480.

23. Elias, *The Civilizing Process*, 123.

24. Elias, *The Civilizing Process*, 152.

25. Elias, *The Civilizing Process*, 477.

26. Fromm, *Escape from Freedom*, 255.

27. Fromm, *Escape from Freedom*, 166, 203.

28. Elias, *The Civilizing Process*, 153.

29. Miller, *Late Modernism*, 33.

30. Belgrad, *The Culture of Spontaneity*, 2.

31. Elias, *The Civilizing Process*, 116.

32. Elias, *The Germans*, 19.

33. Connerton, *How Societies Remember*, 88.

34. Connerton, *How Societies Remember*, 88.

35. Beckett, *Murphy*, 107.

36. Beckett, *Murphy*, 107.

37. Beckett, *Murphy*, 111.

38. Beckett, "Philosophy Notebook," 7-8.

39. Gang, "Mindless Modernism," 120.

40. Beckett, "Philosophy Notebook," 7-9; 7-10.

41. Beckett, *Murphy*, 2, 105.

42. Beckett, *Murphy*, 17.

43. Beckett, *Murphy*, 18.

44. Beckett, *Murphy*, 122.
45. Beckett, *Murphy*, 2.
46. Beckett, *Murphy*, 6, 177.
47. Beckett, *Murphy*, 218.
48. Beckett, *Murphy*, 219.
49. Beckett, *Murphy*, 44.
50. Beckett, *Proust*, 8.
51. Orwell, *Coming Up for Air*, 230.
52. Beckett, *The Unnamable*, 358.
53. Beckett, *The Unnamable*, 375.
54. Beckett, *Murphy*, 49.
55. Beckett, *Murphy*, 185.
56. Begam, *Samuel Beckett*, 46.
57. Beckett, *Murphy*, 122.
58. Lin, "Labor," 250.
59. Beckett, *Murphy*, 107; emphasis added.
60. Beckett, *Murphy*, 179.
61. Beckett, *Murphy*, 1.
62. Gaedtke, *Modernism*, 156.
63. Beckett, "Recent Irish Poetry," 70.
64. Beckett, "Recent Irish Poetry," 70.
65. Beckett would later identify this new artist impulse most prominently in the canvases of Bram van Velde. See Beckett, "Three Dialogues."
66. Miller, *Late Modernism*, 64.
67. Beckett, *Murphy*, 22-23.
68. Astronomy is one of many determinist systems in *Murphy*. Beckett foregrounds it as such in the novel's opening line: "The sun shone, having no alternative, on the nothing new" (1).
69. Murphy refers to the horoscope as a "corpus of deterrents" (Beckett, *Murphy*, 34), a "separation order" (34), a "life-warrant" (31), and a "bull of incommunication" (31). These terms highlight the nativity's status as a surrogate of political institutions; it has the quality of a papal or emperor's "bull," the legal efficacy of a "warrant" or "order," and the juridical power of the *corpus juris*. Beckett's notes bear this out; in a notebook entitled *Whoroscope*, which he began after attending a lecture by Carl Jung, Beckett wrote that the nativity would serve as a "corpus of motives" whose legitimacy would make it "no longer a guide to be consulted but a force to be obeyed" (quoted in Knowlson, *Damned to Fame*, 197).
70. Beckett, *Murphy*, 189.
71. Beckett foregrounds the asylum's place within the political structures of the era in section nine of the novel, which begins, "The Magdalen Mental Mercyseat lay a little way out of town, ideally situated in its own grounds on the boundary of

two counties. In order to die in the one sheriffalty rather than in the other some patients had merely to move up, or be moved up, a little in the bed. This sometimes proved a great convenience" (*Murphy*, 156). What is remarkable about this passage is that it points to the way in which the asylum is situated within and constituted by the legal authority of the state, which had recently brought such institutions under greater control. The Mental Treatment Act 1930 attempted to "normalize" psychiatric institutions by making provisions for voluntary patients, the financial administration of patients by local authorities, and the management of psychiatric documentation. This legislation, Clive Unsworth notes, was "the prelude to a radical expansion of the frontiers of psychiatric medicine" (*The Politics of Mental Health Legislation*, 17) in the United Kingdom. In effect, the 1930 act endowed psychiatrists with the power to regulate society under the aegis of the state. For background on this act and the legal history of psychiatric hospitals in modernist England, see Smith, "Legal Frameworks for Psychiatry."

72. Goffman, *Asylums*, 23.
73. Orwell, *Coming Up for Air*, 231.
74. Waugh, *Brideshead Revisited*, 4.
75. Miller, *Modernism*, 162.
76. Beckett, *Murphy*, 160.
77. Beckett, *Murphy*, 177.
78. Beckett, *Murphy*, 178.
79. Beckett, *Murphy*, 111.
80. Beckett, *Murphy*, 181.
81. Beckett, *Murphy*, 159.
82. Beckett, *Murphy*, 158.
83. Beckett, *Murphy*, 237.
84. Elias, *The Civilizing Process*, 116.
85. Elias, *The Civilizing Process*, 116.
86. Beckett, *Murphy*, 177.
87. Some scholars have read Murphy's lack of knowledge as a form of political critique. Reading Beckett in conversation with Bourdieu's understanding of habitus, Liz Barry has mirrored the analysis of many who have read Murphy as a figure of successful capitalist resistance. Beckett's characters, she writes, preempt habituation to routines of consumption and "therefore fail to absorb the necessary habits of thinking either to negotiate the world, or even to perceive themselves within it; they can recognize neither their own position nor the dispositions that it might entail" (Barry, "Beckett, Bourdieu and the Resistance," 34). It is true that Beckett's characters fail to recognize their own position within social structures and the meaning of their habits. But such forms of un-knowledge in Beckett are almost always indices not of political resistance but of capitulation. See "Beckett, Bourdieu and the Resistance."

88. Bourdieu, *Outline*, 18.
89. Beckett, *Molloy*, 106.
90. Beckett, *Molloy*, 106.
91. Beckett, *The Unnamable*, 341.
92. Beckett, *The Unnamable*, 303.
93. Beckett, *Molloy*, 80-81.
94. Beckett, *Molloy*, 126.
95. Beckett, *Molloy*, 24-25, 105.
96. Beckett, *Molloy*, 27. The desire to locate a self that exists apart from one's conditioning is an enduring problem across much of Beckett's fiction and drama. In his biography of Beckett, *Damned to Fame*, James Knowlson argues that Beckett's entire career can be read as an illustration of a saying by Beckett's mentor at Trinity College, "Every one of us must strive, unflinchingly, to be himself" (quoted in Knowlson, *Damned to Fame*, 66). While Molloy is, in a sense, the very image of the automaton, one way to read the search for his mother is as a symbolic search for an authentic self. Whereas Beckett consciously links paternity to authority in this novel (most notably through Moran's relationship with his son), the maternal figure represents something of the opposite quality—an organic realization of self as opposed to the one "made" by a milieu. That Molloy thinks of his search as something that has been mandated by his "prompters" does not necessarily contradict this hypothesis. Indeed, throughout the trilogy Beckett's characters search for a kind of genuine self-expression, but always under the suspicion that their efforts are themselves mandated—"pensums" (*Molloy*, 27) absorbed from the environments they inhabit. This tension remains a source of energy throughout Beckett's novels (including *Murphy*), where total habituation and radical agency become indistinguishable.
97. Beckett, *The Unnamable*, 337.
98. Jameson, *A Singular Modernity*, 135.
99. Beckett, "Intercessions by Denis Devlin," 91.
100. Beckett, *Waiting for Godot*, 81.
101. Beckett, *Proust*, 516.
102. Beckett, *Proust*, 517.
103. Beckett, *Proust*, 517.
104. Beckett, *Waiting for Godot*, 33.
105. Beckett, *Waiting for Godot*, 10-11.
106. Maude, "Beckett and the Law of Habit," 820.
107. Maude, "Beckett and the Law of Habit," 820.
108. When asked in 1967 if Wyndham Lewis had any influence on his theories of media, McLuhan responded, "Good Heavens—that's where I got it! It was Lewis who put me on to all this study of the environment as an educational—as a teaching machine. To use our more recent terminology, Lewis was the person who

showed me that the manmade environment was a teaching machine—a programmed teaching machine." See McLuhan, "Wyndham Lewis Recalled."

Afterword. Choice Architects, Where Is Your Vortex?

1. Bosanquet, "Social Automatism," 167-168.
2. Thaler and Sunstein, *Nudge*, 6.
3. Thaler and Sunstein, *Nudge*, 3.
4. Thaler and Sunstein, *Nudge*, 3.
5. Thaler and Sunstein, *Nudge*, 3.
6. Kahneman, *Thinking, Fast and Slow*, 13.
7. Thaler and Sunstein, *Nudge*, 19.
8. Thaler and Sunstein, *Nudge*, 37.
9. Thaler and Sunstein, *Nudge*, 20.
10. For more on nudging and the emergence of the experimental approach to politics, see Bennhold, "Britain's Ministry of Nudges," and Issenberg, "Nudge the Vote."
11. One of the most colorful nudges detailed by Thaler and Sunstein regards sanitation in public restrooms. They note that at the Schiphol Airport in Amsterdam, each urinal in the men's rooms is etched with the image of a housefly. In a moment when people tend to be absentminded and thus careless, this image focuses their attention and promotes better aim. Thaler and Sunstein report that this subtle nudge reduces "spillage" by about 80 percent (*Nudge*, 4).
12. Thaler and Sunstein, *Nudge*, 10.
13. James, *The Principles of Psychology*, 122.
14. These kinds of nudges are what choice architecture firms—such as the British nonprofit Behavioural Dynamics Institute and its for-profit arm, SCL—emphasize to the public. In publicly available marketing materials, Nigel Oakes, the founder of both firms, boasts of his ability to create strategic communications that can dissuade youths from joining terrorist groups or curtail those behaviors most injurious to the climate. According to Issenberg, SCL has "developed programs to increase condom use across the Caribbean, improve the effectiveness of tsunami warnings delivered by text message, and guide a Unicef project to discourage child marriage in South Sudan" (Issenberg, "Cruz-Connected Data"). SCL's most notorious and profitable work, however, has not been in the public interest, but rather in the service of American conservative politicians. Its offshoot firm, Cambridge Analytica, played a notorious role in the 2016 American presidential election and England's 2016 Brexit vote.
15. Thaler and Sunstein, *Nudge*, 6.
16. Thaler and Sunstein argue in the conclusion of their book that there are ethical questions raised by choice architecture. Nudges, in their opinion, should

help people, not harm them, particularly when people are making decisions that they are unlikely to fully understand or receive prompt feedback on. They explain, "We should create rules of engagement that reduce fraud and other abuses, that promote healthy competition, that restrict interest-group power, and that create incentives to make it more likely that the architects will serve the public interest" (*Nudge*, 243). However, choice architects are not a group of professionals, like doctors, who could be bound by professional and ethical standards. Furthermore, the most effective nudges are also the most objectionable to them—those that are "invisible and thus impossible to monitor" (249). Taken in the larger cultural context, their stated desire for an ethical standard of this sort is pure posturing, a way of affirming the democratic virtues of their enterprise while undermining values of individual agency and autonomy.

17. White, *The Manipulation of Choice*, 82.
18. Zuboff, *The Age of Surveillance Capitalism*, 8.
19. Zuboff, *The Age of Surveillance Capitalism*, 80-81.
20. This kind of microtargeting relies on what are called "psychometric" models. There is some argument to be made that this approach, popularized by Cambridge Analytica, isn't quite as effective as some firms claim. According to Antonio García Martínez, the original product manager for Facebook's microtargeting tool, social media doesn't allow the precise targeting of psychological states of mind; psychometrics produces models that are too "noisy" to be effective (Martinez, "The Noisy Fallacies"). What really made the 2016 Trump campaign effective, he explains, was simply that it used Facebook's advertising infrastructure to its advantage, more precisely targeting voters and getting more out of their money by making their content controversial, more "clickbaity" (Martinez, "How Trump Conquered Facebook").
21. Quoted in Anderson and Horvath, "Weaponized AI Propaganda Machine."
22. Issenberg, "A More Perfect Union."
23. Issenberg, "A More Perfect Union."
24. Bertoni, "How Jared Kushner Won."
25. Bland, "Picture of Trump's Thumbs Up."
26. Green and Issenberg, "Inside the Trump Bunker."
27. Lippmann, *Public Opinion*, 59.
28. Barbu, "Advertising, Microtargeting and Social Media," 48.
29. Zuboff, *The Age of Surveillance Capitalism*, 8.
30. Zuboff, *The Age of Surveillance Capitalism*, 378-379.
31. Zuboff, *The Age of Surveillance Capitalism*, 379.
32. Cohen, *Configuring the Networked Self*, 167. Though I am focusing here on the problem of targeted influence, there are overtly Orwellian aspects to social media worth noting. In 2016 *Gizmodo* reported that some former Facebook "news curators" accused the company of suppressing conservative news (Nunez, "Former Facebook Workers"), a significant problem when we remember that social media is

often the primary point of access to news for younger users. Real-time surveillance is also a significant problem, one that Bruce Schneier sees as built into the architecture of the internet; he writes that surveillance "is the business model of the Internet" (Schneier, *Data and Goliath*, 49). He explains that this problem is not one of sheer governmental surveillance so much as a "public-private surveillance partnership" (80) between governments and corporations.

33. Cohen, *Configuring the Networked Self*, 172.
34. Cohen, *Configuring the Networked Self*, 182.
35. Harris, "Handful of Tech Companies."
36. Harris, "Handful of Tech Companies."
37. Harris, "Handful of Tech Companies."
38. "Chamath Palihapitiya." There is a growing bibliography about the kind of "self" that networked life enables, variously termed the "networked self," the "algorithmic self," and the "data self." In each of these iterations, ideas of control and surveillance loom large as constitutive features of contemporary subjectivity. For example, Frank Pasquale ties the idea of an "algorithmic self" to ideas of conditioning that are far more subtle than Pavlovian models. He explains that data about behavior is increasingly providing what Watson always dreamed of—a full picture of behaviors that are regular and regularizable. In the data, Pasquale writes, are the routes to sociobiological conditioning: "The platforms are constantly shaping us, on the basis of sophisticated psychological profiles," leading to "whole new kinds of people" (Pasquale, "The Algorithmic Self," 40). For Pasquale, escaping the "Pavlovian cycle of posting, like/faving, being liked/faved" requires something more than just counter-nudging: "Without a stronger sense of commitments that endure above and beyond the feedback and control mechanisms of Big Data and big platforms, we are doomed to selves comprehensively shaped by them" (42). Rob Horning, in a series of articles for *The New Inquiry*, goes even further, suggesting that part of the pleasure of a "data self" is that we can "get rid of" the self in favor of the homogenized non-self configured by data (Horning, "Reparative Compulsions"). See also Cohen, *Configuring the Networked Self*.
39. Freed, "War on Kids."
40. B. J. Fogg quoted in Freed, "War on Kids."
41. Biddle, "Facebook Uses Artificial Intelligence."
42. Biddle, "Facebook Quietly Hid Webpages." It is possible now to see these services as the logical outcome of experiments Facebook has conducted on its own users over the years. In 2010, the company experimented with 61 million user accounts to see how information about friends' reported voting behavior would affect electoral turnout. In a study published in *Nature*, researchers suggested that users who were targeted with information about friends who had reported voting were 2 percent more likely to report the same than those who saw no message about voting at all. According to Zoe Corbyn, "The social message, the researchers

estimate, directly increased turnout by about 60,000 votes. But a further 280,000 people were indirectly nudged to the polls by seeing messages in their news feeds, for example, telling them that their friends had clicked the 'I voted' button" (Corbyn, "Facebook Experiment"). Facebook also controversially ran experiments on users' emotions, as was revealed in 2014; by showing users more "sad" or "happy" content on their feeds, Facebook attempted to gauge the virality or contagion of emotions. Though the soundness of this study has been criticized, Facebook's interest in understanding how networks change the behaviors of users suggests that these experiments laid the groundwork for the services it now offers commercial and political clients. Zuboff offers a compelling overview of these experiments and their place within the economic logic of the twenty-first century in the "Make Them Dance" chapter of *The Age of Surveillance Capitalism*.

    43. Cohen, *Configuring the Networked Self*, 4.

    44. In order for nudging in these ways to be effective, choice architects require a finely grained sense of people's existing cognitive biases, and a robust informational operation that can test, refine, and deploy information en masse. For example, according to Facebook, Donald Trump's 2016 presidential campaign ran 5.9 million unique versions of ads on their platform; those that proved most engaging to users were identified, tweaked, and redeployed (Frier, "Trump's Campaign"). This kind of operation requires teams of data scientists and sophisticated computer engineers not typically available to ordinary citizens.

    45. Watts and Weisburd, "How Russia Wins an Election."

    46. Watts and Weisburd, "How Russia Wins an Election."

    47. McKew, "Putin's Real Long Game."

    48. McKew, "Putin's Real Long Game."

    49. Thomas, "Russia's Reflexive Control Theory," 237.

    50. For more on the history of "reflexive control," including its relationship to cybernetics, see Reid, "*Reflexive Control*."

    51. Thomas, "Russia's Reflexive Control Theory," 253-254.

    52. Philip N. Howard quoted in Dwoskin et al., "Russia Took a Page."

    53. Brad Parscale quoted in Green and Issenberg, "Inside the Trump Bunker."

    54. Zuboff, *The Age of Surveillance Capitalism*, 100, 337.

    55. Lewis, *The Caliph's Design*, 27.

    56. Lewis, *The Caliph's Design*, 30.

    57. Lewis, *The Caliph's Design*, 30.

Works Cited

Adorno, Theodor, Else Frenkel-Brunswik, Daniel Levinson, and Nevitt Sanford. *The Authoritarian Personality*. New York: Harper and Row, 1950.

"Allotropy, n." *Oxford English Dictionary*. Online edition. Oxford University Press, June 2020. www.oed.com/view/Entry/5437?redirectedFrom=allotropic.

Althusser, Louis. "Ideology and Ideological State Apparatus (Notes towards an Investigation)." In *Lenin and Philosophy and Other Essays*. Translated by Ben Brewster, 127-186. New York: Monthly Review Press, 1971. First published 1969.

Anderson, Berit, and Brett Horvath. "The Rise of the Weaponized AI Propaganda Machine." *Medium*, February 12, 2017. https://medium.com/join-scout/the-rise-of-the-weaponized-ai-propaganda-machine-86dac61668b.

Angell, Norman. *The Press and the Organisation of Society*. London: Labour Publishing, 1922.

Anrep, G. V. "Ivan Petrovich Pavlov." *Obituary Notices of Fellows of the Royal Society* 2, no. 5 (December 1936): 1-18.

Anthony, Scott. *Public Relations and the Making of Modern Britain: Stephen Tallents and the Birth of a Progressive Media Profession*. Manchester: Manchester UP, 2012.

Antliff, Mark. *Avant-Garde Fascism: The Mobilization of Myth, Art, and Culture in France, 1909-1939*. Durham, NC: Duke UP, 2007.

———. *Inventing Bergson: Cultural Politics and the Parisian Avant-Garde*. Princeton, NJ: Princeton UP, 1993.

Ardoin, Paul, S. E. Gontarski, and Laci Mattison, eds. *Understanding Bergson, Understanding Modernism*. New York: Bloomsbury, 2013.

Arendt, Hannah. *Eichmann in Jerusalem: A Report on the Banality of Evil*. New York: Penguin, 2006. First published 1963.

———. *The Origins of Totalitarianism*. New York: Schocken, 2004. First published 1951.

Armstrong, Tim. *Modernism, Technology, and the Body: A Cultural Study*. Cambridge: Cambridge UP, 1998.

Arvidson, Heather. "Personality, Impersonality, and the Personified Detachment of Wyndham Lewis." *Modernism/Modernity* 25, no. 4 (November 2018): 791-814.

"Automatic, adj. and n." *Oxford English Dictionary*. Online edition. Oxford University Press, June 2020. www.oed.com/view/Entry/13464?redirectedFrom=automatic.

"Automaton, n." *Oxford English Dictionary*. Online edition. Oxford University Press, June 2020. www.oed.com/view/Entry/13474?redirectedFrom=Automaton.

Ayers, David. *Wyndham Lewis and Western Man*. New York: St. Martin's Press, 1992.

Baars, Bernard J. "I. P. Pavlov and the Freedom Reflex." *Journal of Consciousness Studies* 10, no. 11 (2003): 19-40.

Barbu, Oana. "Advertising, Microtargeting and Social Media." *Procedia: Social and Behavioral Sciences* 163 (2014): 44-49.

Barry, Elizabeth. *Beckett and Authority: The Use of Cliché*. New York: Palgrave Macmillan, 2006.

Barry, Liz. "Beckett, Bourdieu and the Resistance to Consumption." *Modernist Cultures* 2, no. 1 (2007): 31-41.

Beckett, Samuel. "Dante . . . Bruno. Vico . . Joyce." In *Poems, Short Fiction, Criticism*, edited by Paul Auster, 495-510. Vol. 4 of *Samuel Beckett: The Grove Centenary Edition*. New York: Grove Press, 2006. First published 1929.

———. *Disjecta: Miscellaneous Writings and a Dramatic Fragment*. Edited by Ruby Cohn. New York: Grove Press, 1984.

———. "Intercessions by Denis Devlin." In *Disjecta: Miscellaneous Writings and a Dramatic Fragment*, edited by Ruby Cohn, 91-94. New York: Grove Press, 1984. First published 1938.

———. *Malone Dies*. In *Novels*, edited by Paul Auster, 173-281. Vol. 2 of *Samuel Beckett: The Grove Centenary Edition*. New York: Grove Press, 2006. First published 1951.

———. *Molloy*. In *Novels*, edited by Paul Auster, 1-170. Vol. 2 of *Samuel Beckett: The Grove Centenary Edition*. New York: Grove Press, 2006. First published 1951.

———. *Murphy*. New York: Grove Press, 1957. First published 1938.

———. "Philosophy Notebook." MS 10967, Beckett Manuscript Collection. Trinity College Library, Dublin.

———. *Proust*. In *Poems, Short Fiction, Criticism*, edited by Paul Auster, 511-554. Vol. 4 of *Samuel Beckett: The Grove Centenary Edition*. New York: Grove Press, 2006. First published 1930.

———. "Recent Irish Poetry." In *Disjecta: Miscellaneous Writings and a Dramatic Fragment*, edited by Ruby Cohn, 70-76. New York: Grove Press, 1984. First published 1934.

———. "Three Dialogues." In *Disjecta: Miscellaneous Writings and a Dramatic Fragment*, edited by Ruby Cohn, 138-145. New York: Grove Press, 1984. First published 1949.

———. *The Unnamable*. In *Novels*, edited by Paul Auster, 285-407. Vol. 2 of *Samuel*

Works Cited

Beckett: The Grove Centenary Edition. New York: Grove Press, 2006. First published 1953.

———. *Waiting for Godot*. New York: Grove Press, 1954. First published 1952.

———. *Watt*. New York: Grove Press, 2009. First published 1953.

Begam, Richard. *Samuel Beckett and the End of Modernity*. Stanford, CA: Stanford UP, 1996.

Belgrad, Daniel. *The Culture of Spontaneity: Improvisation and the Arts in Postwar America*. Chicago: U of Chicago P, 1998.

Bennhold, Katrin. "Britain's Ministry of Nudges." *New York Times*, December 7, 2013. https://www.nytimes.com/2013/12/08/business/international/britains-ministry-of-nudges.html.

Bergson, Henri. *Creative Evolution*. Translated by Arthur Mitchell. Mineola, New York: Dover Publications, 1998. First published 1911.

———. *Introduction to Metaphysics*. Translated by T. E. Hulme. New York: Knickerbocker Press, 1912. First published 1903.

———. *Laughter: An Essay on the Meaning of the Comic*. Translated by Cloudesley Brereton and Fred Rothwell. New York: Macmillan, 1914. First published 1900.

———. *Matter and Memory*. Translated by Nancy Margaret Paul. New York: Zone Books, 1991. First published 1896.

———. *Time and Free Will: An Essay on the Immediate Data of Consciousness*. Translated by F. L. Pogson. London: George Allen & Unwin, 1910. First published 1889.

Bernays, Edward. *Crystallizing Public Opinion*. Brooklyn: Ig Publishing, 2011. First published 1923.

———. "The Engineering of Consent." *The Annals of the American Academy of Political and Social Science* 250, no. 1 (1947): 113–120.

———. *Propaganda*. Brooklyn: Ig Publishing, 2005. First published 1928.

Bertoni, Steven. "How Jared Kushner Won Trump the White House." *Forbes*, November 22, 2016. https://www.forbes.com/sites/stevenbertoni/2016/11/22/exclusive-interview-how-jared-kushner-won-trump-the-white-house/#6dcc32993af6.

Biddle, Sam. "Facebook Quietly Hid Webpages Bragging of Ability to Influence Elections." *The Intercept*, March 14, 2018. https://theintercept.com/2018/03/14/facebook-election-meddling/.

———. "Facebook Uses Artificial Intelligence to Predict Your Future Actions for Advertisers, Says Confidential Document." *The Intercept*, April 13, 2018. https://theintercept.com/2018/04/13/facebook-advertising-data-artificial-intelligence-ai/.

Bland, Scott. "Picture of Trump's Thumbs Up Proved to Be Fundraising Gold." *Politico*, February 9, 2017. https://www.politico.com/story/2017/02/trump-thumbs-up-fundraising-strategy-234839.

Boakes, Robert. *From Darwin to Behaviourism: Psychology and the Minds of Animals.* New York: Cambridge UP, 1984.

"Books: Circles of Perdition." *Time*, December 8, 1947. 108-118.

Bosanquet, Bernard. "Social Automatism and the Imitation Theory." *Mind* 8, no. 30 (1899): 167-175.

Bourdieu, Pierre. *Outline of a Theory of Practice.* Translated by Richard Nice. New York: Cambridge UP, 2007. First published 1972.

———. *Sociology in Question.* Translated by Richard Nice. London: Sage, 1995. First published 1984.

Braddock, Jeremy. "Tradition and Archive in the Harlem Renaissance." In *A Handbook of Modernism Studies*, edited by Jean-Michel Rabaté, 87-102. Malden, MA: Wiley-Blackwell, 2013.

Brain, Robert Michael. "The Pulse of Modernism: Experimental Physiology and Aesthetic Avant-Gardes circa 1900." *Studies in History and Philosophy of Science* 39 (2008): 393-417.

Brandom, Eric. "Violence in Translation: Georges Sorel, Liberalism and Totalitarianism from Weimar to Woodstock." *History of Political Thought* 38, no. 4 (Winter 2017): 733-763.

Braverman, Harry. *Labor and Monopoly Capital: The Degradation of Work in the Twentieth Century.* New York: Monthly Review Press, 1974.

Burstein, Jessica. *Cold Modernism: Literature, Fashion, Art.* University Park, PA: Pennsylvania State UP, 2012.

Burwick, Frederick, and Paul Douglass, eds. Introduction to *The Crisis in Modernism: Bergson and the Vitalist Controversy*, 1-12. New York: Cambridge UP, 1992.

Camic, Charles. "The Matter of Habit." *American Journal of Sociology* 91, no. 5 (1986): 1039-1087.

Canguilhem, Georges. "The Living and Its Milieu." Translated by John Savage. *Grey Room* 3 (Spring 2001): 6-31.

Čapek, Karel. *R.U.R.* Translated by Ivan Klíma. New York: Penguin, 2004. First published 1921.

Carpenter, William. *Principles of Mental Physiology, with Their Applications to the Training and Discipline of the Mind, and the Study of Its Morbid Conditions.* New York: Appleton, 1874.

Cerullo, J. "A Literary Sorel: 'Diremption' a *Fin de Siècle* Moralist." *History of Political Thought* 24, no. 1 (Spring 2003): 131-149.

"Chamath Palihapitiya, Founder and CEO Social Capital, on Money as an Instrument of Change." *YouTube*, November 13, 2017. https://www.youtube.com/watch?v=PMotykwoSIk.

Chu, Patricia E. *Race, Nationalism and the State in British and American Modernism.* New York: Cambridge UP, 2006.

Cohen, Debra Rae. "Annexing the Oracular Voice: Form, Ideology, and the BBC." In *Broadcasting Modernism*, edited by Debra Rae Cohen, Michael Coyle, and Jane Lewty, 142-157. Gainesville: UP of Florida, 2009.

———. "Sheepish Modernism: Rebecca West, the Adam Brothers, and the Taxonomies of Criticism." In *Rebecca West Today: Contemporary Critical Approaches*, edited by Bernard Schweizer, 143-156. Newark: U of Delaware P, 2006.

Cohen, Julie E. *Configuring the Networked Self.* New Haven: Yale UP, 2012.

Collier, Patrick. *Modernism on Fleet Street*. Hampshire: Ashgate, 2006.

Connerton, Paul. *How Societies Remember*. New York: Cambridge UP, 1989.

Coole, Diana, and Samantha Frost. "Introducing the New Materialisms." In *New Materialisms: Ontology, Agency, and Politics*, edited by Diana Coole and Samantha Frost, 1-43. Durham, NC: Duke UP 2010.

Corbyn, Zoe. "Facebook Experiment Boosts US Voter Turnout." *Nature News*, September 12, 2012. www.nature.com/news/facebook-experiment-boosts-us-voter-turnout-1.11401.

Cottom, Daniel. *Cannibals and Philosophers: Bodies of Enlightenment*. Baltimore: Johns Hopkins UP, 2001.

Crabtree, Adam. "'Automatism' and the Emergence of Dynamic Psychiatry." *Journal of History of the Behavioral Sciences* 39, no. 1 (2003): 51-70.

Crossley, Nick. "Habit and Habitus." *Body and Society* 19, no. 2-3 (2013): 136-161.

Curtis, Adam, dir. *The Century of the Self.* BBC Four, 2002.

Danius, Sara. *The Senses of Modernism: Technology, Perception, and Aesthetics*. Ithaca, NY: Cornell UP, 2002.

Dasenbrock, Reed Way. "Afterword" in *The Art of Being Ruled,* by Wyndham Lewis, 432-445. Santa Barbara, CA: Black Sparrow Press, 1989. First published 1926.

Descartes, René. *Discourse on Method and Meditations on First Philosophy*. Translated by Donald A. Cress. Indianapolis, IN: Hackett Publishing, 1998. First published 1637.

Douglass, Paul. "Bergson, Vitalism, and Modernist Literature." In *Understanding Bergson, Understanding Modernism*, edited by Paul Ardoin, S. E. Gontarski, and Laci Mattison, 108-127. New York: Bloomsbury, 2013.

Dwoskin, Elizabeth, Craig Timberg, and Adam Entous. "Russia Took a Page from Corporate America by Using Facebook Tool to ID and Influence Voters." *Washington Post*, October 2, 2017, http://wapo.st/2xPIDZ6?tid=ss_mail&utm_term=.f4b59e3ebdao.

Dyer, Geoff. "Journeys into History." *Guardian*, August 5, 2006. www.theguardian.com/books/2006/aug/05/featuresreviews.guardianreview2.

Eagleton, Terry. *The English Novel*. Malden, MA: Blackwell, 2005.

———. Introduction to *Samuel Beckett: Anatomy of a Literary Revolution*, by Pascale Casanova, 1-10. New York: Verso, 2006.

Edwards, Paul. *Wyndham Lewis: Painter and Writer*. New Haven: Yale UP, 2000.
Elias, Norbert. *The Civilizing Process*. Translated by Edmund Jephcott. Oxford: Blackwell, 1994. First published 1939.
———. *The Germans: Power Struggles and the Development of Habitus in the Nineteenth and Twentieth Centuries*. Translated by Eric Dunning and Stephen Mennell. Edited by Michael Schröter. New York: Columbia UP, 1996. First published 1989.
Eliot, George. *Middlemarch*. Hertfordshire: Wordsworth Editions Limited, 1994. First published 1872.
Eliot, T. S. *After Strange Gods: A Primer on Modern Heresy*. London: Faber and Faber, 1934.
———. "Tradition and the Individual Talent." In *Selected Prose of T. S. Eliot*, edited by Frank Kermode, 37-44. New York: Farrar, Straus and Giroux, 1975. First published 1919.
———. "*Ulysses*, Order, and Myth." In *Selected Prose of T. S. Eliot*, edited by Frank Kermode, 175-178. New York: Farrar, Straus and Giroux, 1975. First published 1923.
Erlich, Victor. *Russian Formalism: History - Doctrine*. New Haven: Yale UP, 1981. First published 1955.
Esty, Jed. *A Shrinking Island: Modernism and National Culture in England*. Princeton, NJ: Princeton UP, 2004.
Ewen, Stuart. *Captains of Consciousness: Advertising and the Social Roots of the Consumer Culture*. New York: Basic Books, 2001. First published 1976.
———. Introduction to *Crystallizing Public Opinion*, by Edward Bernays, 9-41. Brooklyn: Ig Publishing, 2011.
Fanon, Frantz. *The Wretched of the Earth*. Translated by Constance Farrington. New York: Grove Press, 1963.
Fernihough, Anne. *D. H. Lawrence: Aesthetics and Ideology*. New York: Oxford UP, 1993.
Foster, Michael. *A Textbook of Physiology*. London: Macmillan, 1879.
Freed, Richard. "The Tech Industry's War on Kids." *Medium*, March 12, 2018. https://medium.com/@richardnfreed/the-tech-industrys-psychological-war-on-kids-c452870464ce.
Frier, Sarah. "Trump's Campaign Said It Was Better at Facebook. Facebook Agrees." *Bloomberg*, April 3, 2018. https://www.bloomberg.com/news/articles/2018-04-03/trump-s-campaign-said-it-was-better-at-facebook-facebook-agrees.
Fromm, Erich. *Escape from Freedom*. New York: Henry Holt, 1994. First published 1941.
Gaedtke, Andrew. *Modernism and the Machinery of Madness: Psychosis, Technology, and Narrative Worlds*. Cambridge: Cambridge UP, 2017.
Gang, Joshua. "Behaviorism and the Beginnings of Close Reading." *ELH* 78 (2011): 1-25.

———. "Mindless Modernism." *Novel: A Forum on Fiction* 46, no. 1 (2013): 116-132.
Gibson, Andrew. *Beckett and Badiou: The Pathos of Intermittency*. Oxford: Oxford UP, 2006.
Gillies, Mary Ann. *Henri Bergson and British Modernism*. Montreal: McGill-Queen's University Press, 1996.
Glendinning, Victoria. *Rebecca West: A Life*. New York: Ballantine Books, 1987.
Goffman, Ervin. *Asylums: Essays on the Social Situation of Mental Patients and Other Inmates*. New York: Anchor Books, 1961.
Gramsci, Antonio. *Selections from the Prison Notebooks*. Translated by Quintin Hoare and Geoffrey Nowell Smith. New York: International Publishers, 1971.
Grant, Mariel. *Propaganda and the Role of the State in Inter-War Britain*. Oxford: Clarendon Press, 1994.
Green, Joshua, and Sasha Issenberg. "Inside the Trump Bunker, With Days to Go." *Bloomberg*, October 27, 2016. https://www.bloomberg.com/news/articles/2016-10-27/inside-the-trump-bunker-with-12-days-to-go.
Grierson, John. *Grierson on Documentary*. Edited by Forsyth Hardy. Berkeley: U of California P, 1966.
Hall, Brian. "Rebecca West's War." *New Yorker*, April 15, 1996, 74-83.
Hall, G. Stanley, ed. "A Sketch of the History of Reflex Action." *The American Journal of Psychology* 3, no. 1 (January 1890): 71-86.
Hansen, Lene. *Security as Practice: Discourse Analysis and the Bosnian War*. New York: Routledge, 2006.
Harris, Tristan. "How a Handful of Tech Companies Control Billions of Minds Every Day." TED, April 2017. https://www.ted.com/talks/tristan_harris_how_a_handful_of_tech_companies_control_billions_of_minds_every_day/transcript?language=en.
Hayles, N. Katherine. *How We Became Posthuman: Virtual Bodies in Cybernetics, Literature, and Informatics*. Chicago: U of Chicago P, 1999.
Heywood, Christopher. "'Blood-Consciousness' and the Pioneers of the Reflex and Ganglionic Systems." In *D. H. Lawrence: New Studies*, edited by Christopher Heywood. New York: St. Martin's Press, 1987.
Higham, Charles. *Looking Forward: Mass Education through Publicity*. New York: Knopf, 1920.
Hitchens, Christopher. Introduction to *Black Lamb and Grey Falcon: A Journey through Yugoslavia*, by Rebecca West, xiii-xli. New York: Penguin, 2007.
Horning, Rob. "Notes on the 'Data Self.'" *The New Inquiry*, February 2, 2012. https://thenewinquiry.com/blog/dumb-bullshit/.
———. "Reparative Compulsions." *The New Inquiry*, September 13, 2013. https://thenewinquiry.com/blog/reparative-compulsions/.
Hulbert, Ann. *Raising America: Experts, Parents, and a Century of Advice about Children*. New York: Vintage, 2004.

Hulme, T. E. "Bergson's Theory of Art." In *The Collected Writings of T. E. Hulme*, edited by Karen Csengeri, 191-204. Oxford: Oxford UP, 1993. First published 1922.

———. *The Collected Writings of T. E. Hulme*. Edited by Karen Csengeri. Oxford: Oxford UP, 1993.

———. "A Lecture on Modern Poetry." In *The Collected Writings of T. E. Hulme*, edited by Karen Csengeri, 49-56. Oxford: Oxford UP, 1993. First published 1908.

———. "A Notebook." In *The Collected Writings of T. E. Hulme*, edited by Karen Csengeri, 419-456. Oxford: Oxford UP, 1993. First published 1915-1916.

———. "Notes on Bergson." In *The Collected Writings of T. E. Hulme*, edited by Karen Csengeri, 125-154. Oxford: Oxford UP, 1993. First published 1911-1912.

———. "Notes on Language and Style." In *The Collected Writings of T. E. Hulme*, edited by Karen Csengeri, 23-45. Oxford: Oxford UP, 1993. First published 1907.

Hume, David. *An Enquiry Concerning Human Understanding*. Edited by Eric Steinberg. Indianapolis, IN: Hackett Publishing, 1993. First published 1748.

Hunter, Edward. *Brainwashing: The Story of Men Who Defied It*. New York: Farrar, Straus and Cudahy, 1956.

Huxley, Aldous. *Brave New World*. New York: HarperCollins, 1998. First published 1932.

———. *Brave New World Revisited*. New York: Harper and Row, 1989. First published 1958.

———. "Science and Civilization." In *Complete Essays of Aldous Huxley, Vol. 3, 1930-1935*, edited by Robert S. Baker and James Sexton, 148-155. Chicago: Ivan R. Dee, 2001. First published 1932.

Huxley, Thomas Henry. "On the Hypothesis that Animals Are Automata, and Its History." *Nature*. September 3, 1874, 362-366.

Issenberg, Sasha. "Cruz-Connected Data Miner Aims to Get Inside U.S. Voters' Heads." *Bloomberg*, November 12, 2015. https://www.bloomberg.com/news/features/2015-11-12/is-the-republican-party-s-killer-data-app-for-real.

———. "A More Perfect Union: How President Obama's Campaign Used Big Data to Rally Individual Voters." *MIT Technology Review*, December 16, 2012, https://www.technologyreview.com/s/508836/how-obama-used-big-data-to-rally-voters-part-1/.

———. "Nudge the Vote." *New York Times*, October 29, 2010. https://www.nytimes.com/2010/10/31/magazine/31politics-t.html.

James, William. *The Principles of Psychology*. Cambridge, MA: Harvard UP, 1981. First published 1890.

Jameson, Fredric. *Fables of Aggression: Wyndham Lewis, The Modernist as Fascist*. Brooklyn: Verso, 2008. First published 1979.

———. *The Prison-House of Language: A Critical Account of Structuralism and Russian Formalism*. Princeton, NJ: Princeton UP, 1972.

———. *A Singular Modernity: Essay on the Ontology of the Present*. New York: Verso, 2002.

Joyce, James. *Ulysses*. New York: Random House, 1993. First published 1922.

Joyce, Simon. *Modernism and Naturalism in British and Irish Fiction, 1880-1930*. Cambridge: Cambridge UP, 2015.

Kahneman, Daniel. *Thinking, Fast and Slow*. New York: Farrar, Straus and Giroux, 2011.

Kang, Minsoo. *Sublime Dreams of Living Machines: The Automaton in the European Imagination*. Cambridge, MA: Harvard UP, 2011.

Kenner, Hugh. *Wyndham Lewis*. Norfolk, CT: New Directions, 1954.

Knowlson, James. *Damned to Fame: The Life of Samuel Beckett*. New York: Touchstone, 1997.

Koonz, Claudia. *The Nazi Conscience*. Cambridge, MA: Belknap Press of Harvard UP, 2003.

Laclau, Ernesto, and Chantal Mouffe. *Hegemony and Socialist Strategy: Towards a Radical Democratic Politics*. New York: Verso, 2001. First published 1985.

Lambert, Richard S. *Propaganda*. London: Thomas Nelson and Sons, 1941. First published 1938.

Lasswell, Harold D. *Propaganda Technique in the World War*. London: Kegan Paul, Trench, Trubner & Co., 1927.

Lawrence, D. H. *Aaron's Rod*. Edited by Mara Kalnins. Cambridge: Cambridge UP, 1988. First published 1922.

———. *Apocalypse*. Edited by Mara Kalnins. New York: Penguin, 1995. First published 1931.

———. "Art and Morality." In *Study of Thomas Hardy and Other Essays*, edited by Bruce Steele, 161-168. Cambridge: Cambridge UP, 1985. First published 1925.

———. "Democracy." 1919. In *Reflections on the Death of a Porcupine: And Other Essays*, edited by Michael Herbert, 63-83. Cambridge: Cambridge UP, 1988. First published 1925.

———. "Education of the People." 1920. *Reflections on the Death of a Porcupine: And Other Essays*, edited by Michael Herbert, 87-166. Cambridge: Cambridge UP, 1988. First published 1925.

———. "Enslaved by Civilisation (The Manufacture of Good Little Boys)." In *Late Essays and Articles*, edited by James T. Boulton, 155-159. New York: Cambridge UP, 2004. First published 1928.

———. *Fantasia of the Unconscious*. Mineola, NY: Dover Publications, 2005. First published 1922.

———. "The Future of the Novel [Surgery for the Novel—Or a Bomb]." In *Study of

Thomas Hardy and Other Essays, edited by Bruce Steele, 149-156. Cambridge: Cambridge UP, 1985. First published 1923.

———. *Kangaroo*. New York: Penguin, 1997. First published 1923.

———. *Lady Chatterley's Lover*. New York: Modern Library, 2001. First published 1928.

———. *The Letters of D.H. Lawrence*. Vol. 1. Edited by James T. Boulton. Cambridge: Cambridge UP, 2002.

———. *The Letters of D. H. Lawrence*. Vol. 2. Edited by George J. Zytaruk and James T. Boulton. Cambridge: Cambridge UP, 1981.

———. *The Letters of D. H. Lawrence*. Vol. 4. Edited by Warren Roberts, James T. Boulton, and Elizabeth Mansfield. Cambridge: Cambridge UP, 1987.

———. *The Letters of D. H. Lawrence*. Vol. 5. Edited by James T. Boulton and Lindeth Vasey. Cambridge: Cambridge UP, 1989.

———. *The Letters of D. H. Lawrence*. Vol. 6. Edited by James T. Boulton, Margaret H. Boulton, and Gerald M. Lacy. Cambridge: Cambridge UP, 1991.

———. "Morality and the Novel." In *Study of Thomas Hardy and Other Essays*, edited by Bruce Steele, 169-176. Cambridge: Cambridge UP, 1985. First published 1925.

———. *Mornings in Mexico and Other Essays*. Edited by Virginia Crosswhite Hyde. Cambridge: Cambridge UP, 2009.

———. "The Novel and Feelings." In *Study of Thomas Hardy and Other Essays*, edited by Bruce Steele, 199-206. Cambridge: Cambridge UP, 1985. First published 1925.

———. *The Plumed Serpent*. Edited by L. D. Clark. New York: Cambridge UP, 1987. First published 1926.

———. *Psychoanalysis and the Unconscious*. Mineola, New York: Dover Publications, 2005. First published 1921.

———. *The Rainbow*. New York: Random House, 2002. First published 1915.

———. *Sons and Lovers*. New York: Modern Library, 1999. First published 1913.

———. *Studies in Classic American Literature*. New York: Penguin, 1977. First published 1923.

———. *Study of Thomas Hardy and Other Essays*. Edited by Bruce Steele. Cambridge: Cambridge UP, 1985.

———. "Why the Novel Matters." *Study of Thomas Hardy and Other Essays*, edited by Bruce Steele, 191-198. Cambridge: Cambridge UP, 1985. First published 1925.

———. *Women in Love*. New York: Modern Library, 2002. First published 1920.

Leavis, F. R. *D. H. Lawrence, Novelist*. Chicago: U of Chicago P, 1956.

———. *For Continuity*. Cambridge, UK: Minority Press, 1933.

———. *The Great Tradition*. New York: New York UP, 1963. First published 1948.

———. "Mass Civilisation and Minority Culture." In *For Continuity*, 13-46. Cambridge, UK: Minority Press, 1933. First published 1930.

Leavis, F. R., and Denys Thompson. *Culture and Environment: The Training of Critical Awareness*. London: Chatto and Windus, 1959.

Lehan, Richard. "Bergson and the Discourse of the Moderns." In *The Crisis in Modernism: Bergson and the Vitalist Controversy*, edited by Frederick Burwick and Paul Douglass, 306-329. New York: Cambridge UP, 1992.

Lenin, V. I. *What Is to Be Done? Essential Works of Lenin*. Edited by Henry M. Christman. New York: Dover Publications, 1987. First published 1902.

L'Etang, Jacquie. *Public Relations in Britain: A History of Professional Practice in the 20th Century*. Mahwah, NJ: Lawrence Erlbaum, 2004.

Levenson, Michael H. *A Genealogy of Modernism: A Study of English Literary Doctrine 1908-1922*. Cambridge: Cambridge UP, 1984.

Lewis, Wyndham. *The Art of Being Ruled*. Edited by Reed Way Dasenbrock. Santa Rosa, CA: Black Sparrow Press, 1989. First published 1926.

———. *Blasting and Bombardiering*. Berkeley: U of California P, 1967. First published 1937.

———. *The Caliph's Design: Architects! Where Is Your Vortex?* Edited by Paul Edwards. Santa Barbara, CA: Black Sparrow Press, 1986. First published 1919.

———. *The Childermass*. London: Methuen, 1956. First published 1928.

———. *The Complete Wild Body*. Edited by Bernard Lafourcade. Santa Barbara, CA: Black Sparrow Press, 1982.

———. "Creatures of Habit and Creatures of Change." In *Creatures of Habit and Creatures of Change: Essays on Art, Literature and Society, 1914-1956*, edited by Paul Edwards, 137-161. Santa Rosa, CA: Black Sparrow Press, 1989. First published 1926.

———. "Essay on the Objective of Plastic Art in Our Time." In *The Tyro: A Review of the Arts of Painting, Sculpture and Design*, no. 2, 21-37. London: Egoist Press, 1922.

———. *Hitler*. New York: Gordon Press, 1972. First published 1931.

———. *Men without Art*. Edited by Seamus Cooney. Santa Rosa, CA: Black Sparrow Press, 1987. First published 1934.

———. *Paleface: The Philosophy of the 'Melting Pot.'* New York: Gordon Press, 1972. First published 1929.

———. *Snooty Baronet*. Edited by Bernard Lafourcade. Santa Barbara, CA: Black Sparrow Press, 1984. First published 1932.

———. *Time and Western Man*. Edited by Paul Edwards. Santa Rosa, CA: Black Sparrow Press, 1993. First published 1927.

Leys, Ruth. *From Sympathy to Reflex: Marshall Hall and His Opponents*. New York: Garland Publishing, 1990.

Lifton, Robert Jay. *Thought Reform and the Psychology of Totalism: A Study of "Brainwashing" in China*. New York: W. W. Norton, 1961.

Lin, Lidan. "Labor, Alienation, and the Status of Being: The Rhetoric of Indolence in Beckett's *Murphy*." *Philological Quarterly* 79, no. 2 (2000): 249-271.

Lippmann, Walter. *The Phantom Public*. New Brunswick, NJ: Transaction Publishers, 2009. First published 1925.

———. *Preface to Politics*. New York: Mitchell Kennerley, 1913.

———. *Public Opinion*. New York: Free Press, 1997. First published 1922.

Lovejoy, Arthur O. "The Practical Tendencies of Bergsonism. I." *International Journal of Ethics* 23, no. 3 (April 1913): 253-275.

———. "The Practical Tendencies of Bergsonism. II." *International Journal of Ethics* 23, no. 4 (July 1913): 419-443.

Lukács, Georg. "Realism in the Balance." Translated by Rodney Livingstone. In *Aesthetics and Politics*, 28-59. New York: Verso, 1995. First published 1938.

Luxemburg, Rosa. *The Mass Strike, the Political Party and the Trade Unions*. Translated by Patrick Lavin. New York: Harper & Row, 1971. First published 1906.

MacKay, Marina. *Modernism and World War II*. New York: Cambridge UP, 2007.

Mao, Douglas. *Fateful Beauty: Aesthetic Environments, Juvenile Development, and Literature, 1860-1960*. Princeton, NJ: Princeton UP, 2008.

Marcuse, Herbert. *One-Dimensional Man: Studies in the Ideology of Advanced Industrial Society*. Boston: Beacon Press, 1991. First published 1964.

Martínez, Antonio García. "How Trump Conquered Facebook—Without Russian Ads." *Wired*, February 23, 2018. https://www.wired.com/story/how-trump-conquered-facebookwithout-russian-ads/.

———. "The Noisy Fallacies of Psychographic Targeting." *Wired*, March 19, 2018. https://www.wired.com/story/the-noisy-fallacies-of-psychographic-targeting/.

Matz, Jesse. "T. E. Hulme, Henri Bergson, and the Cultural Politics of Psychologism." In *The Mind of Modernism: Medicine, Psychology, and the Cultural Arts in Europe and America, 1880-1940*, edited by Mark S. Micale, 339-351. Stanford, CA: Stanford UP, 2004.

Maude, Ulrika. "Beckett and the Law of Habit." *Modernism/Modernity* 18, no. 4 (November 2011): 811-821.

———. *Beckett, Technology and the Body*. New York: Cambridge UP, 2009.

Mauss, Marcel. "Techniques of the Body." 1935. In *Sociology and Psychology: Essays*. Translated by Ben Brewster, 97-105. Boston: Routledge & Kegan Paul, 1979. First published 1950.

McGuinness, Patrick. Introduction to *T. E. Hulme: Selected Writings*. New York: Routledge, 2003.

McKew, Molly. "Putin's Real Long Game." *Politico*, January 2017, https://www.politico.com/magazine/story/2017/01/putins-real-long-game-214589.

McLuhan, Marshall. "Wyndham Lewis Recalled: Marshall McLuhan Recalls Lewis." *ArtsCanada* 114 (1967). Flexi disc.

Meerloo, Joost A. M. *The Rape of the Mind: The Psychology of Thought Control, Menticide, and Brainwashing*. New York: World Publishing, 1956.

Miller, Andrew John. *Modernism and the Crisis of Sovereignty*. New York: Routledge, 2008.

Miller, David, and William Dinan. *A Century of Spin: How Public Relations Became the Cutting Edge of Corporate Power*. London: Pluto Press, 2008.

Miller, Mark Crispin. Introduction to *Propaganda*, by Edward Bernays, 9-30. Brooklyn: Ig Publishing, 2005. First published 1928.

Miller, Tyrus. *Late Modernism: Politics, Fiction, and the Arts between the World Wars*. Berkeley: U of California P, 1999.

Moses, Omri. *Out of Character: Modernism, Vitalism, Psychic Life*. Stanford, CA: Stanford UP, 2014.

Münsterberg, Hugo. *The Eternal Life*. Boston: Houghton Mifflin, 1905.

———. *Psychology and Industrial Efficiency*. Boston: Houghton Mifflin, 1913.

Neilson, Brett. "'Dark Page': Narrative Primitivism in *Women in Love* and *The Plumed Serpent*." *Twentieth Century Literature* 43, no. 3 (1997): 310-325.

Nickels, Joel. *Poetry of the Possible: Spontaneity, Modernism, and the Multitude*. Minneapolis: U of Minnesota P, 2012.

Nordau, Max. *Degeneration*. Lincoln: U of Nebraska P, 1993. First published 1892.

North, Michael. *Machine-Age Comedy*. New York: Oxford UP, 2009.

———. *Reading 1922: A Return to the Scene of the Modern*. New York: Oxford UP, 1999.

Nunez, Michael. "Former Facebook Workers: We Routinely Suppressed Conservative News." *Gizmodo*, May 9, 2016. https://gizmodo.com/former-facebook-workers-we-routinely-suppressed-conser-1775461006.

Ogden, C. K., and I. A. Richards. *The Meaning of Meaning: A Study of the Influence of Language upon Thought and of the Science of Symbolism*. New York: Harcourt, 1927. First published 1923.

Olson, Liesl. *Modernism and the Ordinary*. New York: Oxford UP, 2009.

Orwell, George. *Coming Up for Air*. New York: Harvest Books, 1969. First published 1939.

Packard, Vance. *The Hidden Persuaders*. Brooklyn: Ig Publishing, 2007. First published 1957.

Pasquale, Frank. "The Algorithmic Self." *The Hedgehog Review* 17, no. 1 (Spring 2015): 30-45.

Pater, Walter. *The Renaissance: Studies in Art and Literature (The 1893 Text)*. Edited by Donald L. Hill. Berkeley: U of California P, 1980.

Pavlov, Ivan Petrovich. *Conditioned Reflexes: An Investigation of the Physiological Activity of the Cerebral Cortex*. Translated by G. V. Anrep. London: Oxford UP, 1946. First published 1927.

———. *Lectures on Conditioned Reflexes*. Translated by W. Horsely Gantt. New York: International Publishers, 1963. First published 1928.

"Pavlovian, adj. and n.". *Oxford English Dictionary*. Online edition. September 2020. Oxford University Press. www.oed.com/view/Entry/139115?redirectedFrom =Pavlovian.

Phipps, Gregory. *Henry James and the Philosophy of Literary Pragmatism*. New York: Palgrave Macmillan, 2016.

Pound, Ezra. "The Jefferson-Adams Letters as a Shrine and a Monument." In *Selected Prose, 1909-1965*, edited by William Cookson, 147-158. New York: New Directions, 1975.

Prince, Morton. *The Nature of Mind and Human Automatism*. Philadelphia: Lippincott, 1885.

Pritchett, V. S. *The Living Novel*. London: Chatto and Windus, 1961. First published 1946.

Reed, John R. *Victorian Will*. Athens: Ohio UP, 1989.

Reid, Clifford. "*Reflexive Control* in Soviet Military Planning." In *Soviet Strategic Deception*, edited by Brian D. Dailey and Patrick J. Parker, 293-311. Lexington, MA: D. C. Heath, 1987.

Reith, John Charles Walsham. *Broadcast over Britain*. London: Hodder and Stoughton, 1924.

Richards, I. A. "*Behaviorism*." *The New Criterion* 4 (1926): 372-378.

———. "The Niceties of Salvation." *Wyndham Lewis & I. A. Richards: A Friendship Documented, 1928-57*, edited by John Constable and S. J. M. Watson, 60-64. Cambridge, UK: Skate Press, 1989. First published 1952.

———. *Practical Criticism: A Study of Literary Judgments*. New York: Harcourt, Brace, 1960. First published 1929.

———. *Science and Poetry*. London: Kegan Paul, Trench, Trubner & Co., 1935. First published 1926.

Roberts, Ian F. "Determinism, Free Will, and Moral Responsibility in American Literary Naturalism." In *The Oxford Handbook of American Literary Naturalism*, edited by Keith Newlin, 121-138. New York: Oxford UP, 2011.

Rothschuh, Karl. E. *History of Physiology*. Translated by Guenter B. Risse. New York: Robert E. Krieger Publishing, 1973. First published 1953.

Russell, Bertrand. *Portraits from Memory*. New York: Simon and Schuster, 1956.

Rutter, Tasmin, "The Rise of the Nudge—The Unit Helping Politicians to Fathom Human Behavior." *Guardian*, July 23, 2015, https://www.theguardian.com /public-leaders-network/2015/jul/23/rise-nudge-unit-politicians-human -behaviour.

Sachs, Marilyn M. *Marcel Proust in the Light of William James: In Search of a Lost Source*. Lanham, MD: Lexington Books, 2013.

Sand, Shlomo. "Legend, Myth, and Fascism." *The European Legacy* 3, no. 5 (1998): 51-65.

Schmitt, Carl. *The Crisis of Parliamentary Democracy*. Translated by Ellen Kennedy. Cambridge, MA: MIT Press, 1985. First published 1923.

Schneier, Bruce. *Data and Goliath: The Hidden Battles to Collect Your Data and Control Your World*. New York: W. W. Norton, 2015.

Schoenbach, Lisi. "'Peaceful and Exciting': Habit, Shock, and Gertrude Stein's Pragmatic Modernism." *Modernism/Modernity* 11, no. 2 (2004): 239-259.

———. *Pragmatic Modernism*. New York: Oxford UP, 2011.

Schwartz, Sanford. "Bergson and the Politics of Vitalism." In *The Crisis in Modernism: Bergson and the Vitalist Controversy*, edited by Frederick Burwick and Paul Douglass, 277-305. New York: Cambridge UP, 1992.

Schweizer, Bernard. *Rebecca West: Heroism, Rebellion, and the Female Epic*. Westport, CT: Greenwood Press, 2002.

Scott, Walter Dill. *The Psychology of Advertising*. In *Modernism: A Sourcebook*, edited by Steven Matthews, 214-215. New York: Palgrave Macmillan, 2008. First published 1908.

Segel, Harold B. *Pinocchio's Progeny: Puppets, Marionettes, Automatons, and Robots in Modernist and Avant-Garde Drama*. Baltimore: Johns Hopkins UP, 1995.

Selisker, Scott. *Human Programming: Brainwashing, Automatons, and American Unfreedom*. Minneapolis: U of Minnesota P, 2016.

Sherry, Vincent. "Anatomy of Folly: Wyndham Lewis, the Body Politic, and Comedy." *Modernism/Modernity* 4, no. 2 (1997): 121-138.

Shklar, Judith. "Bergson and the Politics of Intuition." *The Review of Politics* 20, no. 4 (October 1958): 634-656.

Shklovsky, Viktor. "Art as Technique." Translated by Lee T. Lemon and Marion Reis. In *The Critical Tradition: Classic Texts and Contemporary Trends*, edited by David H. Richter, 716-726. New York: Bedford/St. Martin's, 1998.

———. *Theory of Prose*. Translated by Benjamin Sher. Norman, IL: Dalkey Archive Press, 1991. First published 1929.

Simmel, Georg. "Metropolis and Mental Life." In *On Individuality and Social Forms*, edited by Donald N. Levine, 324-339. Chicago: U of Chicago P, 1971. First published 1903.

Skinner, B. F. *Walden Two*. New York: Macmillan, 1967. First published 1948.

Smith, Roger. "Legal Frameworks for Psychiatry." In *150 Years of British Psychiatry, 1841-1991*, edited by G. E. Berrios and Hugh Freeman, 137-151. London: Gaskell, 1991.

Sorel, Georges. "Letter to Daniel Halévy." 1907. In *Reflections on Violence*, edited by Jeremy Jennings. Translated by T. E. Hulme and Jeremy Jennings, 3-38. New York: Cambridge UP, 2002.

———. *Reflections on Violence*. Edited by Jeremy Jennings. Translated by T. E. Hulme and Jeremy Jennings. New York: Cambridge UP, 2002. First published 1908.

Spencer, Herbert. "Philosophy of Style." 1852. *Humboldt Library of Popular Science Literature* 34, no. 2 (July 1882): 507-526.

Spitzer, Jennifer. "On Not Reading Freud: Amateurism, Expertise, and the 'Pristine Unconscious' in D. H. Lawrence." *Modernism/Modernity* 21, no. 1 (January 2014): 89-105.

Steel, Richard. Foreword to *Public Opinion*, by Walter Lippmann., xi-xvi. New York: Free Press, 1997. First published 1922.

Sterne, Jonathan. "Bourdieu, Technique and Technology." *Cultural Studies* 17 no. 3-4 (2003): 367-389.

Storer, Richard. *F. R. Leavis*. New York: Routledge, 2009.

Swann, Paul. *British Documentary Film Movement, 1926-1946*. New York: Cambridge UP, 1989.

Szalay, Michael. *New Deal Modernism: American Literature and the Invention of the Welfare State*. Durham, NC: Duke UP, 2000.

Tallents, Stephen. "The Projection of England." In *Public Relations and the Making of Modern Britain: Stephen Tallents and the Birth of a Progressive Media Profession*, by Scott Anthony, 205-235. Manchester: Manchester UP, 2012. First published 1933.

Tarde, Gabriel. "Opinion and Conversation." In *On Communication and Social Influence: Selected Papers*, edited by Terry N. Clark, 297-318. Chicago: U of Chicago P, 2010. First published 1898.

Taylor, Frederick Winslow. *The Principles of Scientific Management*. New York: Harper & Brothers, 1919. First published 1911.

Taylor, Kathleen. *Brainwashing: The Science of Thought Control*. New York: Oxford UP, 2004.

Thaler, Richard H., and Cass R. Sunstein. *Nudge: Improving Decisions about Health, Wealth, and Happiness*. New York: Penguin, 2009. First published 2008.

Thomas, Timothy L. "Russia's Reflexive Control Theory and the Military." *Journal of Slavic Military Studies* 17 (2004): 237-256.

Torgovnick, Marianna. *Gone Primitive: Savage Intellects, Modern Lives*. Chicago: U of Chicago P, 1990.

Trotter, David. *Paranoid Modernism: Literary Experiment, Psychosis, and the Professionalization of English Society*. New York: Oxford UP, 2001.

Uhlmann, Anthony. *Beckett and Post-Structuralism*. Cambridge: Cambridge UP, 1999.

Unsworth, Clive. *The Politics of Mental Health Legislation*. Oxford: Clarendon Press, 1987.

"The Vengeance of Fido." *Sunday Express*, August 12, 1928. Box 31, Folder 1263. Rebecca West Papers, Beinecke Rare Book and Manuscript Library, Yale University Library, New Haven, CT.

Wald, Priscilla. *Constituting Americans: Cultural Anxiety and Narrative Form*. Durham, NC: Duke UP, 1995.

———. "The 'Hidden Tyrant': Propaganda, Brainwashing, and Psycho-Politics in the Cold War Period." In *The Oxford Handbook of Propaganda Studies*, edited by Jonathan Auerbach and Russ Castronovo, 109-130. New York: Oxford UP, 2013.

Wallace, Jeff. *D. H. Lawrence, Science and the Posthuman*. New York: Palgrave Macmillan, 2005.

Watson, John B. *Behavior: An Introduction to Comparative Psychology*. New York: Henry Holt, 1914.

———. *Behaviorism*. 1924. New Brunswick, NJ: Transaction Publishers, 1998.

———. "Psychology as the Behaviorist Views It." *Psychological Review* 20, no. 2 (1913): 158-177.

Watson, Sean. "Bodily Entanglement: Bergson and Thresholds in the Sociology of Affect." *Culture and Organization* 9, no. 1 (2003): 27-41.

Watts, Clint, and Andrew Weisburd. "How Russia Wins an Election." *Politico*, December 13, 2016. https://www.politico.com/magazine/story/2016/12/how-russia-wins-an-election-214524.

Waugh, Evelyn. *Brideshead Revisited*. New York: Back Bay Books, 1999. First published 1944.

Weber, Max. *Economy and Society: An Outline of Interpretive Sociology*. Edited by Guenther Roth and Claus Wittich. Berkeley: U of California P, 1978. First published 1922.

Wells, H. G. "Mr. Wells Appraises Mr. Shaw." *New York Times*, November 13, 1927, SM1-2, 16.

West, Rebecca. *Black Lamb and Grey Falcon: A Journey through Yugoslavia*. New York: Penguin, 2007. First published 1941.

———. "Environment Matters Most." *Daily Express*, June 8, 1928, 10.

———. *Harriet Hume: A London Fantasy*. London: Virago Press, 1987. First published 1929.

———. *The Meaning of Treason*. New York: Viking Press, 1947.

———. "Mind and Materialism." In *The University of Books*, 23-34. London: Newnes, 1936.

———. "The Necessity and Grandeur of the International Ideal." In *Woman as Artist and Thinker*, 42-55. Lincoln, NE: iUniverse, 2005. First published 1935.

———. "Post-Mortem on Radio Propaganda." Box 36, Folder 1356. Rebecca West Papers, Beinecke Rare Book and Manuscript Library, Yale University Library, New Haven, CT.

———. *The Return of the Soldier*. New York: Random House, 2004. First published 1918.

———. *Selected Letters of Rebecca West*. Edited by Bonnie Kime Scott. New Haven: Yale UP, 2000.

———. *The Strange Necessity: Essays and Reviews*. London: Virago Press, 1987. First published 1928.

———. *The Thinking Reed*. New York: Viking Press, 1936.

———. "Woman as Artist and Thinker." In *Woman as Artist and Thinker*, 10-22. Lincoln, NE: iUniverse, 2005. First published 1931.

White, Mark D. *The Manipulation of Choice: Ethics and Libertarian Paternalism*. New York: Palgrave Macmillan, 2013.

Whyte, Lancelot Law. *The Unconscious before Freud*. New York: Basic Books, 1960.

Will, Barbara. *Gertrude Stein, Modernism, and the Problem of 'Genius.'* Edinburgh: Edinburgh UP, 2000.

Wollaeger, Mark. *Modernism, Media, and Propaganda: British Narrative from 1900 to 1945*. Princeton, NJ: Princeton UP, 2006.

Wood, Gabby. *Edison's Eve: A Magical History of the Quest for Mechanical Life*. New York: Knopf, 2003.

Woolf, Virginia. "Modern Fiction." In *The Common Reader*, 207-218. New York: Harcourt, Brace, 1925. First published 1921.

———. *Mrs. Dalloway*. Orlando, FL: Harcourt, 2005. First published 1925.

———. "On Being Ill." In *Selected Essays*, edited by David Bradshaw, 101-110. New York: Oxford UP, 2008. First published 1926.

———. *Three Guineas*. New York: Harcourt, 2006. First published 1938.

Zola, Émile. "The Experimental Novel." In *The Experimental Novel and Other Essays*. Translated by Belle M. Sherman, 1-54. New York: Haskell House, 1964. First published 1880.

———. *Thérèse Raquin*. Translated by Robin Buss. New York: Penguin, 2004. First published 1867.

Zuboff, Shoshana. *The Age of Surveillance Capitalism: The Fight for a Human Future at the New Frontier of Power*. New York: PublicAffairs, 2019.

Index

Adorno, Theodor, 149, 220n103
Alexander I, King (of Yugoslavia), 122
Althusser, Louis, 111, 192n13
Anderson, Benedict, 120
Angell, Norman, 80
animals: as automata, 17, 18, 23
Anrep, G. V., 110
anti-Semitism: in Eliot's writing, 217n58; in France, 67; in Lewis's writing, 102
Antliff, Mark, 205n104
Arendt, Hannah, 113
Aristotle, 144
Armstrong, Tim: *Modernism, Technology, and the Body*, 6, 191–192n10
art: as inhibitor of reflex, 35; as response to automatism, 103–104; West's theories regarding, 115–116. *See also* literature
artificial intelligence (AI): as used by Facebook, 182
Arvidson, Heather, 92
assembly line: and the politics of reflex, 29
asylum: in Beckett's *Murphy*, 157–160, 223–224n71; as symbol of political life, 158
automata: animals as, 17, 18, 23; and brainwashing, 113; humans as, 11, 29, 30, 149, 193–194n4; in Lawrence's works, 43, 52; Lewis's commentary on, 103
automatism/automatic behaviors: Beckett's concerns regarding, 13–14, 36, 141–142, 145, 150–151, 156; and conditioning, 138; Descartes's theories relating to, 17–19; Elias on, 141, 142, 144, 145, 146–149; and Enlightenment philosophy, 9, 17, 21; Lawrence's concerns regarding, 51–57, 59, 60–62; Lewis's concerns regarding on, 2, 73, 74, 82–84; in literature, 3–4, 21–22, 33–40; and mass modernity, 2–5, 14–15; in public life, 171; and public relations, 30–31; reaction against, 42; and sociology, 141; and vitalism, 42–43. *See also* habit; habitus; radical mechanism; reflex, politics of; reflex, science of; reflexes, conditioned
Ayers, David, 98, 213n137

Balzac, Honoré de, 21
Barry, Liz, 224n87
Beaverbrook, Lord, 76
Beckett, Samuel: and automatic behaviors, 13–14, 36, 140–141, 145, 150–151, 156, 161–164; *but the clouds*, 167; *Come and Go*, 167; and environment as influence on behavior in *Murphy*, 151, 152, 153–154, 155; on habit/habitus, 33–35, 39, 138, 150, 154, 161, 164–168, 188; on literature, 139–140; *Malone Dies*, 161; *Molloy*, 161, 162–163, 225n96; *Murphy*, 142, 144–145, 151–160, 161, 162, 188, 192n10, 223n68; *Murphy* as novel of reflex, 151–160, 161; "Philosophy Notebook," 151–152; and post-structuralism, 221n2; *Proust*, 154, 165; *Quad*, 167; "Recent Irish Poetry," 156; reflex psychology as influence on, 151–160, 161, 163; *The Unnamable*, 155, 161, 162, 163; *Waiting for Godot*, 165–167, 188; *What Where*, 167
Begam, Richard, 155

behavioral economics, 173
behaviorism, 11, 13, 24-26, 37, 70, 106; and habit, 143; Lewis's concerns regarding 82. *See also* Watson, John B.
Bekhterev, Vladimir, 151
Belgrad, Daniel, 149, 150
Bell, Charles, 19
Bergson, Henri, 10-11, 12, 33, 55, 58, 186, 203n65, 205n97, 205n104; *Creative Evolution*, 44-45, 49, 202n59; death of, 67-68; on habit, 140; Hulme's critique of, 72-73; as influence on Lewis, 206n4; as influence on modernist writers, 47, 199n19; *Introduction to Metaphysics*, 48; *Laughter*, 199n8; Lewis on, 73; on materialism, 10-11, 45-46, 50, 70-71; *Matter and Memory*, 44; on the sciences, 47; *Time and Free Will*, 44, 47, 200n32; and vitalism, 42, 43, 45-49, 57, 103, 110
Bernard, Claude, 19
Bernays, Edward, 11, 12, 30-32, 33, 78, 105, 111, 187, 195-196n38, 211n89; *Crystallizing Public Opinion*, 79, 208n38; on habit and mass democracy, 88-89; on the "invisible government," 12, 75, 88, 90-92, 93, 94, 101; *Propaganda*, 30, 88, 91, 101-102, 213n135
Bertoni, Steven, 178
Boakes, Robert, 17-18, 109, 112, 214n4
body, the: Bergson's perspective on, 44-45; and consciousness, 140; in Lawrence's fiction, 51, 54-56, 59, 68-70; in Lewis's fiction, 82, 83, 97, 104; and modernist aesthetics, 5-6; and the physiology of reflex, 7, 11, 14, 17-20, 23, 32, 50, 54-56, 59, 116-117, 168, 170-171, 196n39; and social values, 141, 143, 144, 145-146; and technology, 6, 191-192n10; and tradition, 120-121; unconscious operations of, 145; Woolf on, 5-6. *See also* Pavlov, Ivan; vitalism
Bosanquet, Bernard, 2-3, 39, 170
Bourdieu, Pierre, 144, 161
Braddock, Jeremy, 119
Brain, Robert Michael, 23
brainwashing, 24, 112-113, 136, 215n21
Brandom, Eric, 206n105
Braverman, Harry, 195n33

Brecht, Bertolt, 10; *Verfremdungseffekt*, 3, 197n52
British Documentary Film Movement, 11, 84-85
Brown, Curtis, 60
Burstein, Jessica: *Cold Modernism*, 6, 192n10
Business Leagues, 77
Bynner, Witter, 69

Cameron, David, 173
Camic, Charles, 143
Canguilhem, Georges, 21
Čapek, Karel: *R.U.R.*, 16
Capone, Al, 117-118, 124-125
Carpenter, William, 110, 127, 196n39
Chaplin, Charlie, 33
Cherington, Paul, 176
choice: predictable irrationality of, 172-174; science of, 172. *See also* nudging
choice architects, 172, 175, 179; ethical concerns relating to, 226-227n16. *See also* nudging
Chu, Patricia E., 127-128
Clinton, Hillary: presidential campaign of, 178
Cohen, Debra Rae, 86-87
Cohen, Julie E., 180-181, 182
Collier, Patrick, 210-211n81
communication technologies: and automatic behaviors, 14-15
Comte, Auguste, 22
conditioning. *See* Pavlov, Ivan; reflexes, conditioned
Connerton, Paul, 119, 150
Conrad, Joseph, 47
consciousness: Beckett on, 140; Bergson on, 47-48; West's theories regarding, 117
consumption: as reflex behavior, 30-31
Coole, Diana, 7, 192n13
Corbyn, Zoe, 228-229n42
Cottom, Daniel, 17
Crabtree, Adam, 196n39
Crane, Stephen, 21
Crossley, Nick, 143-144, 222n10
cultural hegemony, 28-32

Danius, Sara, 192n10; *The Senses of Modernism*, 6

Index

Darwin, Charles, 20, 21, 22, 44, 50, 108
Dasenbrock, Reed Way, 211n96
data collection: applications of, 175–176; as prediction products, 176; as used in political campaigns, 177–178
de la Mettrie, Julien Offray, 18, 194n6
democracy: mass media's role in, 85–87, 88, 89–91
Descartes, René, 2; on automatic behaviors, 17–19; *Discourse on Method*, 17; *Treatise of Man*, 17
Dewey, John, 33, 38, 149, 174
digital media: data collected from, 176; as used by choice architects, 183–184, 227–228n32
digital technologies: and behavioral science, 181–182; and political campaigns, 177–178, 183–185; and reflex behaviors, 175–177
Dinan, William, 77
Docker, Dudley, 77
Douglass, Paul, 48, 199n19, 200n20
Dreiser, Theodore, 21
du Bois-Reymond, Emil, 19
Durkheim, Émile, 13, 33, 34, 142–143, 145, 147
Dyer, Geoff, 123

Eagleton, Terry, 221n2
Edison, Thomas, 23
Edwards, Paul, 100, 206n4
Eikhenbaum, Boris, 197n51
Elias, Norbert, 33, 36–37, 156; on automatic behaviors, 141, 142, 144, 145, 146–149, 150, 160, 164, 168, 188; *The Civilizing Process*, 13, 138, 141, 146, 148, 160; and reflex psychology, 13, 138, 147–148
Eliot, George, 22, 194–195n15
Eliot, T. S., 43, 47, 63, 73, 217n59; *After Strange Gods*, 204n89, 217n58; on tradition, 119–121, 131, 148, 198n62
embodiment. *See* body, the
Empire Marketing Board (EMB), 85
Enlightenment philosophy: and automatic behaviors, 9, 17, 21; reflex as challenge to, 20, 22, 27; and vitalism, 10, 68
environment/milieu: and habit, 146–147; in Beckett's *Murphy*, 151; as manifested in literature, 21–22; role of in human behavior, 20–21, 22, 26, 41, 82, 121; in West's fiction, 115, 127
Erasmus, 146
Erlich, Victor, 197nn51–52
Esty, Jed, 120, 149
evolutionary theory: Bergson on, 44–45. *See also* Darwin, Charles
Ewen, Stuart, 102, 214n5

Facebook, 175, 176, 182, 228–229n42. *See also* digital technologies; social networks
Fanon, Franz, 58
fascism, 107, 121; and conditioned reflex, 135, 137; gramophonic quality of, 219–220n103; Lewis's leanings toward, 102–103; and vitalism, 68–71, 205n104; West's depiction of, 127–130, 133
Faulkner, William, 47
Fernihough, Anne, 65, 203n64
Flint, F. S., 200n29
Fogg, B. J., 182
Ford, Henry, 3, 29
Foster, Michael, 23, 193–194n4
Frankfurt School, 149
Franklin, Benjamin, 56
Franz Ferdinand, Archduke, 122
Frazer, James George, 119
Freed, Richard, 181
free will: and automaticity, 21; and materialism, 46; West on, 136
Freud, Sigmund, 5, 30, 54, 78, 207n26
Fromm, Erich, 36, 149
Frost, Samantha, 7, 192n13

Gaedtke, Andrew, 84, 99, 156, 213n137; *Modernism and the Machinery of Madness*, 209n53
Gang, Joshua, 6, 37, 152, 192n10
Garnett, Edward, 52, 56
Gillies, Mary Ann, 45–46
Glendinning, Victoria, 215n9
Goldman, Emma, 107
Google, 175, 179–180. *See also* digital technologies
Gramsci, Antonio, 33, 58; and cultural hegemony, 28–32

Grant, Mariel, 77
Grierson, John, 84-85, 209n52
Guinness, Patrick, 49

habit, 222n10; Beckett on, 33-35, 39, 138, 150, 154, 161, 164-168; and behaviorism, 143; Bergson on, 140; and conditioning, 150; and environment, 146-147; William James on, 135; as political force, 38-39, 88-89, 108; Watson on, 143; Weber on, 143; West on, 135. *See also* automatism/automatic behaviors; reflex, politics of; reflex, science of; reflexes, conditioned
habitus, 13; and automatic behaviors, 141-142, 148-149, 150, 161, 188; and the body, 144, 145-146; and sociology, 143-149, 222n10
Hall, Brian, 131-132, 218n73
Hall, Marshall, 19, 50
Hansen, Lene, 132
Hardy, Thomas, 22
Harris, Tristan, 181
Hartley, David, 18, 19
Hayles, Katherine, 182
Helmholtz, Hermann von, 19
Heywood, Christopher, 50
Higham, Charles, 77, 84
Hitchens, Christopher, 122
Horkheimer, Max, 149
Horning, Rob, 228n38
Howard, Philip N., 184-185
Hulme, T. E., 11, 48, 66, 186; on images, 49-50, 67; *Introduction to Metaphysics*, 201n34; "Notes on Bergson," 46; and vitalism, 43, 69, 72-73, 200n28, 206n1
human engineering, 26
human susceptibility, 14-15, 44; to conditioning, 43, 81, 101; to environments, 4, 22, 41, 82; in Lewis's *Childermass*, 95-97; Lippmann on, 79-80; Watson on, 143. *See also* automatism/automatic behaviors
Hunter, Edward, 112, 113, 135, 136, 219n103
Hunter, Walter S., 152
Huxley, Aldous, 114; *Brave New World*, 12, 111, 135; *Brave New World Revisited*, 112, 215n21
Huxley, T. H., 23, 50, 127, 194n14

images/Imagism: emergence of, 49-50, 200n29; Hulme on, 49-50, 67
individuality in mass society, 1-2, 135; Lewis's concerns regarding, 3, 4, 12, 53, 75, 81-82, 83-84, 89, 90-92, 93-100, 102, 104; Pavlov as threat to, 136
intuition: Bergson on, 45, 47-49; and images, 49-50; in Lawrence's works, 43, 51, 55, 62, 65, 66-67; and mass movements, 62; and vitalism, 43-44, 57
invisible government: Bernays's theory of, 12, 75, 88, 90-92, 93, 94, 101
Issenberg, Sasha, 177, 178

James, William, 33, 38-39, 50, 127, 172; *Principles of Psychology*, 208n34
Jameson, Fredric, 36, 96-97, 99-100, 164, 197n52
Joyce, James, 47, 115; *Ulysses*, 120, 217n59; *Work in Progress*, 139
Joyce, William, 217n53, 221n122
Jung, Carl, 223n69

Kahneman, Daniel, 172-173, 175
Kang, Minsoo, 29
Kenner, Hugh, 73, 94, 213n137
Knowlson, James: *Damned to Fame*, 225n96
Koonz, Claudia, 216n25
Kosinski, Michael, 176

Lambert, Richard S., 78; *Propaganda*, 219n95
Lasserre, Pierre, 200n28
Lasswell, Harold, 76-77
Lawrence, D. H., 8, 11, 12, 34, 84, 186, 201n46, 202n62, 203n64, 203-204n72; *Aaron's Rod*, 52; *Apocalypse*, 64; "Art and Morality," 205n94; and automaticity, 11, 51-57, 59, 60-62, 202n50; Bergson as influence on, 198-199n3; on characterization, 56-57; critics of, 68; *Fantasia of the Unconscious*, 51, 54-55, 56; intuition in works of, 43, 51, 55, 62, 65, 66-67; *Kangaroo*, 52, 67, 69; *Lady Chatterley's Lover*, 52, 60; Lewis's critique of, 73-74; "Morality and the Novel," 67; myth in works by, 63-64; *The Plumed Serpent*, 11, 43, 57, 59-67, 69; *Psychoanalysis and the Unconscious*, 54, 55; *The Rainbow*, 51-52,

57, 59, 60, 65, 198-199n3; *Sons and Lovers*, 52, 56-57; and spontaneity, 43, 51-52, 54-57, 59; *Studies in Classic American Literature*, 56; and vitalism, 11, 43-44, 50-57, 68-69; "Why the Novel Matters," 67; *Women in Love*, 51-52, 57, 59, 60, 201n40
Laycock, Thomas, 196n39
Leavis, F. R., 36, 37, 197-198n62; on Lawrence, 59-60, 70, 203n71
Lehan, Richard, 198n3
Lenin, V. I., 58, 112
L'Etang, Jacquie, 79
Levenson, Michael, 49, 69, 200n28
Lewes, George Henry, 22, 108
Lewis, Wyndham, 11-12, 29, 43, 53, 129, 168, 189, 209n51, 213n125, 225-226n108; *Apes of God*, 1, 98; *The Art of Being Ruled*, 1, 12, 73, 74, 82, 83-84, 87, 90-92, 93, 94, 98-99, 211n96; on automatic behaviors, 2, 73, 74, 82-84; Bergson as influence on, 206n4; *The Caliph's Design*, 82, 97, 185-186; *The Childermass*, 1, 12, 93-101, 104, 167, 192n14, 213n137; *Hitler*, 103; on individuality in a mass society, 1-2, 3, 4, 12, 53, 75, 81-82, 83-84, 89, 90-92, 93-100, 102, 104; on Lawrence, 73-74; on mass media, 83-84, 87; *Men without Art*, 104, 212n106; *Paleface*, 93; on politics, 28, 187; on propaganda and public relations, 74-75, 81-84; *Snooty Baronet*, 82, 96; *Time and Western Man*, 1-2, 12, 23, 27-28, 73, 82, 84, 87, 91-92, 93, 94, 99, 106, 192-193n14, 211n96, 212n106, 213n137; on vitalism, 73-74, 103, 206n4; *The Wild Body*, 82
Leys, Ruth, 18-19
Lifton, Robert Jay, 114
Lin, Lidan, 155
Lippmann, Walter, 11, 36, 84-85, 88, 94, 208n38; on democracy, 210n80; on Freud, 207n26; on perception, 179; on mass media, 88, 89-91, 129; on political behaviors, 79-80
literary modernism: and public relations, 80-81; and the rejection of vitalism, 72-73
literature: and automaticity, 3-4, 21-22; and the politics of reflex, 33; and the science of reflex, 34-36; West's theories relating to, 116, 139. *See also* Beckett, Samuel; Lawrence, D. H.; Lewis, Wyndham; West, Rebecca; Woolf, Virginia
Lloyd George, David, 77
London, Jack, 21
Lovejoy, Arthur, 203n65
Luccheni, Luigi, 125
Ludwig, Carl, 19
Lukács, Georg, 99, 101, 213n125
Luxemburg, Rosa, 58

MacKay, Marina, 123, 124
Magendie, François, 19
Mao, Douglas, 31, 78, 115, 131, 195n15; *Fateful Beauty*, 6
Marcuse, Herbert, 149
Marey, Étienne-Jules, 23
Marinetti, Filippo Tommaso, 53
market research: Watson as pioneer in, 106
Martínez, Antonio Garcia, 227n20
Matz, Jesse, 200n32, 206n1
mass culture: literary critics' concerns regarding, 36-37; utopian aspirations for 160-161
mass media: growing influence of, 75-81; Lewis's concerns regarding, 83-84; Lippmann's concerns regarding, 88, 89-91; and public relations, 32, 79-80; I. A. Richards on, 209n48. *See also* public relations
mass modernity: and automatic behaviors, 2-5, 14-15; Bernays on, 88-89; Lewis on, 1-2, 3, 4, 12, 53, 75, 81-82, 83-84, 89, 90-92, 93-100, 102, 104; and literary modernism, 33; and the politics of reflex, 8-10, 13-14, 26-33; and public relations, 11-12, 30-31
materialism/materiality, 42, 51; Bergson on, 10-11, 45-46, 50, 70-71; Lawrence on, 53-54; Pavlov's interest in, 108, 110, 114; and the politics of reflex, 42, 43-44, 46, 51-55, 58-59, 68, 71-74, 79
Maude, Ulrika, 140, 167
Mauss, Marcel, 33, 141, 142, 148; and habitus, 144-146, 168, 188
Mayo, Elton, 33
McGuinness, Patrick, 205n104
McKew, Molly, 183

McLuhan, Marshall, 168; Wyndham Lewis as influence on, 225-226n108
Meerloo, Joost, 112-113, 135
Meyer, Max, 152
microtargeting, 176; as used in political campaigns, 178, 227n20
milieu. *See* environment/milieu
Mill, John Stuart, 194n14
Miller, Andrew John, 158
Miller, David, 77
Miller, Tyrus, 149-150, 156
mind-body dualism, 6, 17, 18-19, 151, 153
Moses, Omri, 47
Müller, Johannes, 19
Münsterberg, Hugo, 33, 45, 198n67; *The Eternal Life*, 41-42
myth: in *The Plumed Serpent*, 63-64

nationalism: and conditioned reflexes, 121-122; West's physiological theories relating to, 123-127, 131
Nazism: associated with conditioned reflexes, 112-114, 121, 126; and human automatism, 216n25
Neilson, Brett, 204n72
nervous system: reflexes of, 18-20
New Criticism, 38
new materialisms, 7
Newton, Isaac, 21, 41
Nickels, Joel, 58
Nordau, Max, 75
Norris, Frank, 21
North, Michael, 78, 81, 89, 206n4, 208n38, 212n117
Northcliffe, Lord, 76
nudging: ethical concerns regarding, 174-175; as factor in making choices, 172-176, 226n14

Oakes, Nigel, 226n14
Obama, Barack: presidential campaign of, 177-178, 183
Ogden, C. K., 37, 208-209n48
Olson, Liesl, 198n67
Orwell, George, 129-130, 135, 215n7; *Coming Up for Air*, 129, 154-155, 158

Packard, Vance, 105, 207n26
Palihapitiya, Chamath, 181

Parscale, Brad, 184-185
Pasquale, Frank, 228n38
Pater, Walter, 196n46
Pavlov, Ivan, 9, 12-13, 23-24, 26, 32, 34, 36, 78, 80, 102, 143, 174, 214n7, 216n33; associated with authoritarianism, 121, 124; Beckett on, 139; changing reputation of, 106-108; *Conditioned Reflexes*, 107, 109, 221n122, 115, 116-117, 118, 127, 138; early research of, 109; as influence on Beckett, 151-152; as influence on West, 12-13, 107-108, 114-118, 121-122, 151; and political applications of his theories, 110-114, 136-137, 187
personality: multiple meanings of, 92
phonograph/gramophone: as metaphor for the mind, 23, 127, 129-130, 133-134; as metaphor for people under fascist regimes, 219-220n103
political campaigns: and digital technology, 177-178, 183-185
politics. *See* reflex, politics of
politics of control: and conditioned reflex, 68, 78-79
Pound, Ezra, 3-4, 49, 218n65
pragmatism, 38, 149, 174
Prince, Morton, 23
Pritchett, V. S., 68
propaganda, 27, 30, 219n95; growing influence of, 76-82; Lewis on, 74-75. *See also* public relations; reflex, politics of
Protocols of the Elders of Zion, The, 102
Proust, Marcel, 33-34, 47, 115, 133
psychology: as applied to public relations, 78-80; of reflex, 19-20
public relations: as established industry, 105-106; as "invisible government," 12, 30, 75, 88, 90-91, 94; Lewis's concerns regarding, 74-75, 81-84, 87, 88, 90-91, 103-104; and the politics of reflex, 11-12, 30-31, 76-82, 105-106, 187; success of, 101-102. *See also* propaganda

radical mechanism, 10, 11, 44-45, 53, 57
radio technology: concerns regarding, 85-87
Ravaisson, Félix, 167
Redfield, Marc, 195n15
Reed, John R., 195n15

Index

reflex, politics of, 4, 7-11, 26, 51, 168-169, 189; ambivalence toward, 39; and the assembly line, 29; and automatic behaviors, 27-33; and Beckett's *Murphy*, 151-160; in contemporary society, 8, 14-15; and the "invisible government," 75, 90-92, 93, 94, 101; in Lewis's *Childermass*, 93, 94, 98; and literature, 33, 34-35, 80-81; Lippmann on, 79-80; and materialism, 42, 43-44, 46, 51-55, 58-59, 68, 71-74, 79; and nudging, 172-176; in *The Plumed Serpent*, 60; and public relations, 11-12, 30-31, 76-82, 105-106; and sociology, 13; in the twenty-first century, 170-189; and vitalism, 10, 11, 12, 42-44, 73

reflex, science of, 5, 9, 10, 14, 143; as applied to politics, 30, 83; as challenge to Enlightenment philosophy, 20, 22, 27; in Lawrence's works, 53-54, 70; and literature, 34-36; and pragmatism, 38-39

reflexes, conditioned, 24-26, 68; as applied to traitors and Nazis, 220-221n122; associated with brainwashing, 24, 112-113, 136; as challenge to democracies, 106-108; and fascism, 125; in literature, 135-136; and nationalism, 121-122, 217n53; and Nazism, 113-114, 121; Pavlov's study of, 106-108, 109-114, 187; political applications of, 110-114, 136-137; psychology of, 19-20; and repressive regimes, 108; social implications of, 22-26. *See also* habit; Pavlov, Ivan

Reith, John, 86

Richards, I. A., 37-38, 101, 106, 208-209n48; *Science and Poetry*, 197n59

Richardson, Dorothy, 47

robot: as metaphor, 16-17, 40, 193n4

Russell, Bertrand, 68, 106

Russia: interference in foreign elections perpetrated by, 183-184; and reflexive control, 184

Russian Formalism, 35-36, 38, 197n51

Rutter, Tamsin, 173

Schmitt, Carl, 27, 30
Schoenbach, Lisi, 4, 34, 38, 39, 193n14
Schwartz, Sanford, 42, 48
Schweizer, Bernard, 123
scientific management, 29

Scott, Walter Dill: *The Psychology of Advertising*, 211n89
Sechenov, Ivan, 19-20, 108; *Reflexes of the Brain*, 20, 23
Selisker, Scott, 113, 193n19, 215n7
Seltzer, Adele, 60
Seltzer, Thomas, 60
Shaw, George Bernard, 47, 114
Sherry, Vincent, 206n4
Shklar, Judith, 58, 205n97
Shklovsky, Victor, 4, 35, 38, 49, 67
Shuttleworth, Sally, 195n15
Simmel, Georg, 31-32
Skinner, B. F., 102, 106, 181
social engineering, 111
social networks: data generated by, 180-182
sociology: early debate surrounding, 34, 142-143; and habitus, 143-149; and the politics of reflex, 13, 34, 138, 141, 143-148
Sorel, Georges, 12, 42, 57, 59, 69, 73, 205n104, 206n105; "Letter to Daniel Halévy," 63; on myth, 63; *Reflections on Violence*, 10-11, 43, 62, 66
Spencer, Herbert, 22, 35, 50, 108
Spitzer, Jennifer, 54, 201n46
spontaneity: Lawrence's concerns regarding, 43, 51-52, 54-57, 59; in mass society, 3, 11, 58-59
Steel, Richard, 210n80
Stein, Gertrude, 39, 47, 192-193n14, 198n67
Stevens, Wallace, 47
Storer, Richard, 203n71
Sunstein, Cass, 173. *See also* Thaler, Richard, and Cass Sunstein
Szalay, Michael, 149

Tallents, Stephen, 85
Tarde, Gabriel, 76
Taylor, Frederick Winslow, 3, 28, 29
Taylor, Kathleen, 113
Thaler, Richard, and Cass Sunstein: *Nudge: Improving Decisions about Health, Wealth, and Happiness*, 171-173, 174, 175, 226n11, 226-227n16
Thomas, Timothy, 184
Thompson, Denys, 36, 37
Thorndike, Edward, 152

Trotter, David, 84; *Paranoid Modernism*, 209n51
Trump, Donald: presidential campaign of, 178, 183, 229n44
Tversky, Amos, 172-173, 175

unconscious, the: and automatic behavior, 32, 140, 145; early conceptions of, 6, 31-32; and public relations, 78, 81; role of in daily life, 78
Unsworth, Clive, 224n71

Vaucanson, Jacques de, 194n6
vitalism, 10, 110; appeal of, 58-59, 69-70; and automaticity, 42-43; and Bergson, 42, 43, 45-49, 57; and fascism, 68-71, 205n104; and Hulme, 43; and intuition, 43-44; in Lawrence's works, 11, 43-44, 50-57, 68-69; and the politics of reflex, 10, 11, 12, 42-44, 186; and public relations, 12
Vorticism, 1, 185-186

Wald, Priscilla, 78
Wallace, Jeff, 50
Watson, John B., 9, 11, 24-26, 28, 32, 34, 36, 46, 70, 78-79, 99, 102, 138, 174, 182, 193n19, 214nn4-5; as advertising executive, 106, 176; Beckett on, 152; and behaviorism, 105-106; *Behaviorism*, 37, 106, 127, 214-215n7; on habit, 108, 143, 198n62; and Pavlov, 110, 214n7; on personality, 92
Watson, Sean, 198-199n3
Watts, Clint, 183
Waugh, Evelyn: *Brideshead Revisited*, 158
Weber, Eduard, 19-20
Weber, Max, 13, 33, 34, 142-143, 145
Weisburd, Andrew, 183

Weiss, A. P., 152
Wells, H. G., 114, 116
West, Rebecca, 8, 34, 219n95; aesthetic theories of, 115-117; Beckett on, 139, 140; *Black Lamb and Grey Falcon*, 12-13, 23, 108, 115, 117, 118, 121-135, 218n73, 220n119; and environment as influence on behavior, 117-118, 127, 131; fascism as depicted by, 127-130, 133; *Harriet Hume*, 115; and material culture, 132; *The Meaning of Treason*, 118, 221n122; on nationalism, 123-127, 131, 217n53; on Nazism, 121, 126; Pavlov as influence on, 12-13, 107-108, 114-118, 121-122; and the politics of reflex, 81, 107-108, 187-188; *The Return of the Soldier*, 115; *St. Augustine*, 118, 136; *The Strange Necessity*, 115-117, 123, 124, 125, 126, 130, 131, 137, 139, 216n33; *The Thinking Reed*, 118, 216n37; on tradition, 118, 132-133, 134-135, 148; and Yugoslavia, 122-127, 131-133, 134-135, 167, 218n73
White, Mark: *The Manipulation of Choice*, 174-175
Whyte, Lancelot Law, 196n39
wireless. *See* radio technology
Wollaeger, Mark, 81, 94
Woolf, Virginia, 47, 129; on atmosphere, 133-134; "Modern Fiction," 5, 6; *Mrs. Dalloway*, 191n9; "On Being Ill," 5; *Three Guineas*, 13, 133-134, 191n9, 220n119

Yerkes, Robert, 26, 106
Yugoslavia: West's interest in, 122-127, 131-133

Zola, Émile, 21, 116
Zuboff, Shoshana, 175-176, 179-180, 185, 229n42

www.ingramcontent.com/pod-product-compliance
Lightning Source LLC
Chambersburg PA
CBHW030120240426
43673CB00041B/1339